Sons and Daughters of Labor

SONS AND DAUGHTER

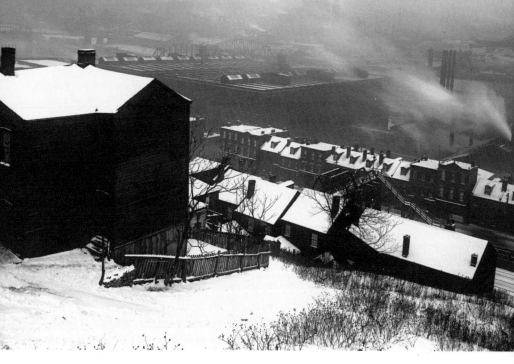

F LABOR

Class and Clerical Work in

Turn-of-the-Century Pittsburgh

Ileen A. DeVault

Cornell University Press   *Ithaca and London*

This book has been published with the aid
of a grant from the Hull Memorial
Publication Fund of Cornell University.

First published 1990 by Cornell University Press.
First printing, Cornell Paperbacks, 1995.

International Standard Book Number 0-8014-2026-1 (cloth)
International Standard Book Number 0-8014-8307-7 (paper)
Library of Congress Catalog Card Number 90-55134
Printed in the United States of America
Librarians: Library of Congress cataloging information
appears on the last page of the book.

⊗ The paper in this book meets the minimum requirements of
the American National Standard for Information Sciences—
Permanence of Paper for Printed Library Materials, ANSI Z39.48-1984.

Frontispiece: Southside mills and downtown Pittsburgh from South Hill
neighborhood, 1909. Photo courtesy of the Archives of Industrial Society,
University of Pittsburgh.

Contents

Illustrations, Figures, and Tables

Illustrations

Figures

Tables

Preface

Historians have long been fascinated by the dramatic changes in the economic structure of the United States in the late nineteenth century. At that time the development of monopoly capitalism transformed the workplaces, life-styles, and aspirations of American workers, native-born and immigrant, male and female. The changing patterns of life in the United States at the turn of the century raise familiar questions: Why did some sectors of the economy expand more rapidly than others? Which groups of workers filled the new jobs? What was the significance of growing numbers of women in the paid labor force, and what was their impact on the industries they entered? What did the future hold for the children of workers in contracting sectors of the economy? How did the people involved in these changes understand and react to their situation? This book addresses these and other questions by investigating the people who filled the rapidly growing clerical occupations at the turn of the century. Who were the young people who entered these new jobs, and how did their decisions to do so grow out of and affect their families and communities?

I first became interested in these issues while writing my senior thesis as a women's studies major at the University of California, Berkeley in 1978. My thesis was about clerical workers, and I found that when I told people my topic, most of them responded, "Oh, yes. You're writing about middle-class women, then." Having once worked as a clerical worker, I knew this characterization did not seem to fit most of the people who had worked beside me in Oakland's large offices. I became intrigued with the question of the class background and status of clerical workers. The next year, as a graduate student at the University of Pittsburgh, I stumbled across the enrollment records of the Pittsburgh public high school programs in the 1890s. This book is the result of that discovery.

Over the past ten years many people and institutions have aided me in this work. At the University of Pittsburgh, Yale University, the University of Maryland–College Park, and the School of Industrial Relations at Cornell University, communities of scholars and activists contributed to this project in diverse ways. I am especially grateful to Carolyn Schumacher, who first told me about the Pittsburgh high school enrollment records. My thinking about history and theory has been influenced by sharing ideas and work with, among others, Peter Albert, Ava Baron, James Barrett, Jeanne Boydston, Cecelia Bucki, Nancy Cott, Thelma Crivens, Tony Fels, Julie Greene, Maurine Greenwald, Linda Hassberg, Douglas Koritz, Gale McGloin, John Merriman, John A. Miller, Priscilla Murolo, Steven Sapolsky, Patricia Simpson, Amy Stanley, and Richard von Glahn. In addition, my students have consistently contributed more than they probably realize.

The research for this book profited from the assistance of many library staff members, friends, and institutions. The staff of the Sterling and Mudd libraries at Yale University were always helpful. Special thanks go to Frank Zabrosky, Frank Kurtik, and Katie Kerwin of the Archives of Industrial Society at the Hillman Library of the University of Pittsburgh and to the staff of the Pennsylvania Room at the Carnegie Library of Pittsburgh. Richard Strassberg of the Labor-Management Documentation Center and other staff members of Catherwood Library at Cornell University provided invaluable assistance through the final years of my work on this book. The people I stayed with on research trips were equally important. Thanks go to Linda Hassberg, Doug Koritz, and Joshua, as well as Peter Albert, Gay Gullickson, and Amy Stanley in Washington, D.C. In Pittsburgh the Greenwald family—Maurine, Mickey, and Marla—put up with me for an entire summer, and Gale McGloin survived a week of last-minute checking.

My research was funded by a Lena Lake Forrest Fellowship from the Business and Professional Women's Foundation, a Ralph Henry Gabriel Fellowship from Yale University, a Whiting Fellowship in the Humanities from the Mrs. Giles Whiting Foundation, as well as by the Affinity Group Foundation and the School of Industrial and Labor Relations at Cornell University. The School of Industrial and Labor Relations also provided me with research assistants, including Sue Kline, Alice Oberfield, C. Michael Roland, and Daria Steigman.

The computer research for this project would have been impossible without the aid of friends and colleagues. Nora Faires first introduced me to SPSS and its benefits and complications. At several crucial stages Thomas Dublin gave me long-distance advice and ideas on record linkages. William Cronon provided continuing help as well as last-minute consultations. Tim Nolan and Eileen Driscoll helped me transfer my data and text from Yale to Cornell, a task that should have been much simpler than it was. Ali Hadi of Cornell's Department of Economic and Social Statistics helped me with the figure that appears in chapter 4. Research assistants also helped with data collection and coding, including Cara Grigsby, Ken Packman, Ken Pomeranz, Alice Oberfield, and James Rundle. Any shortcomings in my numbers appear in spite of these people's valiant efforts.

I am sure that my editor at Cornell University Press, Peter Agree, sometimes despaired at my stubbornness as he prodded and pushed me to finish this book. Amazingly, we have managed to become and remain good friends. Roger Haydon, also at the Press, and Lise Rodgers, my copyeditor, used their skills and good humor to improve my final round of revisions. Susan Porter Benson provided helpful comments and support; she has given me a model of thoughtful collegiality. Jackie Dodge typed and retyped, cheered me up, and provided support and inspiration in ways she'll never know. I only wish this book could have translated into a well-deserved raise in her salary.

Four people deserve special thanks. When I was very young, Marjorie DeVault began to teach me the meaning of "sisterhood"; she has continued to do so, not only in the personal sense but also politically and intellectually. I am thrilled to find that I still learn so much from her. Dana Frank and I have remained friends ever since we were both labeled "Californians" at Yale. She has always supported me and reminded me of the vital connection between clarity of thought and clarity of writing. Over almost a decade Lori Ginzberg has always come through with the hardest questions, the sharpest insights, and the most unquestioning support. My debts to her go far beyond anything I could ever say here. Finally, David Montgomery not only served as my academic adviser but provided incisive comments throughout this project. He is a formidable role model—as a historian, a teacher, a political actor, and a person. I have been aided in my research by all these people; in addition, my parents, brother, and grandparents provided crucial insights and support over the years.

I have never met any of the people who appear—however opaquely—

Sons and Daughters of Labor

Introduction

White Collar/Blue Collar

In its June 1905 issue the national stenographers' monthly, *Phonographic World,* reprinted a short blurb from the Pittsburgh *Dispatch:* "Many readers will be surprised to learn that there are more typewriting machines in use in Pittsburg than in any other American city except New York." The magazine's editors then went on to comment sarcastically, "Yes, not only surprised, but amused."[1] At the time many in the United States would probably have agreed. Pittsburgh was "the Iron City," a place of brawny male workers engaged in heavy industry. The image of the typewriter—a word used for both the machine and its operator— would have seemed incongruous with the "Smokey City's" reputation. Despite the snide comment of the *Phonographic World*'s editors, however, Pittsburgh's industrial base in fact made that city home to some of the nation's earliest and most famous corporations, among them Westinghouse Electric (founded in 1886), the U.S. Glass Company (1891), and U.S. Steel (1901), as well as the financial institutions of the Mellon family. Beneath the smoke of Pittsburgh's famous factories lay the offices of the corporations that ran them. Within those offices worked the members—both male and female—of the fastest-growing sector of the labor market.

By 1951 C. Wright Mills could state that "by their rise to numerical importance, the white-collar people have upset the nineteenth-century expectation that society would be divided between entrepreneurs and

---

1. *Phonographic World* 25 (June 1905), 449. The spelling of Pittsburgh's name changed during the years covered in this book. I have used the modern spelling in the text while preserving the original spelling in quotations.

wage workers."[2] Most ordinary people understood the distinction implied by the phrases "white collar" and "blue collar." This distinction operated in their daily lives, in their working comprehension of the social structure in which they lived. Post–World War II social scientists also began to use and analyze this new bifurcated model of industrial society. Social mobility studies, for example, traced the movement of individuals and generations from blue-collar into white-collar occupations and pronounced such movement "upward."

As scholars began to examine this model more closely, however, they began to run into difficulties. Individuals in "low-level" white-collar jobs, it turned out, did not always receive—or perceive—greater benefits, either material or psychic, than individuals in blue-collar occupations. Social theorists began to talk about the "ambiguities" of the social status of clerical work. Some, emphasizing work situations, have argued that nonmanual occupations have been increasingly "proletarianized" over time, creating a "new working class" made up of both manual and nonmanual workers; others have focused on status and maintained that the "collar line" remains the crucial point of division between manual and nonmanual workers.

Whichever theory they use, scholars continue to puzzle over the situation of low-level white-collar workers, that is, clerical and sales workers. For advocates of the proletarianization argument, this group provides a clear case of white-collar wage workers controlling nothing but their labor power. In any division of society into owners and workers, clerical and sales employees clearly belong to the latter group. In addition, examination of workplace conditions reveals a substantial decline across the twentieth century in these workers' control over the work process, as well as an increase in mechanization and routinization. Nonetheless, scholars have had to come to grips with a continuing status differential between low-level white-collar workers and manual workers. Their analyses have often foundered upon the problems involved in evoking "false consciousness" as an explanatory tool. The "proletarians in false collars" seem to have missed subjectively the decline in their objective conditions.[3]

On the other hand, scholars focusing on status and differences in

2. C. Wright Mills, *White Collar: The American Middle Classes* (New York: Oxford University Press, 1951), p. ix.

3. Emile Lederer (1912), quoted in Michel Crozier, *The World of the Office Worker,* trans. David Landau (New York: Schocken, 1973), p. 25; see also Harry Braverman, *Labor and Monopoly Capital: The Degradation of Work in the Twentieth Century* (New York: Monthly Review Press, 1974), and Mark Stuart Sandler, "Clerical Proletarianization in Capitalist Development," diss., Michigan State University, 1979.

consciousness have had a difficult time dealing with the deterioration of low-level white-collar workers' material conditions. Over and over they find themselves unable to explain how these clerical and sales workers maintained a sense of superior status despite the increasingly irrefutable fact that they were, when all was said and done, employees—wage workers. Faced with the contradictions of this sector of the work force, they have looked outside the office, arguing that the ambiguity arises in large part from the "embourgeoisement of the blue-collar employee rather than the proletarization of the white-collar employee."[4]

Both groups of scholars, in positing a process by which the status of white-collar workers has changed over time, assume an earlier time at which the division between manual workers and clerical workers was explicit and absolute. Historians, whose work by definition explores changes over time, could be expected to have studied this transition from an earlier state of collar-line clarity. Some historians of clerical work have attempted to do just this, most particularly those exploring the proletarianization of clerical workers. Central to their thesis is a description of the "nineteenth-century office," a workplace in which a small number of employees shared bonds of common interest and personal relationships with their employers. While these studies describe an increasingly depersonalized office, they do not completely account for the sudden and dramatic increase in the numbers of clerical workers in the late nineteenth century. At the same time they often slight the larger economic changes which engendered that explosion of a previously insignificant portion of the work force.[5]

Virtually all examinations of the changing social status of clerical workers have passed over the ways in which gender operated in the clerical sector. Historians and sociologists often note the growing feminization of clerical work as the nineteenth-century "golden age" of the office waned; however, few of them go beyond a few sentences suggesting possible implications for the promotional opportunities of male office

---

4. Crozier, *World of the Office Worker*, p. 38; see also David Lockwood, *The Blackcoated Worker: A Study in Class Consciousness* (London: Allen & Unwin, 1958). Jürgen Kocka, *White Collar Workers in America, 1890–1940: A Social-Political History in International Perspective* (London: Sage, 1980), combines aspects of both analyses.

5. See Lockwood, *Blackcoated Worker*, pp. 19–35; Braverman, *Labor and Monopoly Capital*, p. 294; Margery W. Davies, *Woman's Place Is at the Typewriter: Office Work and Office Workers, 1870–1930* (Philadelphia: Temple University Press, 1982); and Sandler, "Clerical Proletarianization in Capitalist Development." See also Stuart M. Blumin, "The Hypothesis of Middle-Class Formation in Nineteenth-Century America: A Critique and Some Proposals," *American Historical Review* 90 (1985), 299–338.

workers.[6] In fact, acknowledgment of the growing numbers of women in clerical work is often accompanied by the systematic dismissal of female office workers from further analysis. This unfortunate tendency obscures not only the connection between organizational changes in clerical work and the feminization of the work force, but the nature of the social position of clerical work as well.

Recent work by women's historians has begun to reverse this trend by focusing on both the dynamics of the feminization of the office work force and the sexual stratification of office jobs. These studies grew out of questions about the sexual segregation of the labor market as a whole as feminists attempted to explain how women ended up in occupations popularly labeled "women's jobs." Margery Davies and others have clarified the process of feminization in the office and its connection to organizational changes in, and the mechanization of, clerical work. It is, however, intriguing but ultimately inadequate for Davies to tell us that "the nineteenth-century clerk had not turned into a proletarian; he had merely turned into a woman."[7]

Despite feminization, large numbers of male workers also entered the clerical work force during the years before World War I. As Cindy Aron has demonstrated in her study of the atypical office workers of the U.S. government during and after the Civil War, feminization of the office work force affected both male and female workers.[8] One of our challenges is to combine the examination of class and status conducted by those interested in male clerical workers with the insights gained from those who focus on feminization and other gender-related interests.

Examining the determinants of class for women and the ways men

6. Crozier, *World of the Office Worker*, p. 16; Lockwood, *Blackcoated Worker*, p. 125; Kocka, *White Collar Workers in America*, pp. 98–101.

7. Davies, *Woman's Place Is at the Typewriter*, p. 175. See also Elyce J. Rotella, *From Home to Office: U.S. Women at Work, 1870–1930* (Ann Arbor: UMI Research Press, 1981); Samuel Cohn, *The Process of Occupational Sex-Typing: The Feminization of Clerical Labor in Great Britain* (Philadelphia: Temple University Press, 1985); Cindy S. Aron, " 'To Barter Their Souls for Gold': Female Clerks in Federal Government Offices, 1862–1890," *Journal of American History* 67 (1981), 835–853; Evelyn Nakano Glenn and Roslyn L. Feldberg, "Proletarianizing Clerical Work: Technology and Organizational Control in the Office," in Andrew Zimbalist, ed., *Case Studies on the Labor Process* (New York: Monthly Review Press, 1979), pp. 51–72; Martin Oppenheimer, "Women Office Workers: Petty-Bourgeoisie or New Proletarians?" *Social Scientist* 40–41 (November–December 1975), 55–75; Jane E. Prather, "When the Girls Move In: A Sociological Analysis of the Feminization of the Bank Teller's Job," *Journal of Marriage and the Family* 33 (1971), 777–782.

8. Cindy Sondik Aron, *Ladies and Gentlemen of the Civil Service: Middle-Class Workers in Victorian America* (New York: Oxford University Press, 1987).

experienced gender will help clarify some of the ambiguous status of the clerical sector, but it will still not answer all of our questions. To understand the place of clerical work in the class structure, we need to examine more than just clerical work itself. A major argument of this book is that understanding the impact of clerical work on overall social stratification requires understanding stratification within the manual working class as well. The status of clerical work would perhaps be much clearer in contrast to that of the working class if that working class were itself a monolithic group. However, as the "new labor history" has demonstrated over the past twenty years, the working class did not act or see itself as a seamless whole. The ways in which divisions within the working class affected workers' perceptions of clerical occupations—and clerical workers' perceptions of manual work—highlight many of the ambiguities of the social status of clerical work.

Historians have paid careful attention to the ways that overlapping waves of immigration necessitated not a single "creation of a working class" in the United States, but a continuous process of working-class formation. Ethnicity and its attendant complications have been crucial for understanding society in the United States at least since the beginning of the nineteenth century. Labor historians, beginning with John R. Commons himself, have always been keenly aware of ethnic divisions in the labor force. In recent years the boundary has often blurred between labor history and ethnic history. The resulting exchange of ideas and information has produced a more nuanced view of the working class than would be possible without such cross-fertilization. We need to remember, though, that just as gender refers to both women and men, ethnicity informs the lives of those who are native-born or assimilated as well as those who wear their ethnic identity on the sleeves of their native costumes.

The continuous processes of migration and assimilation in the United States have often obscured other changes within and around the working class. Not only the country's workers, but also the work they were performing, has changed. Differences in skill, reinforced by ethnicity, gender, and race, divided the working class. Because of the strength of ethnic and racial divisions in the United States, historians of the American working class have had greater difficulty dealing with issues of skill than have European historians. Unhampered by as many coinciding cultural divisions, these scholars have described the ways in which distances between highly skilled and lesser skilled workers have determined a range of organizational, political, and social forms of expression and action. In particular, they have described how skilled workers have played dual roles, sometimes as the self-conscious leaders of a militant working class and sometimes as the self-interested defenders of the status quo.[9] In the United States skilled workers have demonstrated these same contradictory tendencies.[10] The result has been an ambiguity within the working class at least as great as that seen in clerical workers on the other side of the collar line.

Jürgen Kocka has called upon historians of the working class to use the techniques and findings of social mobility studies in order to explore the question, "What is the relative weight of the 'class line,' the outer boundary of the working class, in structuring social reality?"[11] Both scholars of social mobility and labor historians have generally assumed that this "class line" equals the "collar line" between manual and non-manual occupations. The central goal of this book, however, is to explore the very validity of this equation. Did the collar line function as a major social marker for the turn-of-the-century working class? To begin to uncover the answer to this question, we must understand the context in which the rise of the clerical sector took place, a context that included many competing identities arrayed in constellations of varying complexity.

What we are examining, then, is how the rise of the clerical sector influenced the social organization of class at the turn of the century. By "social organization of class" I mean the combination of objective condi-

9. See Eric Hobsbawm, "The Labour Aristocracy in Nineteenth-Century Britain," in his *Labouring Men* (New York: Basic Books, 1965), pp. 277–315; Geoffrey Crossick, *An Artisan Elite in Victorian Society: Kentish London, 1840–1880* (London: Croom Helm, 1978); John Foster, *Class Struggle and the Industrial Revolution* (London: Weidenfeld & Nicolson, 1974); Robert Q. Gray, *The Labour Aristocracy in Victorian Edinburgh* (Oxford: Clarendon Press, 1976); as well as the essays in Eric Hobsbawm, *Workers: Worlds of Labor* (New York: Pantheon, 1984), pp. 214–272; James Hinton, *The First Shop Stewards' Movement* (London: Allen & Unwin, 1973); and Michael P. Hanagan, *The Logic of Solidarity: Artisans and Industrial Workers in Three French Towns, 1871–1914* (Urbana: University of Illinois Press, 1980).

10. See Peter R. Shergold, *Working-Class Life: The "American Standard" in Comparative Perspective, 1899–1913* (Pittsburgh: University of Pittsburgh Press, 1982); Andrew Dawson, "The Paradox of Dynamic Technological Change and the Labor Aristocracy in the United States, 1880–1914," *Labor History* 20 (1979), 325–351; Dawson, "The Parameters of Craft Consciousness: The Social Outlook of the Skilled Worker, 1890–1920," in Dirk Hoerder, ed., *American Labor and Immigration History, 1877–1920s: Recent European Research* (Urbana: University of Illinois Press, 1983), pp. 135–155; and Ronald Schatz, "Union Pioneers: The Founders of Local Unions at General Electric and Westinghouse, 1933–1937," *Journal of American History* 66 (1979), 586–602.

11. Jürgen Kocka, "The Study of Social Mobility and the Formation of the Working Class in the 19th Century," *Le Mouvement Sociale* 111 (April–June 1980), 107.

tions and social perceptions that make up people's ideas about how they fit into the socioeconomic structure of their society.[12] Such an analysis requires investigating overlapping sets of issues; that is, defining our interest as the collar line entails identifying and examining both "sides" of that line. This means studying not only what was happening to office jobs at the turn of the century, but also what was happening to manual jobs at the same time, as well as how all of these changes interacted. In addition, the feminization of some office occupations further demands that we pay special attention to how gender operated on either side of— and across—the collar line.

During the 1890s over a thousand teenagers from the families of manual workers entered the Commercial Department of the Pittsburgh, Pennsylvania, public high school. They enrolled in such courses as bookkeeping, commercial law, penmanship, business customs and correspondence, typewriting, and stenography. While many dropped out of the program within months, almost half graduated two or three years after their entrance. Most of the students were boys, though the proportion of girls rose steadily over the course of the decade. These working-class students joined other students from diverse backgrounds in striving to attain jobs as members of Pittsburgh's expanding office work force.

What did it mean to Pittsburgh's working class—and to individual working-class families—to have its sons and daughters enter clerical positions? Pittsburgh provides a microcosm of the most dramatic effects of monopoly capitalism on life in the United States at the turn of the century. As one commentator proclaimed, "In the revolution that has gone on in the iron trade in the past two and a half years, the changes as they have affected operating and sales departments have had most attention in current trade literature. But in the accounting department the upheaval has been just as great."[13] These simultaneous revolutions in work processes reverberated throughout working-class life in Pittsburgh.

The working-class students of the Commercial Department grew up in Pittsburgh's working-class neighborhoods. However, the working world they eventually entered differed not only from that of their parents but also

---

12. I am indebted to many conversations with Marjorie L. DeVault for my understanding of the social organization of class. See Dorothy E. Smith, "Women, Class and Family," in Ralph Miliband and John Saville, eds., *The Socialist Register 1983* (London: Merlin, 1983), pp. 1–44, esp. p. 7.

13. R. R. Shuman, "The Malcontent in Office Organization," *Iron Trade Review,* August 15, 1901, p. 19.

from that of previous office workers. The transformation of clerical work—and workers—at the turn of the century requires that we rethink occupational mobility and its implications for workers in the United States. These women and men took into the office the inheritance of their class and gender, their values and aspirations. The ways in which their work experiences changed them would affect not only their own lives but the entire class structure of the country.

Not all of the young people who enrolled in the Commercial Department actually became clerical workers, but their educational choice in itself is significant. Examining who these young people were can help us to discover the significance of the collar line. Without access to questionnaires, diaries, interviews, or other sources that would tell us more explicitly how students within the Commercial Department viewed their options, we can only let their actions speak for them. Educational choices, by exposing beliefs about which occupations are desirable and which are open, begin to make the social organization of class accessible. Proceeding from this assumption, we can uncover, through their actions, the students' own perceptions of the collar line.

The first chapter of this book sets the stage for this inquiry by describing the transformation of clerical work in the decades surrounding the turn of the century. Within this changing economic context Pittsburgh's Commercial Department provided the city's young people with increasingly important skills, as chapter 2 explains. Chapter 3 examines how the new office jobs fit into Pittsburgh's overall job market. The ways in which family structure and expectations combined with new opportunities for clerical employment are explored in the fourth chapter. The fifth chapter contains studies of two working-class neighborhoods that sent disproportionate numbers of skilled workers' children to the Commercial Department. Finally, chapter 6 follows the students of the Commercial Department into their working lives, foreshadowing the impact of the development of the clerical sector on twentieth-century social structure.

1 /

Clerical Work

"The growing complexity of business"

When Willis Larimer King began working for the Jones and Laughlin Steel Company in Pittsburgh in 1869, the entire office force consisted of six men. One was Jones and two were the Laughlin brothers; two others did the firm's bookkeeping and miscellaneous clerical work. Some seventy years later King recalled the intimate and personal nature of the business:

> There were no telephones, stenographers or typewriters, and business was done face to face. A man would travel hundreds of miles to buy a carload of iron (15 tons), rather than write because he could see all the iron manufacturers, and felt he could more than save his expenses in getting the lowest price. There were probably more callers at our office then than there are today. . . . Business hours began at seven in the morning and six in the evening was recognized as quitting time only if the day's work was finished, and it was not unusual to continue work after supper.[1]

In this business atmosphere, future steel magnates like Andrew Carnegie and Henry Oliver could begin their careers as messenger boys and, through such face-to-face interactions, develop the contacts that propelled them into business on their own.[2] King himself would reach the board of directors and a vice presidency of Jones & Laughlin. However, as King hinted in the opening sentence of the foregoing quotation, a myriad of changes soon transformed the everyday business world.

1. Willis Larimer King, "Recollections and Conclusions from a Long Business Life," *Western Pennsylvania Historical Magazine* 23 (1940), 226.
2. See Henry Oliver Evans, *Iron Pioneer: Henry W. Oliver, 1840–1904* (New York: E. P. Dutton, 1942).

1. Order Department, Pittsburgh Dry Goods Co., Pittsburgh. From Edward White, ed., *Pittsburgh the Powerful* (Pittsburgh: Industry Publishing Co., 1907), p. 52.

Pictures published in 1907 illustrate some of these changes. A "General View of the Offices" of a Pittsburgh carpeting firm reveals three men, working at various tasks, and two women literally surrounded by office machines—typewriters, an adding machine, a postage scale.[3] Photographs of the offices of the Joseph Horne Pittsburgh Dry Goods Company, one of the city's first and largest department stores, include one described as the "Order Department": "In the foreground is one of Mr. Rodger's Assistants dictating correspondence, and to the left are two Typewriter Operators transcribing the dictation for the department managers throughout the house; average letters sent out by each of the operators is over 100 daily." The assistant dictator is male, and the typewriter operators female. The accompanying narrative explained that speed was crucial to the business, necessitating the systematization of this sort of work.[4]

By 1919 a writer could proclaim that "the file clerk is just as essential to

3. Edward White, ed., *Pittsburgh the Powerful* (Pittsburgh: Industry Publishing Co., 1907), p. 86. The fact that this photograph appears to have been spliced together only reinforces the point: offices separated women and men in more ways than one.

4. White, *Pittsburgh the Powerful*, pp. 52, 46.

2. A general view of the offices, Geo. Wehn, Son & Co., Pittsburgh. From Edward White, ed., *Pittsburgh the Powerful* (Pittsburgh: Industry Publishing Co., 1907), p. 86.

the steel business, under modern conditions, as the puddler." In the same year Pittsburgh steel companies averaged office staffs of over 200, including 190 "clerks," of whom a quarter were women.[5] Although the city's most famous corporations, such as U.S. Steel, Westinghouse, and the U.S. Glass Company, did not write about their office practices, they, too, instituted new procedures. Large corporate offices required precise delineation of the work of each clerk. Complex organizational charts clarified the lines of command and illustrated the intense division of labor. Photographs of such offices picture young women and men seated at carefully aligned and identical desks, often equipped with the latest office "appliances" such as typewriters or adding machines.[6]

5. Lee Galloway, *Office Management: Its Principles and Practice* (New York: Ronald, 1919), p. ix; U.S. Department of Commerce, Bureau of the Census, *Manufactures 1919: Reports for States, with Statistics for Principal Cities*, vol. 9 (Washington, 1923), table 5, pp. 1342–1343.

6. An example of a typical organization chart can be found in William Schulze, *The American Office: Its Organization, Management and Records* (New York: Key Publishing Co., 1913), chart V, p. 105.

Table 1. Clerical occupations and women as percentage of clerical work force, United States and Pittsburgh, 1870–1920 (absolute numbers and percentages)

	Clerical workers in work force			Women as clerical workers		
	United States[a]		Pittsburgh[b]		United States[c]		Pittsburgh[b]
1870	81,619	0.6%	121	0.4%	1,823	2.6%	5	4.1%
1880	160,480	0.9	341	0.7	6,610	4.7	4	1.2
1890	468,586	2.0	5,946	6.2	73,603	19.4	750	12.6
1900	737,486	2.5	10,683	8.1	179,345	29.2	2,182	20.4
1910	1,718,458	4.6	22,788	9.8	575,792	37.7	6,748	29.6
1920	3,111,836	7.3	36,298	14.5	1,401,105	45.0	15,238	42.0

Sources:

a. Alba M. Edwards, *Comparative Occupation Statistics for the U.S., 1870–1940,* U.S. Department of Commerce, Bureau of the Census (Washington, 1943), pp. 101, 112.

b. These numbers were derived from the following U.S. Census figures, using the procedure described in Edwards, Appendix A.

U.S. *Census,* 1870, vol. I, table XXXII, p. 795.
U.S. *Census,* 1880, vol. I, table XXXVI, p. 895.
U.S. *Census,* 1890, pt. II, table 118, pp. 712–713.
U.S. *Census Occupations,* 1900, table 43, pp. 682–683.
U.S. *Census,* 1910, vol. IV, table VIII, pp. 591–592.
U.S. *Census,* 1920, vol. IV, table 19, pp. 204, 220.

c. The number of women office workers cited combines the figures in U.S. Department of Labor, Women's Bureau, *Women's Occupations through Seven Decades,* Bulletin no. 218 (Washington, 1947), pp. 75 and 78.

Just fifty years after Willis King entered the office of the Jones and Laughlin Steel Company, Pittsburgh's business practices—and the businesses themselves—had been transformed in fundamental and dramatic ways. In these years a virtually new sector of the labor force had developed, not only in Pittsburgh but throughout the United States. The clerical sector in the decades around the turn of the century was new in three main ways. First, it had grown substantially in size. Second, the people who made up the clerical sector had changed: many more of them were women (see table 1). Finally, the content of clerical work itself had changed in significant ways.

By 1920 the U.S. work force had increased to over three times its 1870 size. Some of the new industrial sectors had grown even more rapidly: jobs in iron and steel had increased by fourteen times, and jobs in rubber by thirty-five times. But the fastest growing sector of the work force was the clerical sector, which increased by more than thirty-eight times during these same decades. Changes in business procedures, spurred by the development of larger and more concentrated concerns, brought about this expansion of clerical work.

3. A portion of the Cost Department of a large electric supply manufacturer in Pittsburgh. From E. St. Elmo Lewis, *Efficient Cost Keeping* (Detroit: Burroughs Adding Machine Co., 1914), p. 112.

The "modern business enterprise" described by Alfred Chandler, Jr., in *The Visible Hand* not only separated the professional managerial control of businesses from actual ownership of them, but also called forth new needs for clerical work. Chandler has described how the emergence of the modern corporation required the "administrative coordination" of business activities. Such administrative coordination called forth not only a new managerial level, but also a constant flow of information upon which managers could base their decisions.[7] As businesses elaborated management hierarchies, an increasingly complex layer of clerical work-

7. Alfred D. Chandler, Jr., *The Visible Hand: The Managerial Revolution in American Business* (Cambridge: Harvard University Press, 1977), pp. 6–8, 109.

4. A section of the Cost Accounting Department of the Westinghouse Machine Co., Pittsburgh. From E. St. Elmo Lewis, *Efficient Cost Keeping* (Detroit: Burroughs Adding Machine Co., 1914), p. 78.

ers provided this information. Since the paramount justification for middle management's existence lay in its ability to realize greater profits, the most crucial escalation of information took the form of accounting reports. As managers called for exact statistical reports on every aspect of the processes under their control, accounting procedures and analyses were applied to ever-greater areas of business.[8] In 1870 the United States Census reported fewer than 39,000 bookkeepers and accountants in the entire country. By 1920 there were almost 735,000.[9]

8. See Ileen A. DeVault, "Sons and Daughters of Labor: Class and Clerical Work in Pittsburgh, 1870s–1910s," diss., Yale University, 1985, pp. 26–28.

9. Margery W. Davies, *Woman's Place Is at the Typewriter: Office Work and Office Workers, 1870–1930* (Philadelphia: Temple University Press, 1982), pp. 178–179.

5. A section of a busy Cost Department. From E. St. Elmo Lewis, *Efficient Cost Keeping* (Detroit: Burroughs Adding Machine Co., 1914), frontis.

Other types of office work increased in similar ways. For example, the need for both external and internal correspondence became greater as businesses grew and developed. By 1919 businesses were so far from the face-to-face transactions of the 1860s that a business advice author could claim undisputedly that "without [correspondence] the operation of the business would cease." External communications included those between businesses (for example, between manufacturers and their suppliers, or manufacturers and wholesalers) and those between businesses and their customers (the most striking example is that of mail-order retailing). Another author, calling correspondence work "as important as the manufacturing department" of a business, reminded businessmen that "your stenographic department is the bridge between your business and your customers."[10]

10. "as important . . . ," Galloway, *Office Management,* p. 525; "without [correspondence] . . . ," *How to Become a Successful Stenographer: For the Young Woman Who Wants to Make Good* (n.p.: Stenographic Efficiency Bureau, Remington Typewriter Co., 1916), p. 5 (hereafter cited as *Successful Steno*).

At the same time the elaboration of internal communication networks also called for expanding correspondence work. This correspondence aimed not at communicating with the outside world, but at coordinating the processes within the corporation itself. Lee Galloway described it dramatically:

> As the subdivisions of work increase the necessity grows for continual communication between the various ranks of authority. Letters and memos, production orders and work tickets, speaking tubes and telautographs, cost statistics and controlling accounts, time clocks and messenger boys, multiply to keep pace with the growing complexity of business.[11]

This "growing complexity of business" existed not only within individual production units, but also between central offices and outlying production facilities, and between the varied components of the huge trusts and merged corporations.

The proliferation of correspondence called forth a proliferation of stenographers and typists, job categories that grew faster than any other clerical occupations. In 1870 there were only 154 individuals so listed in the census; by 1920 the census recorded over 600,000 stenographers and typists. Other clerical job categories increased numerically in analogous ways.[12]

But the growth in numbers was not the only change in clerical work during these years; such work also became increasingly feminized, though the pace of feminization varied across job categories. Already a majority of stenographers and typists by 1890, for example, by 1920 women dominated these jobs, making up 92 percent of the category. The feminization of other occupations was neither so rapid nor so complete. Women entered bookkeeping jobs steadily, at about the same rate as they were entering clerical occupations in general. Until the 1890s women comprised but a small portion of the increasing numbers of bookkeepers. In both the 1890s and the 1900s, however, women contributed over 48 percent of the total increase in the job category. By the 1910s women entered bookkeeping in even greater numbers, accounting for almost 70 percent of the increase during that decade. In 1920 almost half (49 percent) of the bookkeepers and accountants in the United States were women.[13]

A variety of factors played central roles in women's increasing par-

11. Galloway, *Office Management*, p. vii.
12. Davies, *Woman's Place Is at the Typewriter*, pp. 178–179.
13. DeVault, "Sons and Daughters of Labor," p. 23.

ticipation in clerical work. These factors can be grouped into three general categories: (1) women's education and the wage-earning positions it prepared them for; (2) women's "suitability," both experiential and ideological, for routinized, dead-end employment; and (3) the features of the female job market which lowered women's wages in comparison to men's. These elements operated, to a greater or lesser extent, in all the occupations making up the clerical sector.

All clerical jobs required basic literacy skills and some amount of knowledge at a high school level—grammar and spelling, arithmetic, geography—as well as training in specific business applications, such as bookkeeping or stenography and typewriting. Throughout the nineteenth century high school attendance rates rose for both men and women. Women's rates rose relative to men's, however, and (at least from 1870 when reliable records began to be kept) more women than men graduated from high school.[14] As Margery Davies has pointed out, the years of clerical work's greatest expansion were also years when other occupations for men which required higher education also increased. Male high school students and graduates therefore encountered a range of options for using their education. Young women faced fewer alternatives. For these women clerical employment quickly became "the other thing" they could do besides teaching school.[15]

This trend grew as opportunities for women's business training increased from the 1870s on, with the help of advertising and sales strategies used by the new typewriter manufacturers. When the Remington company began to market the first commercially feasible typewriters in 1874, it used women to demonstrate the operation of the new machines. Because the company often promised typewriter purchasers that it would supply an operator as well as a machine, the role of typist (or "typewriter," as she was called at the time) was consequently identified as female.[16] Private business schools quickly picked up this identification. Silas Sadler Packard, New York City's foremost business educator, introduced instruction in stenography into his school in 1872, followed by

14. Elyce J. Rotella, *From Home to Office: U.S. Women at Work, 1870–1930* (Ann Arbor: UMI Research Press, 1981), pp. 153, 156; Davies, *Woman's Place Is at the Typewriter,* table 2, p. 180.

15. Davies, *Woman's Place Is at the Typewriter,* pp. 71, 73; "Stenography in the Public Schools," *Phonographic World* 1 (October 1885), 27 (hereafter cited as *PW*). Also see Susan B. Carter and Mark Prus, "The Labor Market and the American High School Girl, 1890–1928," *Journal of Economic History* 42 (March 1982), 163–171. Chapter 3 discusses job-market options for women and men in more detail.

16. See DeVault, "Sons and Daughters of Labor," pp. 63–64.

typewriting in 1873. He thus created the increasingly popular "amanuensis course," combining the study of shorthand and typewriting for a specifically female student body.[17] These courses, available in an increasing number of educational formats, provided young women with the technical skills necessary for office employment.

As female stenographers and typists poured into business offices, debate raged over their suitability for such employment. Ideologues of all stripes took sides, incorporating the controversy over women's office employment into the larger debate about the advisability of any sort of waged work for women.[18] Both supporters and detractors of "the pretty typewriter" tended to view women office workers as neither equal to nor inferior to men, but as different. As one woman argued in an address to female students at Packard's Business College in New York City, the successful "business woman" did not require the "mental capacity" of a businessman, but only "concentration and the right kind of endurance."[19] Advocates of female office workers also frequently praised the neatness and manual dexterity of women as particularly suited to clerical work.

The central gender issue in the debate over women's business employment, however, involved something very different from women's aptitudes or lack thereof. One of the most famous articles arguing against such employment emphasized this issue. In "The Incapacity of Business Women," first published in the *North American Review* but widely reprinted elsewhere, Marion Harland maintained that a woman viewed her business employment merely "as a stop gap against the tide of impecuniosity until she can wed a bread-and-bonnet-winner." Because they viewed their work as only temporary, Harland continued, women did not apply themselves to business with the same rigor and discipline as did men.[20] Indignant supporters of "business women" responded quickly, attempting to change the terms of the debate. Rather than address the question of single women's temporary status as wage earners, they tried to undercut the basis for Harland's conclusions. One article, for example, argued that Harland's use of salesladies, stenographers, typewriters, and nurses to represent businesswomen in general was akin to using elevator boys, porters, and waiters when discussing businessmen. Another re-

17. Janice Harriet Weiss, "Educating for Clerical Work: A History of Commercial Education in the United States since 1850," thesis, Harvard Graduate School of Education, 1978, p. 55.

18. Margery Davies has supplied a fine analysis of this interconnection. See Davies, *Woman's Place Is at the Typewriter,* pp. 79–96.

19. "The Woman in Business," *PW* 8 (March 1893), 231.

20. Marion Harland, "The Incapacity of Business Women," *North American Review* 397 (December 1889), 707–712 (reprinted in *PW* 5 [January 1890], 157).

spondent pointed out that "so far as comparison is to be made, the faults of the lowest order of women-workers are precisely the same as those of the same order among men."[21]

In fact, both sides of the debate ignored the realities of the clerical job market and workplace. Business offices were already filled with male clerks and bookkeepers seeking promotion or self-employment. However, the increasingly pyramidic organizational structure of offices diminished such opportunities for male employees. Businesses welcomed women workers for exactly the reason Harland had decried their employment. Young, single women presumably looking forward to marriage would not be likely to demand substantive promotions, businessmen assumed. One author noted approvingly that while a male stenographer would want to move on to a higher position in the business, a woman would remain in a job indefinitely with only periodic wage increases. Another argued that "when the girls marry, openings are provided for others just as efficient and deserving, and the promotion is beneficial to all who remain."[22] The introduction of women into offices seemed to build flexibility into the new office hierarchies.

This aspect of women's "suitability" for office work is directly related to the third major factor encouraging women's employment as stenographers and typists: the low wages at which they could be hired. The difference between a $15-a-week male bookkeeper and an $8-a-week female clerk provided a powerful incentive for businessmen to hire women whenever possible.[23]

Contemporary discussions of male versus female wages often ignored the continuing transformation of the work actually performed in offices, while discussions of job content masked the growing feminization of those jobs. The most obvious changes in office work processes came about through the mechanization of clerical tasks. After its introduction in the 1870s, the typewriter both sped up the pace of office correspondence work and virtually abolished the old job of the clerk-copyist, who had laboriously written letters in elegant handwriting, making a second copy for the business's records.[24] The invention of adding machines and other calculating mechanisms from the 1880s on left intact the occupational

21. "The Business Capacity of Women," *PW* 5 (April 1890), 243–244. This article reprinted the arguments of the Rev. D. P. Livermore in the *Union Signal*, 2/13/1890, and Helen Campbell in the *New York Herald*, 3/2/1890.
22. *PW* 35 (April 1910), 231; H. A. Harris, "How I Choose and Train Stenographers," *System* 25 (1914), 532.
23. Wages for male and female office workers are discussed in chapter 3.
24. John Allen Rider, "A History of the Male Stenographer in the United States," diss., University of Nebraska, 1966, p. 11.

titles of bookkeepers, but lessened the skill necessary to perform the work. The promotional literature of the Burroughs Adding Machine Company often provided examples of the savings possible when businesses used their machines: "Suppose you have 1000 extensions a day to be made on piece-work tickets, and a $15-per-week bookkeeper does the work in 3½ hours, and thus cost [sic] you $1.15. A Burroughs cost keeping machine and an $8-a-week cost clerk could do the same work in 2 hours at a cost of $0.36, and thus save you $237 a year on this one item."[25] Examples such as this not only avoided mention of workers' gender, but also implied new and less variable standards of work. Adding machines, like other office machines, minimized differences between individual clerical workers, leading managers to expect all of their workers to handle similar work loads.

Mechanization was not the only change in the content of clerical work. Beginning in the 1890s, and picking up greatly through the 1910s, office advice books urged businessmen to reorganize their offices along "scientific" lines. One of the first steps toward a scientific organization involved separating correspondence work from other tasks. Beyond that, complex organizational charts specified both the chain of command and the work to be done throughout the business. Advocates of "scientific office management" also delineated further subdivision of tasks. One author, for example, designated nine basic tasks, to be performed by nine different individuals, in the accounting department. The purchase bookkeeper would oversee the work of the purchase order and invoice clerk, the disbursement clerk or cashier, the payroll clerk, and a security or auditing clerk, while the sales bookkeeper managed the order and sales record clerk, a cashier, and a security and auditing clerk.[26]

In the correspondence department office managers found a different way to specialize the work, creating what we know today as the stenographic or typing pool.[27] Once again, advocates of scientific office management recommended going even further. One of the most famous, W. H. Leffingwell, suggested that large companies, sending out numbers of similar letters, might adopt a "paragraph system" for their correspondence. In such a system dictators would compose model paragraphs fitting various common situations, and typists would then merely combine

25. E. St. Elmo Lewis, *Efficient Cost Keeping* (Detroit: Burroughs Adding Machine Co., 1914), pp. 166–167.
26. Frank N. Doubleday, ed., *Accounting and Office Methods* (Chicago: System Co., 1911), p. 10.
27. Remington Typewriter Company, *Cutting the Cost of Stenographic Service* (N.p., 1914), p. 12; Galloway, *Office Management*, p. 200.

the appropriate paragraphs. Leffingwell stressed the system's positive features: "I have seen a system consisting of over 600 paragraphs easily handled by high-school girls who glibly discussed the relative merits of a letter consisting of paragraphs 'A2, B14, J26' as compared with 'A12, B22, J26.' " Leffingwell also instigated motion studies in the office. Complaining that "there has been very little real motion study done," he provided the new generation of office managers with information such as the amount of time that a proper typist should spend inserting paper into her machine (three-hundredths of a minute).[28]

Aside from bringing a modicum of order to the large office and increasing efficiency, the various schemes for dividing office tasks had two other important functions. One author described the effects possible in the accounting department: "Modern business methods have greatly systematized and simplified the work of the accounting department. Many of the complications and much of the elaboration of the old-time methods have been done away with, making most of the work of a clerical and mechanical character, requiring less expert bookkeeping and accounting."[29] As in the factory, scientific management in the office gave managers greater control over the work process itself and enabled them to replace relatively skilled workers with less skilled and therefore cheaper workers.[30]

At the same time that more openings were being created for low-paid (usually female) workers with minimal training, a small elite began to grow within the clerical ranks. This group, often but not always synonymous with middle management, included both managers of the newly distinct office departments and, increasingly, individuals with specialized training, possibly even at the college level. The distinction between bookkeepers and accountants provides the clearest example. "Accounting" and "accountant" had always had a more general sense than "bookkeeping" and "bookkeeper," implying an understanding not just of a firm's records but of the wider context for those books, both within the

28. W. H. Leffingwell, *Scientific Office Management* (Chicago: A. W. Shaw Co., 1917), pp. 94, 36, 130. See Harry Braverman, *Labor and Monopoly Capital: The Degradation of Work in the Twentieth Century* (New York: Monthly Review Press, 1974), pp. 306–311, for a discussion of the work of Leffingwell and Galloway.

29. Doubleday, *Accounting and Office Methods*, pp. 10–11.

30. See, for example, Daniel Nelson, *Managers and Workers: Origins of the New Factory System in the United States, 1880–1920* (Madison: University of Wisconsin Press, 1975), and David Montgomery, *The Fall of the House of Labor: The Workplace, the State and American Labor Activism, 1865–1925* (Cambridge: Cambridge University Press, 1987), chaps. 4 and 5.

firm and across firms. Managers at the top of the new business hierarchies required more than just copies of bookkeeping ledgers; they needed to receive an *analysis* of the contents of the books, a digested version of the business's transactions.[31] This contrast between bookkeeping records and accounting analysis is at the heart of the increasing differentiation between bookkeepers and accountants. By the end of the 1910s, one group, accountants, was firmly established as a profession within middle-management hierarchies. Bookkeepers, on the other hand, were equally firmly established as nonmanagement clerical workers.[32]

As the new clerical sector emerged, the combination of these changes in the content of the work, the feminization of some occupations, and the sheer growth in numbers, combined to create a three-tiered structure of workers within business offices. Near the top, just below corporate officers, sat the ranks of middle management, whose development Alfred Chandler has outlined so well.[33] Here were the office managers of various sorts, both general and in charge of the different departments of the business. These ranks included some accountants and other male clerical workers who had risen through the ranks. Below these middle managers lay those Chandler calls "lower management," a layer that began to overlap with the upper ranks of clerical employees, such as the skilled male bookkeepers. At the bottom of the hierarchy were the least skilled and most poorly remunerated workers, performing narrow and routinized tasks. By the 1910s women predominated in this bottom stratum of the office.

Within the nation's offices divisions between clerical workers on the basis of gender obscured the growing distance between middle-management positions and clerical positions. Businesses increasingly drew management personnel from colleges rather than from the ranks, while male and female clerical workers shared a common narrow, technical training for their jobs. Male clerical workers nonetheless continued to identify with the male managers above them rather than with their female co-workers, a tendency that was reinforced in at least two ways. First, prevailing ideas about men and women and their different roles in the work force prevented male clerical workers from regarding women as workers of equal standing. Male office workers, who considered their employment a lifelong undertaking, continued to hope for managerial or ownership positions, despite the diminution of their promotional oppor-

---

31. Chandler, *Visible Hand*, p. 109.
32. See DeVault, "Sons and Daughters of Labor," pp. 25–46.
33. Chandler, *Visible Hand*, pp. 381–414.

tunities. Women, isolated in single-sex job categories and generally not planning on long-term employment, identified with each other and with their family roles. Furthermore, the distinct labor markets faced by male and female clerical workers further reinforced their separate identities by insuring considerable wage differences. Thus, although men and women did share a number of common work experiences within corporate offices, they tended to view even their commonalities in divergent ways.

The clerical sector may have appeared monolithic in its growth, but it was actually deeply divided—by gender, by workers' expectations, by the work performed, and by the training necessary to perform it. Any attempts to understand how this new clerical sector fit into the overall structure of the work force—and people's experiences of that structure— must take into account not only these divisions within the nation's offices but also the ways in which they echoed, transformed, or reinforced divisions in the world beyond the office walls. In order to understand the significance of the collar line between white-collar and blue-collar occupations at the turn of the century, we must look beyond the new corporate structures and examine the wider social world that supplied the context and the opportunity for changes in the clerical work force. As offices grew and were reorganized, new institutions began to offer training for the new clerical jobs.

The School

"From inclination or necessity"

> In business, the evolution of new methods has exploded the old-time idea that the office was the place where the boy must obtain his elementary schooling for business pursuits.
> —*Shorthand World,* August 1895

Clerical workers in the United States had always needed a facility with the English language, including knowledge of business conventions of grammar and form. From an early time many office jobs also required more specific skills, such as bookkeeping. As long as the clerical work force was not expanding very rapidly, the requisite skills could be attained through a combination of grammar school education, a smattering of special classes, and on-the-job training in the form of informal apprenticeships. By the late nineteenth century, however, the demand for office workers began to exceed the ability of these limited means to provide appropriately trained workers. With the development of large corporate bureaucracies at the turn of the century, informal training became increasingly anachronistic.

In response to these job-market pressures, several interrelated forms of business education developed over the course of the nineteenth century. Private "business colleges" provided the most important means of instruction from the 1850s through the 1880s. By the 1890s public high schools across the country began to take over this role. These public programs often sought to emulate the success of the private business schools.

During the 1890s and early 1900s, hundreds of Pittsburgh's young people gained clerical skills in that city's public school system each year. Unlike many other high school programs around the country, however, by the 1890s Pittsburgh's program already had a long history. Established in 1868, the Pittsburgh high school's Commercial Department was one of the earliest public business programs in the nation. Janice Weiss has argued that these early programs developed in response to criticisms that a narrow focus on college preparation disqualified high schools from the support of general tax revenues. Commercial programs, then, were attempts to broaden the function and clientele of the high school.[1] The Pittsburgh program conforms to this model. Thus the Pittsburgh superintendent of schools described the goal of the public high school's Commercial Department in 1873: "The object of this Department is to prepare for business those who, from inclination or necessity, do not desire to take the Academical Course."[2]

The establishment of the Pittsburgh high school's Commercial Department, then, must be understood in the context of the development of the high school itself. The city's grammar schools had developed on a ward-by-ward basis during the 1830s. Although some citizens had opposed the imposition of taxes to support these schools, efforts to repeal school legislation were unsuccessful. By the 1840s Pittsburghers accepted the existence of the ward grammar schools. Some wards even established evening schools, and one school principal instituted a series of lectures for adults. The enthusiastic response to these lectures led to the creation of a committee to develop a proposal for a unified city school system that would include a high school.[3] The city held a referendum on the issue in 1849. Although some of the city's newer, largely working-class, wards voted in favor of the unified system, the proposal was defeated.[4] Dis-

1. Janice Harriet Weiss, "Educating for Clerical Work: A History of Commercial Education in the United States since 1850," thesis, Harvard Graduate School of Education, 1978, p. 95.

2. Pittsburgh Central Board of Education, *5th Annual Report of the Superintendent of Public Schools for the School Year Ending June 1, 1873* (Pittsburgh: Jackson & McEwen, 1874), p. 56. School board reports are hereafter cited as Pittsburgh Board of Education, *-th Annual Report* (year).

3. William D. McCoy, "Public Education in Pittsburgh, 1835–1950," *Western Pennsylvania Historical Magazine* 34 (1951), 220–221, 225.

4. [Pittsburgh] *Daily Gazette*, 6/6/1849, p. 3. Of the most heavily working-class wards, the 5th ward voted 65 percent in favor; the 9th ward, 93 percent in favor; the 8th ward, 45 percent in favor. On composition of wards, see Michael F. Holt, *Forging a Majority: The Formation of the Republican Party in Pittsburgh, 1848–1860* (New Haven: Yale University Press, 1969), pp. 320, 322. The 9th ward led the referendum move,

agreement over control of and taxation for the schools would continue throughout the nineteenth century.

When the state legislature passed an act establishing a unified city school system for Pittsburgh in 1855, one of the local papers editorialized: "That those who dread every improvement in our common schools that costs money should oppose the new law, was to be expected. They are opposed to all school laws, and public education." Nonetheless, without the hindrance of a popular referendum this time, the legislation established a Central Board of Education for Pittsburgh. This central board, made up of a representative from each of the ward, or subdistrict, boards, decided on textbooks, determined the number of teachers necessary in each of the subdistricts, and allocated salaries for those teachers. Ward-level school directors retained control of their local grammar schools, holding real estate and property for the schools and appointing teachers. Thus the act did not substantially change the grammar or common schools of Pittsburgh. The act did, however, add a citywide high school to the school system.[5]

The central board held its first organizational meeting in February 1855 and appointed a High School Committee in March. Throughout that summer the board members busied themselves with readying the high school, renting rooms in a downtown building and hiring a principal. During the month of August the principal and the president of the board toured eastern cities, gathering information on the organization of other high schools.[6] When the high school opened on Tuesday, September 25, 1855, one hundred fourteen students attended, instructed by the principal, two professors, and one "Female Assistant."[7] The Pittsburgh High School seemed to be off to a grand start, but the next few years would not proceed so smoothly.

Opposition to public high schools was common across the nation at this time. Opponents employed varied and often contradictory arguments. Andrew Burtt, a ward grammar school principal and well-known Pitts-

according to Marguerite Renner, "Who Will Teach? Changing Job Opportunity and Roles for Women in the Evolution of the Pittsburgh Public Schools, 1830–1900," diss., University of Pittsburgh, 1981, pp. 100–101.

5. [Pittsburgh] *Daily Morning Post*, 2/22/1855, p. 2. See chapter 5 for details on the functioning of local ward schools.

6. Pittsburgh Central Board of Education, Minutes, vol. A, 2/20/1855 (this and all other unpublished Pittsburgh school records cited are in the Archives of Industrial Society, Hillman Library, University of Pittsburgh); [Pittsburgh] *Daily Morning Post*, 3/14/1855; 6/22/1855; 7/24/1855; Pittsburgh, Central Board of Education, Minutes, vol. A, 8/21/1855, p. 27.

7. [Pittsburgh] *Daily Morning Post*, 9/26/1855.

burgh labor advocate, later claimed that the Pittsburgh High School resulted from a contest between the "friends of liberal common schools" and the "pernicious conservative element."[8] As another observer noted, "the experiment of establishing a High School in this city was, to a certain extent, hazardous. It was long opposed by a large class of influential citizens, who contended that the duty of the public was performed when it provided means for a simple elementary education."[9] Members of Pittsburgh's upper class, sending their own children to private academies, saw no need for a public high school. At the same time they could easily enlist some working-class support for their opposition by pointing to the increase in taxes necessary to support the school. Some workers equated public schools of any kind with "pauper schools," and believed that they provided education inferior to the private schools of the rich.[10] The high school's first graduation ceremony in 1859 gave fuel to the complaints. Two boys and one girl had successfully completed the high school's course. This meager turnout raised to new heights public doubts about the high school's worth.[11]

By 1869, however, the Pittsburgh superintendent of schools could report that "the Public School tax is coming to be considered, not an unnecessary burden, but a good investment." While the sheer passage of time and the continuance of the high school contributed in part to this change in opinion, the central board and the school administration also worked actively at "popularizing education." They argued that the public school system, with the high school as its crown, was not meant to educate a privileged elite, but "to fit every man [sic] for his chosen sphere of future action."[12] The development of business education within the school was closely linked to this goal.

The high school's curriculum always included some commercial subjects. When the school opened in 1855, bookkeeping was a required course for all students. In short order the board of education added penmanship to the course of study as well. For the 1856–57 school year,

8. Pittsburgh Board of Education, *3rd Annual Report* (1871), p. 44; on Burtt, see David Montgomery, *Beyond Equality: Labor and the Radical Republicans, 1862–1872* (New York: Vintage, 1967), pp. 389–392.

9. Pittsburgh Board of Education, *13th Annual Report* (1881), p. 53.

10. Renner, "Who Will Teach?" pp. 48–49, 81; Pittsburgh Board of Education, *1st Annual Report* (1869), p. 76; B. Jeannette Burrell and R. H. Eckelberry, in "The High School Controversy in the Post–Civil War Period: I. Political, Social, Moral, and Religious Arguments," *School Review* 42 (1934), 606–614, discuss how school legislation was often seen as "class" legislation—by both sides.

11. McCoy, "Public Education in Pittsburgh," p. 228.

12. Pittsburgh Board of Education, *1st Annual Report* (1869), pp. 8, 12.

the board's Committee on Studies and Textbooks presaged future developments by introducing the study of phonography (stenography) into the high school as well.[13]

During the high school's first decade, there were no other major additions or changes in the school's business offerings. There were, however, several changes of leadership for the high school. In 1858, Philotus Dean became the first principal of the school to remain in the post for more than two years. For the next thirteen years, Dean's educational philosophy guided the development of the high school. He repeatedly emphasized the importance of "extending the usefulness of the school." At the high school's semicentennial celebration in 1905, speakers praised Dean for his crucial role in shifting public opinion in favor of the high school.[14] It was during Dean's principalship that the Commercial Department was established as an entity in its own right.

Despite problems gaining public acceptance for the high school, the board of education did not take up the issue of expanding the school's program along more "practical" lines until 1868. On June 9, 1868, the board resolved "that the Committee on High School be authorized to confer with the Faculty on the expectency [sic] of incorporating Normal and Commercial Departments with the High School, and report at next meeting." The High School Committee at the time consisted of three members of the board: a hardware merchant and a physician, both of whom represented old wards in the central city, and John J. Covert, a druggist from the newly annexed Lawrenceville area. Covert gave the committee's report in favor of establishing the two programs at the July 14 board meeting. The board accepted the committee's recommendation and instructed the committee "to prepare details for the introduction of these departments and the necessary qualifications of students to be admitted to those branches."[15]

In late August the High School Committee presented its plans to the full board. Two separate "schools" would be set up under the auspices of the regular high school, a Normal School and a Commercial School. The

---

13. Pittsburgh Central Board of Education, Minutes, vol. A, 9/21/1855, p. 34; 10/9/1855, p. 44; 7/8/1856, p. 89. Stenography was not yet widely accepted as a business practice in the 1850s; see Ileen A. DeVault, "Sons and Daughters of Labor: Class and Clerical Work in Pittsburgh, 1870s–1910s," diss., Yale University, 1985, pp. 53–55.

14. Pittsburgh Board of Education, *1st Annual Report* (1869), Dean's appointment, p. 40; "extending the usefulness . . . ," p. 47; semicentennial, Pittsburgh Board of Education, *37th and 38th Annual Reports* (1905–6), p. 48.

15. Pittsburgh Central Board of Education, Minutes, vol. B, 6/9/1868, p. 138; 7/14/1868, p. 144.

Commercial School's course of study would include "Commercial Arithmetic, Bookkeeping, Business Forms, Commercial Law, Ethics, and Customs, and writings." The school would meet on weekdays like the regular high school, but its hours of instruction would be from 2:30 to 4:30 P.M. and from 7:00 to 9:00 P.M. For admittance into the daytime session of the program, students would have to "bring a certificate from the City Superintendent, of being of legal school age, and of graduation from the Grammar Department." The night sessions of the program would admit anyone at least twelve years old and with "a sufficient knowledge of reading, writing, the four fundamental rules of arithmetic, United States Money, Denominate Numbers, and Fractions." The professor of the department would examine candidates for admission, and students wishing to attend both sessions of the school had to obtain special permission. Pittsburgh residents could attend the program free of charge, while nonresidents would have to pay a twenty-dollar tuition fee. Diplomas would be awarded when the student passed "a thorough examination in the studies of the commercial course." The board passed the report unanimously and moved immediately to hire Robert Johnston, a bookkeeping instructor at the private Iron City Commercial College, as commercial professor.[16]

Several characteristics of the program merit specific attention. First, the department offered only business subjects. Its creators did not intend the Pittsburgh High School's Commercial Department to be an amalgam of classical academic subjects and business courses. In fact, as superintendent of schools George Luckey pointed out, "in the Commercial School the course of study embraces the same studies, to the same extent, as are pursued in the best Commercial Colleges." Like other public school experiments with commercial courses at the time, the Pittsburgh Board of Education hoped to copy the enrollment successes of contemporary private business colleges.[17]

Secondly, the hours of teaching in the department reveal the school's concern with serving a wider clientele. Unlike the Normal School established at the same time, which held courses concurrently with the academic portion of the high school, the Commercial School's hours were

16. Description of program and requirements, Pittsburgh Central Board of Education, Minutes, vol. B, 8/27/1868, pp. 154–155; Board passes report, p. 156, and hires Johnston, p. 157. Information on Johnston comes from the Pittsburgh City Directories for 1867–1870.

17. Pittsburgh Board of Education, *1st Annual Report* (1869), p. 47; Weiss, "Educating for Clerical Work," p. 101.

explicitly set outside the regular school session. The afternoon hours began immediately after the regular academic sessions ended, allowing students to follow the commercial course in addition to their academic studies. At the same time, these afternoon hours were clearly not meant solely for erstwhile academic students. For one thing, bookkeeping, penmanship, and phonography continued to be taught in the academic program as well, and by the Commercial Department faculty.[18] Academic students therefore had some opportunity to continue to gain business skills without enrolling in the new department. The Commercial School, after all, was designed to supplement, not supplant, the high school's regular offerings.

The program's entrance requirements reflect the import of its hours of instruction. Entrance into the academic course of the high school required both a diploma from one of the ward grammar schools and a stiff admissions examination, but students of the Commercial Department's afternoon program (as well as pupils in the Normal School) were not required to pass such an examination. Furthermore, the entrance requirements of the program's night sessions did not even include proof of grammar school graduation. Thus the public school increasingly came to resemble private business schools. Few private schools had either age requirements or academic standards; even the high school's nighttime Commercial School would have been comparable to the most rigorous private programs of the time.[19] As Principal Dean pointed out, the "department meets a great want of that extensive portion of our population which cannot attend day schools, or, at least, cannot pursue their complete list of studies."[20] Clearly, the Commercial Department's establishment was compatible with the board's attempts to broaden the public appeal of the high school.

Judging solely from the department's initial enrollment figures, the board had succeeded. During the program's first two years, 488 students enrolled in the classes of the Commercial Department; only 438 students attended the academic course during the same years. Both the Commercial Department and the academic program had low graduation rates. Eleven students graduated from the commercial course in 1869, and 20

18. For example, see Pittsburgh Central Board of Education, "Reports fr. the Principal of the H.S. to the Central Board of Education," vol. 1, November 1871, pp. 58–59, and July 1871, p. 50 (hereafter cited as Pittsburgh Central Board of Education, "Principal's Reports").

19. Weiss, "Educating for Clerical Work," pp. 25–26.

20. Pittsburgh Central Board of Education, "Principal's Reports," vol. 1, July 1871, p. 50.

more in 1870. (The academic program graduated only 24 and 29 students in these same years.) The early commercial students included 60 young women, 4 of whom graduated.[21] Unfortunately, published school records did not break down the department's enrollment according to afternoon or evening attendance, so it is impossible to speculate how many of the students could not attend the regular school.

The superintendent's annual report for 1870 does indicate the kinds of courses the students took. The report listed the 20 graduates of the program that year, along with the "studies named in [their] diploma[s]." All 20 graduates attended classes in writing, single-entry, and double-entry bookkeeping. Almost all took arithmetic, business forms, and "actual business." Other courses indicate the program's specialization; for example, 10 students took bank bookkeeping, while 13 enrolled in railroad bookkeeping, and 8 in forwarding. Only one student had phonography (shorthand) named in his diploma. This kind of specialization also reflected the practices of private business colleges, which would often personalize instruction to serve different students' career plans.[22]

That the Commercial Department's success was integral to the public acceptance of the high school as a whole is symbolized by the fact that 1868 witnessed both the inception of the department and the erection of a central high school building for the city of Pittsburgh. Thus the same High School Committee that established the commercial and normal departments quite literally laid the groundwork for the institution's permanent structure.[23] In his speech at the high school building's cornerstone ceremony in 1869, Principal Dean outlined his educational beliefs, declaring that

> the obtuseness of the lukewarm and the opposition of the hostile have not changed his conviction, that whatever is worth having at all is worth being made good; that the people's schools should be capable of imparting to the people's children that which is, in the world's estimate, an education; . . . that the people themselves, who must be educated by their own system, if at all, shall not be looked upon as a pariah caste in education, shut out from knowledge held only by a favored few; that the talented of the people shall have a chance of development in the people's own institutions.[24]

21. Pittsburgh Board of Education, *1st Annual Report* (1869), p. 71; *2nd Annual Report* (1870), p. 58; *14th Annual Report* (1882), p. 39.
22. Pittsburgh Board of Education, *2nd Annual Report* (1870), p. 57; Weiss, "Educating for Clerical Work," p. 29.
23. Pittsburgh Board of Education, *1st Annual Report* (1869), p. 77; *3rd Annual Report* (1871), pp. 20–21.
24. Pittsburgh Board of Education, *3rd Annual Report* (1871), pp. 26–27.

For Dean the Commercial Department was an important part of his overall vision for the high school. In his 1870 report he declared: "It is to be hoped that the advantages of a People's Commercial College, open on the same terms as a public school, will continue to be appreciated more and more by those who can give their children no higher education."[25]

Over the next two decades the Commercial Department faced many problems: the resignations or deaths of its strongest supporters, controversies over the program's hours and entrance requirements, overcrowding, difficulties in retaining qualified instructors. At the same time, however, changes made in these years reflected both educational developments and the transformation of the clerical sector itself. These changes remained at the core of the Commercial Department program into the twentieth century.

The first major modification in the program came in 1871, after the resignation of the department's instructor and the untimely death of Philotus Dean.[26] The new principal, Benjamin Cutler Jillson, proposed altering the schedule so that commercial classes would be offered from 8:45 A.M. to 2:30 P.M., at the same time as the academic classes. He argued that afternoon commercial classes "wasted" the rest of the day for the students.[27] Enrollment in the Commercial Department subsequently plummeted from 270 students in the 1869–70 school year to only 57 in 1871–72, and did not top 270 again until the 1890s.[28]

This change in the Commercial Department's hours of instruction marked a new era during which Jillson and a new professor of commercial science, Charles Cochran, shifted the program's concerns from serving the largest possible clientele to instituting higher standards. From the mid-1870s on, the high school itself was firmly established as a permanent institution in Pittsburgh, and its supporters and administrators no longer found it necessary to concern themselves with increasing enrollment.

Accordingly, at the beginning of the 1872–73 school year, Jillson, on behalf of Cochran, asked the board to establish entrance exams for commercial students. The exams would cover only arithmetic and spelling, but would be equal in rigor to the same exams for academic students.

25. Pittsburgh Board of Education, *2nd Annual Report* (1870), p. 58.

26. Pittsburgh Central Board of Education, Minutes, vol. B, 11/8/1870, p. 363; 1/10/1871, p. 377; 8/8/1871, p. 454.

27. Pittsburgh Board of Education, *4th Annual Report* (1872), p. 18. Evening sessions for the program disappeared sometime during the 1870–71 year, probably when Johnston fell ill.

28. Pittsburgh Board of Education, *6th Annual Report* (1874), pp. 26–27.

Cochran's request reflects a central concern of business educators at the time, many of whom attempted to respond to criticisms that their schools turned out substandard workers. While private business schools were often forced to concentrate on collecting as much tuition as possible, the public school system was free from the constraints of a profit-making enterprise. Cochran wanted more than filled classrooms; he wanted quality students and graduates. The board granted his request for the entrance examinations.[29]

While entrance exams for the Commercial Department persisted for the next three decades, one crucial difference distinguished them from the Academic Department's exams. The schools held entrance exams for the high school's academic course only once a year, limiting entrance into the program to the month of September. Entrance exams for the Commercial Department, however, were given on the first Monday of each month. Thus students could enter the Commercial Department at any time during the year, creating seasonal rises in enrollment. Time and again the Commercial Department admitted students who had failed the academic entrance exam.[30] While this practice appears to have increased the program's appeal for some students, it also helped create and sustain well into the twentieth century an image of second-class status for the program.

As participation in the Commercial Department decreased due to the new hours and the institution of entrance exams, Cochran set up the basic curriculum of the department, which held sway, with only minor changes in scale and scope, through the next quarter century. The program's combination of higher standards and attention to practical job-market needs ultimately overcame the forces diminishing its clientele.

Cochran divided the program's course of study into three separate "departments." Students spent their first three months in the Department of Theory, taking courses in bookkeeping, arithmetic, and if they wished, phonography. They attended lectures on commercial law, business customs, business ethics, and political economy. In addition, they received "Theoretical Training in Penmanship," with "black-board analysis and lectures." During their second three months, students continued with the same basic courses in the Intermediate Department. Commercial law focused on "Partnership and Agency" now, and lectures on business

29. Pittsburgh Central Board of Education, "Principal's Reports," vol. 1, September 1872, p. 81; Weiss, "Educating for Clerical Work," pp. 45–50; Pittsburgh Central Board of Education, Minutes, vol. C, 9/10/1872, p. 66.

30. Pittsburgh Central Board of Education, Minutes, vol. D, 7/8/1879, p. 241; Pittsburgh Central Board of Education, "Principal's Reports," vol. 2, September 1882, p. 98.

correspondence replaced business ethics. They also began to practice penmanship for themselves rather than listening to lectures and watching demonstrations.[31]

The pride of the program was the third department, the Department of Practice. For the four months they attended this department, students bent their efforts to the practical. "Commercial Calculations" replaced arithmetic; "Actual Business" bookkeeping provided students with "*real* transactions" to record. Even penmanship focused specifically on "Business Forms and Letter Writing." Crowning it all were the department's offices,

> furnished in first-class business style, viz: A Post Office, a Transportation Office, a Real Estate Office, the Wholesale and Importing Office of B. C. Jillson & Co., the Commission and Forwarding Office of C. C. Cochran & Co., and the Students National Bank. No student can receive the Diploma of this Department until he has remained the specified time in each of these Offices, and done satisfactory work therein.

Rather than simply studying books describing business activities, students actually replicated those activities. Once again, this was not an innovation of the public school program, but an imitation of private business schools, which often set up such "model businesses."[32]

In fact, Cochran's Commercial Department maintained a close relationship with at least one private business school. By 1874 the high school students carried on a "business correspondence" with the students of Packard's Business College in New York City. S. S. Packard's prominence in business education gives this development particular significance. Packard began his business education career as the principal of the seventh school in the large Bryant and Stratton chain, breaking off from the chain in 1867. In 1878 he became the first president of the Business Educators' Association (BEA). Throughout his career he remained concerned with public criticism of commercial education. Packard wanted to maintain high standards for both public and private commercial programs, but he also had a keen sense of the realities of clerical work. Unlike many other business educators, Packard acknowledged and ac-

31. Handbook of Pittsburgh schools appended to Pittsburgh Board of Education, *5th Annual Report* (1873), p. 11.

32. Handbook, Pittsburgh Board of Education, *5th Annual Report* (1873), p. 11; Pittsburgh Board of Education, *5th Annual Report* (1873), p. 56; Weiss, "Educating for Clerical Work," p. 23. Masculine pronouns from this and the following quotes are all from the original text.

cepted that the mission of the commercial schools was the training of clerical workers rather than business executives. In fact, his school had pioneered the typewriting and shorthand "amanuensis course."[33] The association of Cochran with Packard, both through the schools and within the BEA, reflects Cochran's emphasis on practicality and his attention to possible criticism.[34]

The Pittsburgh faculty continued to be very proud of their "department of actual business," and the superintendent's 1887 annual report included a detailed description of its operation. The high school program reflected two simultaneous trends in the economic world of the 1880s. Despite continued economic stagnation, many people experienced the 1880s as a relief from the devastation of the 1870s' depression. To them the decade appeared to offer new opportunities for independent entrepreneurs. In reality, corporate business structures were beginning to develop, increasing the number of clerical-level positions.[35]

These developments gave the Commercial Department two distinct goals. On the one hand, the department wanted to enable its students to establish businesses of their own. The ethos of the small business community permeated the program, and its transmittal constituted a not-so-hidden curriculum. The 1887 description of the "department of actual business" encapsulated this idea: "During the foregoing business career [in the department] the pupil has frequent opportunities to show his shrewdness. If he is thoughtful, capable and quick at seeing results he winds up business more than whole, otherwise he is invariably the loser."[36] On the other hand, the program also needed to prepare students for the growing numbers of jobs in business hierarchies. The Jobbing and Commission houses "employed" managers, cashiers, bookkeepers, and clerks; the banks were "officered with a president, cashier, paying and receiving tellers, discount clerk and messenger."[37]

The faculty of the commercial program managed to combine these two

33. Pittsburgh Board of Education, *6th Annual Report* (1874), p. 31; on Packard, see Benjamin R. Haynes and Harry P. Jackson, *A History of Business Education in the United States* (Cincinnati: South-Western, 1935), p. 29, and Weiss, "Educating for Clerical Work," pp. 50–52.

34. Cochran headed the shorthand section of the July 1885 BEA meeting. *Packards Short-hand Reporter and Amanuensis* 1 (August 1885), p. 242.

35. Alfred D. Chandler, Jr., *The Visible Hand: The Managerial Revolution in American Business* (Cambridge: Harvard University Press, 1977), p. 289; James Livingston, "The Social Analysis of Economic History and Theory: Conjectures on Late Nineteenth-Century American Development," *American Historical Review* 92 (1987), 72–75.

36. Pittsburgh Board of Education, *19th Annual Report* (1887), p. 20.

37. Pittsburgh Board of Education, *19th Annual Report* (1887), p. 18.

employment routes in their "practical" department. While maintaining an aura of emphasis on entrepreneurial skills, the program instilled a strong sense of the appropriateness of business hierarchies as well. Students began as mock capitalists, but ended up as office workers. The 1887 annual report describes this transformation:

> On entering this department of practice the pupil brings with him the marks received in his previous studies, the total of which constitutes his capital for business. . . . He makes the usual arrangements with the bank. . . . The next step is to . . . rent a store. . . . He next orders goods from the jobbing house, receives them through the transportation office and pays the freight. He is now fairly started in business and forthwith proceeds to sell, buy, make invoices, accept drafts, pay when due, give notes, take notes, pay taxes, advertise business, advertise for clerks, ship goods to commission house to be sold on his own account and risk, or on joint account, receives account of sales, draws for the net proceeds, and has the draft collected by his banker. . . . He is at times an individual dealer and several times in partnership—each time on a different plan. . . . If his work is satisfactory he is finally allowed to retire from business and take a position in the bank or jobbing house. He fills in succession every position in the various offices, and as business is on a much larger scale his business experience is greatly enlarged.[38]

After completing this course of action, the student was examined in nine topics. If successful in the examination, the student received a diploma from the Commercial Department.

As business bureaucracies became more firmly established over the course of the 1890s, and as increased initial capitalization requirements reduced small-business opportunities, the corresponding dual goals of the department, so prominent in the 1880s, merged almost imperceptibly. The program's rhetoric of the individual entrepreneur diminished as it found its niche in training workers for the middle and lower echelons of the office world. By 1897 the high school announced: "It is the aim of the department to give a thorough business training so that the graduate may not only be able to keep books and make out bills but may have facility in correspondence and a general knowledge of business laws and customs and laws of trade with the restrictions thereof." The program added typewriting to its curriculum in 1894, and though the subject was officially optional, everyone enrolled in it. The "Practical Department" still featured model cities and businesses, but it also included a "type-writing

38. Pittsburgh Board of Education, *19th Annual Report* (1887), pp. 19–20.

room" and an "office of expert accountant." While the department still wanted to provide "such training as will best and most immediately prepare [students] for business pursuits," the definition of "business pursuits" had changed to reflect economic reality.[39]

Despite the pronouns used in descriptions of the program, the Commercial Department also began to reflect (and to some extent to anticipate) another transformation underway in the clerical sector. As the number of women working in offices increased, so did their numbers in the high school program. Over the course of the 1880s, the number of women enrolled in the Commercial Department increased from 13 percent to 30 percent of the student body. However, the program's two-pronged approach in these years was less useful to young women than to young men. Women entering clerical occupations at the time rarely could aspire to running businesses. Since much of the final department's training was therefore irrelevant to their future work lives, fewer women than men graduated from the program.[40] Given the gender divergence in job opportunities, female students would find the department's early courses useful, but would not need the emphasis of the "department of actual business" on setting up partnerships or managing banks. This incipient gender differentiation reinforced the split goals of the early Commercial Department.

The number of young women entering the department doubled from 1894 to 1895, coincident with the introduction of typewriting into the curriculum. Women students outnumbered men for the first time in the entering class of 1899. Through the first decade of the twentieth century, female students consistently made up about half of the student body.[41] This influx of women reflects both the increased opportunities for women as clerical workers and the Commercial Department's clarified focus. As the department more exclusively emphasized training workers for business hierarchies, it became more appealing to the women who would fill the lowest rungs of those hierarchies.

Thus, despite many changes in the program, the Commercial Depart-

39. "It is the aim . . . ," Pittsburgh Central Board of Education, *Catalogue 1897–98*, p. 53; typewriting added, Pittsburgh Board of Education, *26th Annual Report* (1894), p. 2; all enrolled, Enrollment Records and Pittsburgh Board of Public Education, Central High School, Commercial Department Grade Books, vols. 1–7, 1884–91; description of "Practical Department," Pittsburgh Central Board of Education, *Catalogue 1897–98*, p. 57, and Pittsburgh Board of Education, *28th Annual Report* (1896), p. 23; "such training . . . ," Pittsburgh Central Board of Education, *Catalogue 1897–98*, p. 53.

40. Only 19 percent of the women in the program in the 1880s graduated, whereas 25 percent of the men did.

41. See the description of the 1890s' students later in this chapter.

ment remained pertinent enough to the office job market that overcrowding was a major problem from the 1870s on. After several temporary locations for the department, the central board in 1893 finally began to address permanent solutions to overcrowding.[42] The members of the board decided to erect a new high school building, to be used solely for the commercial and normal departments. The board purchased a lot for the school on Fifth Avenue, within a mile of the central business district, and selected an architect for the project. However, plans for the new building were soon embroiled in school-board politics.

The central board's Building Committee presented the plans for the new high school early in 1894. Original estimates had placed the building's cost at $150,000; now the chosen plan turned out to be a $400,000 proposition. Opposition to the plan erupted immediately. Some opponents objected to the manner in which the architect had been selected and to the inclusion of a large public auditorium and offices for the central board. The most sustained attack, however, came from residents of the city's South Side and East End. Led by the South Side Board of Trade, these groups argued that the money would be better spent on branch high schools in these neighborhoods far from the city center. Many of the outlying subdistrict school boards instructed their central board representatives to vote against the Fifth Avenue High School. At the board meeting called to discuss the issue, the Building Committee faced an unusually large audience. When committee members explained the history of the decision to build the new school, tracing the growth pattern of Normal and Commercial Department enrollments, the representative for the South Side Board of Trade agreed that the new building did have a justifiable and specific purpose. However, he argued that $400,000 was still too extravagant a price for housing the central board and "a couple of school departments," and he repeated his call for branch high schools. In this charged atmosphere, the central board voted to reconsider the high school plan at its next meeting.[43]

In the meantime, however, work had already begun at the Fifth Avenue site. Ultimately the storm over the new building died down, although virtually every step in its erection provoked dissent and discussion within

42. Pittsburgh Central Board of Education, Minutes, vol. C, 2/8/1876, p. 362; 7/13/1876, pp. 401–402, 404; Pittsburgh Board of Education, *14th Annual Report* (1882), p. 19; *17th Annual Report* (1885), p. 10; *21st Annual Report* (1889), p. 23; *26th Annual Report* (1894), p. 2.

43. [Pittsburgh] *Dispatch*, 3/14/1894, 3/17/1894, 3/18/1894, 3/29/1894, 4/4/1894; Pittsburgh Howard (16th-ward) Sub-District School Board, Minute Book, 4/6/1894; *Dispatch*, 4/11/1894. Also see chapter 5.

the central board.[44] The building, completed in April 1896, provided a permanent home for the Commercial Department. The Fifth Avenue High School's "more commodious and convenient quarters" seated over a thousand students. In 1900 Principal Wood reported that the Commercial Department's new accommodations had definitely affected its enrollment. Commercial students had previously made up 28 percent of the entire high school enrollment, a number that had dropped to 24 percent when the department moved to an unused grammar school. When the Fifth Avenue building opened, however, the percentage quickly rose to 33 percent.[45]

In 1870, the second year of its existence, the Commercial Department had boasted an enrollment of some 270 students. That figure was not topped until 1895. By the 1890s, however, no new crises within the Commercial Department or the high school as a whole led to any more precipitous drops in the student body. In September of 1905, Pittsburgh's Central Board of Education held a celebration of the high school's semi-centennial in the Fifth Avenue school building.[46] Like the high school itself, the Commercial Department was by then considered a permanent part of the city, contributing to its economic growth and well-being.

The Commercial Department was no longer the cutting edge of innovation for the high school. At the turn of the century, Pittsburgh educators directed their attention to "education of the masses," viewing their teaching staff as a "great standing army, of peace, maintained to fight foreignism, illiteracy and vice." They focused most of their effort on establishing evening and industrial trade schools for immigrants and manual workers. These were the programs of the hour throughout the United States, as historians of vocational education have noted.[47] By 1906 the Pittsburgh superintendent of schools expressed his concern that Pittsburgh was falling behind other communities in instituting such programs:

44. For example, see [Pittsburgh] *Dispatch*, 3/13/1895, for debate over what kind of blackboards to use.

45. Pittsburgh Board of Education, *28th Annual Report* (1896), p. 17; *32nd Annual Report* (1900), p. 46; *28th Annual Report* (1896), table B. The board also heeded the South Side's calls for its own high school, opening Pittsburgh's first branch high school in September 1898. South Side Commercial Department students spent their first year of commercial study in the South Side High School and then transferred to the Fifth Avenue building to complete the course. Pittsburgh Board of Education, *32nd Annual Report* (1900), p. 46.

46. Pittsburgh Board of Education, *37th and 38th Annual Reports* (1905–06), p. 48.

47. Pittsburgh Board of Education, *37th Annual Report* (1905), pp. 7, 8. See Paul Violas, *The Training of the Urban Working Class* (Chicago: Rand McNally, 1978), and David John Hogan, "Capitalism and Schooling: A History of the Political Economy of Education in Chicago, 1880–1930," diss., University of Illinois at Urbana-Champaign, 1978, among others.

6. Home of the Commercial Department: Fifth Avenue High School, Pittsburgh. From Pittsburgh School Board, *41st and 42nd Annual Report* (1909 and 1910), frontis.

> We are really behind our times in our recognition of the demands made upon us. . . . Flooded with foreigners, we have not equalled many other cities in efforts to assimilate them to our American civic ideals; the leader of the world in industrial activities, we do not lead in the hand and eye training of instruction; . . . having in our midst hundreds of day workers asking for night instruction we give, compared with other cities, very little attention to night schools.[48]

In the context of this new array of concerns, the Commercial Department played a unique role. Situated between the academic program, which catered to college-bound students, and the industrial education programs designed for the new immigrants, the Commercial Department attracted a middle group of students. The appeal of clerical work for

48. Pittsburgh Board of Education, *37th and 38th Annual Reports* (1905–06), p. 8.

young men and women from native-born and old-immigrant groups ensured that the program served a particular clientele.

When the Pittsburgh School District was reorganized in 1912, the high schools offered seven separate courses of study. The college preparatory, general, and technical courses all prepared pupils for further education; the commercial, arts and crafts, and sex-segregated industrial arts courses were designed as terminal education. With this array of options facing its pupils, the high school also established a Department of Vocational Guidance. The guidance staff initially focused on retaining students in the school system. Their research indicated the central role that the Commercial Department played in the high school. In a 1912 survey of 290 eighth-grade students who were not planning to go on to the high school, 42 percent of those who had chosen a vocation wanted to go into "Stenography, Bookkeeping and Office Work."[49]

The evening high school was designed to meet some of these students' needs. Opened in October 1907, it enrolled over 1,000 students during its first year. Commercial offerings dominated the evening program; in 1907 only English language classes had higher enrollments than did typing, shorthand, and bookkeeping. These topics continued to command "the greatest interest" in the evening schools. By 1913 over 2,000 students were enrolled in evening classes on commercial subjects.[50]

Without major curriculum changes or a great deal of discussion, Pittsburgh's Commercial Department fit easily into the new organization of the high school in the early twentieth century. Because the program had maintained a narrowly vocational nature from its inception, it conformed to the schemata of progressive education. At the same time the continued expansion of the clerical work force provided an enduring economic justification for the program. From its beginnings as an attempt to broaden the appeal of the high school, to its incorporation into the tiered structure of the twentieth-century school system, the Commercial Department trained workers for a business community in transition. An early emphasis on business law and partnerships had thus devolved into shorthand and typing for an increasingly female student body. Pittsburgh's education for clerical work was just that: an education for the economy's changing

49. Pittsburgh Board of Public Education, *1st Annual Report* (1912), p. 48; *2nd Annual Report* (1913), pp. 123, 128. See chapter 5 for discussion of the 1911 reorganization of the Pittsburgh school system.

50. Pittsburgh Board of Education, *39th and 40th Annual Reports* (1907–08), pp. 10, 52; Pittsburgh Board of Public Education, *1st Annual Report* (1912), p. 77; *2nd Annual Report* (1913), p. 113.

needs. This fact becomes even clearer when we look at the students who enrolled in the program.

Commercial Department enrollment records survive for the years 1890 through 1903. During this fourteen-year period over 3,000 students enrolled in the program. Who were these students? The following collective portrait is based on a sample of 1,844 of these individuals. A subsample of about 500 of the students found in the 1900 census provides information on their ethnicity and family structures.[51]

Despite the Commercial Department's careful curriculum planning, only 40 percent of its 1890–1903 entrants actually graduated; 60 percent dropped out after varying lengths of attendance.[52] Graduates actually outnumbered dropouts in the first six years of the fourteen-year period, making up 51 percent of these early students. In 1896 nongraduates took a substantial lead over the graduates and maintained that lead for the rest of the period.[53] This trend was consistent with ongoing changes in clerical education and within the clerical work force itself. The increase in the number of clerical positions in Pittsburgh over the course of the 1890s meant that a diploma from the Commercial Department became less important. Competing with students from private business schools offering short six-month courses and moving into increasingly specialized positions, students from the public school program had fewer reasons than ever for completing the entire course of study.[54]

Meanwhile, the feminization of the Commercial Department student body began to outstrip the incipient feminization of clerical work. During the fourteen years of the collective portrait, young women made up 43 percent of the department's student body, far in excess of their representation in Pittsburgh's clerical work force. From 1891 through 1898 men

51. See Appendix, Description of Data.

52. In general, graduation rates for students in the high school were not high. For example, in 1900, for all high school departments, 70 percent of the students returned the second year, 49 percent the third year, and only 36 percent eventually graduated. The low graduation rates for the Commercial Department thus were not unusual. (Pittsburgh Board of Education, *32nd Annual Report* [1900], p. 60). In chapter 6 the significance of graduation status is discussed in more detail.

53. If records were also available for the South Side High School's commercial course, the number of nongraduates after 1898 would be much higher. As it is, individuals who left the school system after their year in the South Side school never show up in the records. Even without this information nongraduates substantially outnumbered graduates of the Commercial Department at the turn of the century. The impact on future employment of both receiving a diploma and leaving the program without one is discussed in chapter 6.

54. See, for example, Jeannette Eaton and Bertha M. Stevens, *Commercial Work and Training for Girls* (New York: Macmillan, 1915), pp. 36–37.

outnumbered women in the high school program, with the ratio of women to men ranging from 3:7 to 4:6. The school year 1899–1900 was the first in which more women than men entered the department. The sex ratio then hovered around 1:1 for the remaining years up to 1903. In contrast, women made up only 13 percent of the city's clerical workers in 1890 and increased their participation to only 20 percent in 1900. The Commercial Department, then, was ahead of the workplace trend toward feminization. These figures are at least partially due to women's relatively shorter periods of participation in the labor force. More important, though, is the fact that the program provided an economical and respected vehicle for women to obtain clerical skills, consonant with many young women's ideas about both education and wage earning. In other words, women attending the program found what they wanted and needed to compete in the clerical job market. By providing the basic skills most in demand by the city's businesses, such as bookkeeping, stenography, and typewriting, the Commercial Department both foreshadowed and contributed to the further transformation of the clerical work force.

The most obvious difference between the young men and women in the Commercial Department lay in their prior educational experiences. In Pittsburgh, female adolescents faced two educational options: a nonvocational general education or a vocational education for teaching or clerical work. Academic high school programs, while providing a very small number of women with college preparatory education, served mainly to inculcate dominant cultural values into future wives and mothers.[55] While an academic degree did not automatically preclude employment as a teacher or as a clerical worker, the presence of specific programs for each of these occupations placed women from the academic program at a disadvantage in the job market. Without providing specific skills such as typewriting and bookkeeping, the academic program contributed little to young women's job-market value, since employers did not want to spend time training women they regarded as relatively short-term employees. Ten percent of the women in the sample transferred to the Commercial Department from the Academic Department, thus moving toward a narrower vocational application for their education. Another 10 percent transferred from the school's Normal Department. For this group the shift

55. Joseph F. Kett, *Rites of Passage: Adolescence in America, 1790 to the Present* (New York: Basic Books, 1977), p. 138. Popular fiction often ridiculed the idea of high school education for working-class girls. See [John Hay], *The Breadwinners* (New York: Harper, 1884), for an example of an upper-class author arguing that high school made working-class girls think they were "too good" for their class position.

represented a change in their specific job aspirations, but not in their general desire for waged employment.

Young men's educational options, like their wage-earning options, were both more varied and more ambiguous. The high school's academic program had two goals for its male students: to prepare them for higher education or to assist them in obtaining white-collar employment. The academic course might give a young man an edge over others in securing white-collar employment; some employers were quite willing to invest time and energy in training male employees, hoping to benefit from their more general education as well.[56] Young men in the Commercial Department, then, moved between that program and the academic program without necessarily changing their long-term goals. Fifteen percent of the program's male students transferred from the Academic Department. For these young men the Commercial Department represented one of several paths toward white-collar employment, while it involved a more specific and narrow choice for their female counterparts.

The Commercial Department's structure and curriculum thus sometimes mirrored and sometimes masked the different experiences of women and men both in offices and in the overall job market. The high enrollment level of women during the 1890s reflected the program's emphasis on training individuals for the middle to lower ranks of the office work force. The nativity of students enrolled in the Commercial Department in 1900 suggests that the program also served a middle group of the city's population. Almost half (49 percent) of the program's students were the native-born children of native-born parents. Children with foreign-born parents comprised the second largest group, with 42 percent. Foreign-born students made up only 6 percent of the student body, and 3 percent of the students were black. Compared to the population of the city as a whole, foreign residents were greatly underrepresented in the department, while Pittsburghers born in the United States were overrepresented (see table 2, columns 3 and 4).

Table 2 compares the commercial students' nativity with that of Pittsburgh's clerical workers in 1890, 1900, and 1910 (columns 1, 2, and 5). In 1900 the native-born children of native-born parents made up a smaller proportion of the student body than of clerical workers, even though this group was gaining within the clerical occupations. At the same time the

56. David B. Tyack, *The One Best System: A History of American Urban Education* (Cambridge: Harvard University Press, 1974), p. 58; Reed Ueda, "The High School and Social Mobility in a Streetcar Suburb: Somerville, Massachusetts, 1870–1910," *Journal of Interdisciplinary History* 14 (Spring 1984), 751–771; Kett, *Rites of Passage*, pp. 153–154.

Table 2. Nativity of clerical workers, Pittsburgh population, and students of the Commercial Department (percentages)

	(1) All clerical workers in Pittsburgh (1890)[a]	(2) All clerical workers in Pittsburgh (1900)[b]	(3) Population of Pittsburgh (1900)[b]	(4) Commercial Department students (1900)[c]	(5) All clerical workers in Pittsburgh (1910)[d]
Native-born, native-born parents	47%	51%	33%	49%	52%
Native-born, foreign-born parents	39	39	37	42	39
Foreign-born, foreign-born parents	13	10	25	6	8
Nonwhite	1	*	5	3	1

Sources:

a. U.S. *Census,* 1890, pt. II, table 118, pp. 712–713.

b. U.S. *Census Occupations,* 1900, table 43, pp. 682–683.

c. Record linkage of Commercial Department enrollment records with manuscript census. See Appendix: Description of Data.

d. U.S. *Census,* 1910, vol. 4, table VIII, pp. 591–592.

*Less than 0.5 percent.

proportion of native-born students of foreign parentage exceeded their representation in the clerical work force, while that of foreign-born students was actually less than their appearance in the city's offices. The Commercial Department students thus represented a middle portion of the population in terms of nativity, coming from neither the higher-status native-born group nor the lower-status foreign-born group at quite the expected levels.

The socioeconomic background of the school's students reinforces this picture. Table 3 depicts the distribution of students in nine basic economic categories.[57] Using guardians' occupations for all 1,844 students reveals that working-class parents (unskilled and skilled manual workers) made up 46 percent of the program's student body. If we examine only fathers' occupations, this predominance of working-class students becomes even clearer, with 19 percent of the fathers in the unskilled category and 35 percent in the skilled category, for a total of 54 percent.[58] Thus at least

57. See Appendix, Description of Data.

58. Female guardians make up most of the difference in the two sets of numbers; 70 percent of mothers listed as students' guardians fell into the "unknown" category. Virtually all of these women were widowed.

Table 3. Distribution of Commercial Department students by
guardians' occupations, 1890–1903

Occupational category	All guardians*		Fathers only	
	N	%	N	%
Unskilled	300	16	236	19
Skilled	549	30	449	35
Foremen	121	7	89	7
Public-service	53	3	37	3
White-collar	202	11	139	11
Proprietors	320	17	232	18
Professionals	52	3	32	3
Agricultural	4	**	3	**
Unknown	243	13	54	4
Total	1,844	100	1,271	100

Source: See Appendix: Description of Data.
*All individuals listed as "guardians" in the Commercial
Department records, including fathers, mothers, other rela-
tives, and nonrelated individuals.
**Less than 0.5 percent.

half of the Commercial Department's students came from working-class
families, a lower percentage than in the city's general population, as an
estimated 72 percent of Pittsburgh's male wage earners were of the
working class. But if the Commercial Department underrepresented the
working class as a whole, it had an extremely high level of skilled workers
among its clientele. Historians have found that about 19 percent of
Pittsburgh's men held skilled jobs at this time, compared to the 35 percent
of Commercial Department fathers.[59] The class makeup of the Commercial Department can also be compared with that of the high school's
academic program. In 1890, 46 percent of that program's students came
from manual workers' families, while 36 percent came from the ranks of
professionals and proprietors, a group making up only 20 percent of the
Commercial Department students.[60]

59. John Bodnar, Roger Simon, and Michael P. Weber, *Lives of Their Own: Blacks,
Italians, and Poles in Pittsburgh, 1900–1960* (Urbana: University of Illinois Press, 1982),
table 4, p. 64; from a 20 percent sample of the manuscript census for 1900. See also
Andrew Dawson, "The Paradox of Dynamic Technological Change and the Labor Aristocracy in the United States, 1880–1914," *Labor History* 20 (1979), 325–351.
60. Carolyn Schumacher, "Education and Social Mobility: Class and Occupation of
Nineteenth-Century High School Students," unpub. paper, University of Pittsburgh, 1970,
p. 5. Her figures are not exactly comparable to mine. She uses different occupational
groupings in addition to examining an earlier time.

The Commercial Department, then, did not precisely reflect the class background of all Pittsburgh's residents. The least advantaged members of the population, unskilled workers, were unlikely to have children attending the program. Home ownership figures for the students' families reinforce this impression. While only 26 percent of the city's population owned homes in 1900, 49 percent of the Commercial Department students' parents owned their residences in that year.[61] At the same time, the Commercial Department was not as elite an institution as the high school's Academic Department. However, the high representation of skilled workers' children suggests that the Commercial Department served an elite group within the working class itself. With stable employment and a sense of their own economic worth, these skilled workers took advantage of a high school education for their children. Specifically, they found in the Commercial Department a form of higher education which provided their children with specific and highly marketable skills for desirable jobs.

The Commercial Department can thus be seen as a site for the meeting of the two sides of the collar line. Focused on creating workers for the new white-collar jobs, the program's raw materials consisted of students from a range of economic backgrounds. Did the Commercial Department sharpen the collar line or blur it? Or create it? The meaning Commercial Department students might have invested in their education only gained significance in circumstances beyond the high school itself.

61. U.S. Department of Commerce, Census Office, *Twelfth Census of the United States, Taken in the Year 1900: Population, Part II*, vol. 2 (Washington, 1902), table 107, p. 709.

3 /

The Clerical Job Market
"Many workshops"

By the turn of the century, the Commercial Department had established itself within the Pittsburgh High School. However, high school attendance was still a relatively rare phenomenon; only about 5 percent of Pittsburgh's eligible teenagers attended public high school as late as 1910.[1] So how and why did the young men and women of the Commercial Department decide to attend the program? Since attending high school was both uncommon and involved delaying other, often remunerative, activities, a decision to attend the Commercial Department required looking carefully at the existing job market and clerical work's place within that job market. Each prospective student and his or her family had to decide if the benefits of future office employment outweighed the sacrifice of other options. In order to understand why different groups of students chose to attend the Commercial Department, we must attempt to recreate these decisions.

Though this type of historical decision-making process is often hard to uncover, clerical work is an ideal occupation to examine. Families—especially working-class families—did not necessarily sit down and make "career decisions," as we think of them today, with and for their children. Many, perhaps most, did not enjoy the material conditions necessary for such a luxury; others took for granted progressions within occupations or from one occupation to another. However, when a young person decided to seek office employment, it *was* a decision, since clerical work required specific "off-the-job" training. Thus, while it would be very difficult to

---

1. Lila Ver Planck North, "Pittsburgh Schools," in Paul Underwood Kellogg, ed., *The Pittsburgh District: Civic Frontage* (New York: Survey Associates, 1914), p. 295.

discuss, for example, individual or family "choices" to have young working-class men become common laborers, the movement of similarly placed young men into office work allows us to discuss, albeit gingerly, a range of conscious choices and decisions.

We cannot know exactly what information about the job market was available to Pittsburgh's young people and their families. But through family members, friends, and neighbors, as much as if not more than through the printed media, individuals gained a working knowledge of at least portions of the job market. These kinds of informal information networks passed along knowledge of objective conditions of various jobs. The information received was then filtered through people's various ideological assumptions.

Setting aside these caveats for the moment, it is possible to identify the main factors involved in a young person's choice of an occupation. Any individual considered jobs with both immediate and long-range objectives in mind. First, it was important to gain employment and contribute to the economy of one's family of origin.[2] But young people also held long-range objectives, assuming that they would eventually have their own families. Necessity forced many of them (even those aspiring to clerical employment) to focus principally on the first objective; immediate earning power, at almost any level, outweighed considerations of long-term benefits. Others enjoyed material conditions that allowed them to consider the second objective, participating in extended training in order to gain future benefits. For these the first objective became incidental, or, in some cases, at least temporarily irrelevant.

When either of these objectives was pursued, four kinds of considerations came into play. The first was the material benefits of a job—not only wages, but also working hours and other working conditions. These material benefits had both short- and long-term implications; beginning wages often varied widely from possible peak earning rates, and peak earnings were reached after differing intervals. Training was also a consideration: Was it required? How was it acquired? How did it affect the

2. Peter R. Shergold, *Working-Class Life: The "American Standard" in Comparative Perspective, 1899–1913* (Pittsburgh: University of Pittsburgh Press, 1982), assumes that children stop contributing to family income at twenty-one years of age (p. 80). Other recent research has found that while most people married in their early twenties, half remained single into their late twenties: John Modell, Frank F. Furstenberg, Jr., and Theodore Hershberg, "Social Change and Transitions to Adulthood in Historical Perspective," in Hershberg, ed., *Philadelphia: Work, Space, Family, and Group Experience in the Nineteenth Century: Essays toward an Interdisciplinary History of the City* (New York: Oxford University Press, 1981), p. 324.

course of earnings over time? A third consideration was promotional opportunities: Were low beginning wages or a long and possibly expensive training period eventually rewarded by compensatory remuneration of one sort or another? Finally, the status associated with various occupations also played a role in job decisions. People's perceptions of occupational status were influenced by the interplay of competing cultural values arising from class and ethnicity, as well as from the rapidly changing ideals of the dominant culture.

These considerations, however, provide only the barest outline of decisions involving job selection. All of them operated not only in conjunction with individuals' preferences and desires but also in the context of a gendered society. Two sets of issues need to be addressed here. First of all, men's and women's decisions were influenced by their very different expectations for their futures. While both young women and young men weighed decisions against their dreams for the future, those dreams rested on quite different projected family roles. Men and women, therefore, emphasized different considerations when making job choices. Although some women might not end up marrying, most young women assumed that they would. Because of this, they paid less attention to long-term wages and more attention to the often nebulous indicators of "respectability." To help a woman meet her long-term goals, a job needed either to preserve or to increase her marriage prospects. Young men's plans led in different directions. While they, too, paid attention to issues of status and propriety, their marriageability depended much more on their future earnings. Men's perceptions of their future familial role as primary breadwinner thus led them to focus more on long-term economic considerations when choosing occupations. Only by doing so would they prove themselves "worthy" of their "respectable" female counterparts.

The second set of issues that needs to be addressed is the sexual segregation of the turn-of-the-century job market: women and men simply did not face the same options in making job choices. This segregation in the work force was a result of both blatant employer discrimination and a complex of assumptions about men's and women's abilities, assumptions shared by most women and men, their employers, and their co-workers. Thus job options for women were extremely limited. Because of these and other differences, women's and men's job choices, and in particular their decisions to become clerical workers, must be examined separately.

In Pittsburgh as elsewhere in the country, women faced a labor market in which only a few jobs were open to them—jobs highly segregated by sex. Although domestic service and the needle trades remained the top two female occupations in 1900, a range of other industries and occupations employed over half of Pittsburgh's women workers.[3] Despite the city's reputation as a male-dominated bastion of heavy industry, increasing opportunities existed for women's wage earning. As Elizabeth Beardsley Butler reminded her readers in the introduction to her 1909 book, *Women and the Trades,*

> Pittsburgh is not only a great workshop, it is many workshops; and in these workshops women stand beside the men. . . . The influence of climate, the commercial wants of a rich producing district and the demands of a great laboring force as consumers, can readily be seen in tracing the development of the trades which employ [these women].[4]

In order to recreate the choices as perceived by young women preparing for clerical work, office jobs can be compared with the three other occupations most commonly held by sisters of the aspiring female clerical workers in the Commercial Department: sales, the needle trades, and teaching.[5] These three occupations were repeatedly mentioned in late-nineteenth-century discussions of the female jobs "replaced" by office work. They also illustrate the class nature of women's clerical work, since this constellation of occupations places clerical work firmly among working-class options, albeit among the most privileged and prestigious of those options. What benefits did office jobs provide relative to these other jobs?

During the 1890s women clerical workers in Pittsburgh received an average wage between $8.00 and $9.00 a week.[6] This general average,

3. U.S. Department of Commerce and Labor, Bureau of the Census, *Occupations at the Twelfth Census, 1900* (Washington, 1904), table 43, pp. 682–683. (Hereafter cited as U.S. *Census Occupations, 1900*).

4. Elizabeth Beardsley Butler, *Women and the Trades: Pittsburgh, 1907–1908* (1909; rpt. Pittsburgh: University of Pittsburgh Press, 1984), pp. 17–18.

5. Over two-thirds of the women entered these three occupations. Out of the total group of 261 sisters, 41 percent were employed in clerical occupations. See Appendix, Description of Data.

6. That is, $8.22. This estimate is derived from wages listed in Pennsylvania Secretary of Internal Affairs, *Annual Report of the Secretary of Internal Affairs of the Commonwealth of Pennsylvania,* pt. III, *Industrial Statistics, 1894,* sect. A, hereafter cited as Pennsylvania, *Industrial Statistics* (year); U.S. Bureau of Labor, *Work and Wages of Men, Women, and Children,* 11th Annual Report of the Commissioner of Labor, 1895–96 (Washington, 1897), hereafter cited as U.S., *Work and Wages;* and U.S. Bureau of Labor, *A Compilation of Wages in Commercial Countries from Official Sources,* 15th Annual Report of the Commissioner of Labor, 1900 (Washington, 1900), hereafter cited as U.S., *Wages in*

however, represents wide variations, both within and among specific occupations. In the mid-1890s the weekly wages of Pennsylvania's female "clerks" ranged from a minimum of $2.50 to a maximum of $12.00, averaging $6.92. Stenographers fared better, with a minimum of $5.00 a week, a maximum of $18.00, and an average of $9.55. Women hired as bookkeepers averaged less than stenographers ($9.08/week), but had within their ranks a highly paid minority who earned as much as $20.00 to $25.00 a week.[7] Working hours averaged 54 to 57 hours a week, or about 9¼ hours a day, 6 days a week. In general, 48-hour weeks were the shortest to be found.[8]

Both hours worked and wages received varied not only by job title, but also according to the nature of the employing business. Clerical workers usually worked during the same daytime hours that their employer's factory was operating or store was open; this was particularly true for clerks and bookkeepers whose work involved keeping track of production or sales. Furthermore, bookkeepers in particular often found "official" working hours deceptive, since, as one commented in 1894, "We are frequently kept at night when the ledgers are not in balance."[9] Stenographers and typists usually enjoyed shorter hours, more often working only 48 hours and rarely enduring the 60-hour weeks reported by some others. Presumably these clerical workers' shorter hours approximated "business hours" as we think of them today; their presence was necessary only when the employer was present, and they had no ledgers to balance at the end of the day.

Clerical work also provided fairly steady work for women wage earners. Both the 1890 and 1900 censuses reported that Pittsburgh's female clerical workers enjoyed lower rates of unemployment than did women wage earners in general. Fewer than 5 percent of women clerical workers were unemployed for some period of time in 1890; in 1900 this figure rose to 9.5 percent. The unemployment figures for all female wage earners were 10.5 percent in 1890 and almost 17 percent in 1900.[10]

Commercial Countries. See Ileen A. DeVault, "Sons and Daughters of Labor: Class and Clerical Work in Pittsburgh, 1870s–1910s," diss., Yale University, 1985, pp. 88–91. Elyce J. Rotella reached the same figure for 1890; Rotella, *From Home to Office: U.S. Women at Work, 1870–1930* (Ann Arbor: UMI Research Press, 1981), p. 199.

7. U.S., *Wages in Commercial Countries;* Pennsylvania, *Industrial Statistics* (1894); U.S., *Work and Wages.*

8. Pennsylvania, *Industrial Statistics* (1894), pp. A.134–135, A.88–91, 74–75; U.S., *Wages in Commercial Countries;* U.S., *Work and Wages.* See DeVault, "Sons and Daughters of Labor," pp. 91–92.

9. Pennsylvania, *Industrial Statistics* (1894), p. A.40, case no. 398.

10. U.S. Department of the Interior, Census Office, *Report on Population of the United States at the Eleventh Census: 1890,* pt. II (Washington, 1897), table 118, pp. 712–713

How did these material conditions of clerical work for Pittsburgh's female wage earners compare with other available employment? A fifth of the aspiring clerical workers' sisters worked as teachers in 1900. As early as 1885 proponents of office work for women proclaimed that stenography had become "the other thing" educated women could do besides teaching school.[11] What benefits accrued to Pittsburgh's teachers? Before 1905 wages for grammar school teachers in the city ranged from $300.00 to $650.00 for the school year. Paid over a 36-week session, these wages amounted to $8.33 a week and $18.06 a week, respectively. If averaged over a full 50-week working year, they fell to $6.00 and $13.00 a week.[12] The greatest disadvantage of teaching was not the salary, however, but the crowded conditions of the job market. According to the census Pittsburgh had 592 more female teachers in 1900 than in 1890. During the same decade the public high school's Normal Department produced 636 new graduates. These new graduates comprised only a portion of those competing for the city's teaching jobs.[13] Unemployment figures for teachers reflected this competitive job market. For both 1890 and 1900 the rate of unemployment for teachers out of work between 4 and 12 months exceeded that of all employed women in Pittsburgh. Teachers were also the only group of female workers to show a substantially larger number unemployed for 7 to 12 months than for 4 to 6 months.[14]

Saleswomen experienced a very different competitive situation. Almost a quarter of the aspiring clerical workers' sisters worked as saleswomen in 1900, compared to less than 7 percent of Pittsburgh's female work force. Unlike teaching, sales employment expanded rapidly at the turn of the century, as the mass production of consumer goods necessitated their mass distribution as well. By 1910 over 5,000 saleswomen sold a wide variety of products to the city's growing labor force.[15] Despite the season-

---

(hereafter cited as U.S. *Census*, 1890, pt. II); U.S. *Census Occupations*, 1900, table 43, pp. 682–683.

11. *Phonographic World* (hereafter cited as *PW*) 1 (October 1885), 27.

12. North, "Pittsburgh Schools," p. 269.

13. U.S. *Census*, 1890, pt. II, table 118, pp. 712–713; U.S. *Census Occupations*, 1900, table 43, pp. 682–683; Pittsburgh Board of Education, *32nd Annual Report* (1900), p. 58.

14. Teachers' unemployment for four to twelve months in 1890 and 1900 was 7.4 percent and 8.5 percent, respectively. For all women workers in Pittsburgh the equivalent figures were 4.8 percent and 7.9 percent. U.S. *Census*, 1890, pt. II, table 118, pp. 712–713; U.S. *Census Occupations*, 1900, table 43, pp. 682–683.

15. U.S. *Census*, 1910, vol. IV, table VIII, pp. 591–592; Harry Braverman, *Labor and Monopoly Capital: The Degradation of Work in the Twentieth Century* (New York: Monthly Review Press, 1974), p. 371; Susan Porter Benson, " 'The Clerking Sisterhood': Rationalization and the Work Culture of Saleswomen in American Department Stores, 1890–1960," *Radical America* 12 (March/April 1978), p. 42; Susan Porter Benson, *Counter*

ality of some sales positions, unemployment rates were relatively low, with only 8 percent of Pittsburgh's saleswomen reporting periods of unemployment in 1890, and only 13 percent in 1900.[16]

The image of retail work as cleaner and more "respectable" than factory work drew throngs of young women to apply for positions, thereby lowering wages. According to an 1894 study Pittsburgh saleswomen commonly received only $6.00 a week, though reported wages ranged between $2.00 and $20.00 a week.[17] When Butler surveyed female occupations in Pittsburgh in 1908, she found that almost three-quarters of Pittsburgh's saleswomen earned less than $7.00 a week.[18] Low wages were not the only problem facing the city's saleswomen, however. Responding to the state's 1894 survey, more saleswomen complained about their long hours than about any other issue. Almost 80 percent of them worked between 54 and 60 hours a week; during the Christmas season and January inventory, hours were even longer.[19] The converse of seasonally long hours, of course, was off-season short hours. Layoffs during the slow summer months were reportedly widespread.[20] Poor working conditions exacerbated the problem of long hours. All too often stores violated Pennsylvania's 1887 law requiring mercantile institutions to provide seats behind the counters for saleswomen.[21]

In 1888 *Phonographic World* heralded the impending replacement of "the ill-paid seamstress and the overworked shop-girl of former years" with stenographers and typewriters.[22] The needle trades were as common for clerical workers' sisters as were sales positions. Seamstresses, dressmakers, and milliners accounted for almost 24 percent of the Commercial Department students' sisters. Once again this percentage exceeded the prominence of the occupations in the city's female work force as a whole. Although the needle trades decreased in importance in the female job market over time, they remained a mainstay of women's employment.[23]

Cultures: Saleswomen, Managers, and Customers in American Department Stores, 1890–1940 (Urbana: University of Illinois Press, 1986), pp. 12–27.

16. U.S. *Census*, 1890, pt. II, table 118, pp. 712–713; U.S. *Census Occupations*, 1900, table 43, pp. 682–683.

17. Pennsylvania, *Industrial Statistics* (1894), pp. A.115–133.

18. Butler, *Women and the Trades*, p. 408.

19. Pennsylvania, *Industrial Statistics* (1894), pp. A.43, 46; Butler, *Women and the Trades*, p. 302.

20. U.S. *Census*, 1890, pt. II, table 118, pp. 712–713; U.S. *Census Occupations*, 1900, table 43, pp. 682–683; Pennsylvania, *Industrial Statistics* (1894), p. A.42.

21. Pennsylvania, *Industrial Statistics* (1894), p. A.4.

22. *PW* 3 (June 1888), 204.

23. Nineteen percent in 1890, 14 percent in 1900, 10 percent in 1910: U.S. *Census*, 1890, pt. II, table 118, pp. 712–713; U.S. *Census Occupations*, 1900, table 43, pp. 682–683; U.S. *Census*, 1910, vol. IV, table VIII, pp. 591–592.

Pittsburgh's needleworkers plied their trades in a variety of settings. Some, including those listed in the census as "tailoresses" and many of the dressmakers, worked out of their homes, providing custom-made clothing. Others worked in factories, ranging from large-scale "modern" concerns to the small "contract shops," which Butler found dominated by the newest immigrants. Still others performed piecework in their homes, while a few, such as those surveyed by the 1894 study, worked for the large department stores.[24]

In the 1890s female needleworkers, including dressmakers, seamstresses, milliners, and garment factory operatives, averaged about $6.00 a week in wages.[25] Butler found that Pittsburgh garment work was less seasonal than comparable work in East Coast cities, but the vagaries of fashion and climate still produced substantial periods of unemployment for the city's needleworkers.[26] In both 1890 and 1900 proportionally more needleworkers experienced some unemployment than did all female wage earners.[27] While they were employed, these women worked long hours nearly equal to those of the "overworked shop-girl," with an average of just over 58 hours weekly, or between 9 and 10 hours a day. By 1908 Butler could report that garment workers in factories worked 9 to 9½ hours a day at the longest, and that most had shorter hours; but her figures allowed neither for the women employed by the department stores, whose hours matched the torturous hours of saleswomen, nor for the home pieceworkers, whose hours stretched as far as their endurance lasted.[28]

Table 4 summarizes the objective conditions of these four occupations: clerical work, teaching, sales, and the needle trades. Teaching provided the highest wages, though teachers also experienced the highest levels of unemployment. Clerical wages and working conditions compared favorably to both sales work and the needle trades. Both clerical work and teaching required some sort of formal training before entering the job

24. Butler, *Women and the Trades*, p. 128. In 1910, 16.5 percent of the city's needleworkers worked in factories. U.S. *Census*, 1910, vol. IV, table VIII, pp. 591–592. (This breakdown was not given in censuses for earlier years.) Pennsylvania, *Industrial Statistics* (1894), pp. A.132–135; Butler, *Women and the Trades*, pp. 297–298, pp. 131–140.

25. Pennsylvania, *Industrial Statistics* (1894); U.S., *Wages in Commercial Countries;* U.S., *Work and Wages;* Butler, *Women and the Trades*, p. 409; U.S., *Work and Wages,* pp. 157, 292–293.

26. Butler, *Women and the Trades*, p. 122.

27. 1890: needle trades = 11.13 percent, all = 10.47 percent; 1900: needle trades = 21.29 percent, all = 16.85 percent. U.S. *Census*, 1890, pt. II, table 118, pp. 712–713; U.S. *Census Occupations*, 1900, table 43, pp. 682–683.

28. Pennsylvania, *Industrial Statistics* (1894); U.S., *Wages in Commercial Countries;* U.S., *Work and Wages;* Butler, *Women and the Trades*, p. 122.

Table 4. Working conditions and benefits for four female occupational groups in the 1890s

	Weekly wages[a]	Weekly hours[a]	Unemployment[b] 1890	Unemployment[b] 1900	Benefits/conditions[c]
Clerical workers	$8.00–9.00	54–57	5%	9%	Might be paid for
Clerks	6.92		4	7	vacations, ill-
Stenographers					ness
and typists	9.55		8	13	Safe, clean work-
Bookkeepers	9.08		5	9	ing conditions
Teachers	12.00	32.5	38	58	Summers off
	(50 wks.)	(school hrs.)			Crowded market
	16.67				Supervision of
	(36 wks.)				personal life
Saleswomen	6.00–7.00	58	8	13	Seasonal overtime and unemploy- ment
					Poor working con- ditions
Needle trades	6.00	58	11	21	Seasonal
Milliners	7.24		—	26	(Wide range of
Dressmakers	6.50		—	18	working condi-
Seamstresses	5.50		—	19	tions)
Factory					
operatives	4.84		—	—	

Sources:
a. Pennsylvania, *Industrial Statistics* (1894), section A; U.S. Bureau of Labor, *Work and Wages of Men, Women, and Children,* 11th Annual Report of the Commissioner of Labor, 1895–96 (Washington, 1897); and U.S. Bureau of Labor, *A Compilation of Wages in Commercial Countries from Official Sources,* 15th Annual Report of the Commissioner of Labor, 1900 (Washington, 1900). For saleswomen and the needle trades, also see Butler, *Women and the Trades,* pp. 408–409. For teachers' wages, North, ''Pittsburgh Schools,'' p. 269; Pittsburgh Board of Education, *37th–38th Annual Report* (1905–06), pp. 11–12.
b. U.S. *Census,* 1890, pt. II, table 118, pp. 712–713; U.S. *Census Occupations,* 1900, table 43, pp. 682–683.
c. See DeVault, ''Sons and Daughters of Labor,'' pp. 87–105.

market. In return for this investment in time, energy, and money, women in these jobs gained material benefits in terms of both wages and working conditions. Although average wages were not as high for clerical workers as for teachers, there were many more office jobs available, and office employment did not entail the level of community scrutiny attached to a public or parochial school position. Investment in clerical training pro- vided a more sure ''return.''

Young women's job choices were based on much more than material conditions, however. As opportunities for wage earning increased, ethnic

Table 5. Nativity of Pittsburgh's female labor force: 1890, 1900, 1910

	Native-born (native parents)	Native-born (foreign parents)	Foreign-born	Nonwhite
1890				
Total female work force	25.1%	36.5%	34.3%	4.1%
Clerical workers	40.3	51.1	8.3	.4
Teachers	47.6	44.9	6.8	.7
Saleswomen	35.2	54.7	10.0	.2
Needle trades	30.4	49.1	18.4	2.1
Servants	18.6	27.1	48.6	5.7
Female population	31.3	38.5	27.5	2.7
1900				
Total female work force	28.4	37.6	26.7	7.3
Clerical workers	50.1	42.5	6.9	.5
Teachers	46.5	45.5	7.5	.5
Saleswomen	35.3	51.5	13.0	.2
Needle trades	31.4	47.8	17.7	3.1
All manufacturing occupations	27.9	49.2	20.6	2.3
Servants	17.8	28.4	41.0	12.8
Female population	33.2	39.1	23.5	4.2
1910				
Total female work force	30.6	36.6	24.6	8.3
Clerical workers	50.7	43.5	5.5	.4
Teachers	49.0	41.1	9.4	.5
Saleswomen	37.8	50.4	11.2	.6
Needle trades	35.1	41.2	19.1	4.7
Servants	15.6	21.1	46.2	17.1
Female population	34.0	37.7	23.6	4.7

Sources: U.S. *Census*, 1890, pt. II, table 118, pp. 712–713.
U.S. *Census Occupations*, 1900, table 43, pp. 682–683.
U.S. *Census*, 1910, vol. IV, table VIII, pp. 591–592.

divisions contributed to and reinforced the hierarchy of desirability within the female job market. Table 5 illustrates these divisions. Immigrant women dominated the ranks of domestic servants and of specific manufacturing occupations, such as tenement cigar workers. Other manufacturing jobs drew most heavily upon native-born women with immigrant parents. Sales work also attracted women of foreign parentage, though native-born women with native-born parents were represented in this occupation beyond their proportion in the female work force as a whole. Teachers included almost equal proportions of native-born women with native-born and with foreign-born parents. The city's clerical workers were virtually all born in the United States; in 1900, 50 percent of them had American-born parents, while the parents of another 42 percent were immigrants, mostly of German and Irish stock.[29] These divisions developed out of a convoluted interaction of employers' prejudices and desires for malleable work forces and the preferences and prejudices of the women workers and their families.[30]

These ethnic variations highlight less tangible qualities: namely, the tensions inherent in the female labor market due to the widening economic and social gap between native-born or old-immigrant group workers and the city's new immigrants from southern and eastern Europe. The ethnic identifications associated with certain occupations encouraged native-born women and those from the old-immigrant groups from northern Europe to enter the labor force. Both clerical occupations and teaching provided waged work virtually untainted by any peer contact with the new immigrants.[31] Given the limited employment opportunities and crowded applicant pool of the teaching profession, the rapid growth of clerical work made it an ideal aim for young native-born women.

Several other qualities of clerical work also insured its respectable social status in the female working-class job market. The presence of a stenographer or typist in a working-class family reflected the family's material well-being. If not exactly the conspicuous consumption of the middle classes, it was a kind of "conspicuous employment," representing a family's investment in time, education, and accoutrements. Clerical work required above all else a specific and relatively high level of education. At a time when only a small portion of teenagers attended school after the eighth grade, sending a child to school beyond the compulsory age of fourteen suggested to friends and neighbors a secure and comfortable standard of living.[32] It demonstrated that a family could afford to forgo a daughter's household work and still take advantage of the ready-

29. U.S. Department of Commerce and Labor, Bureau of the Census, *Statistics of Women at Work* (Washington, 1907), table 28, pp. 286–289.

30. See Mary P. Ryan, *Womanhood in America: From Colonial Times to the Present*, 2d ed. (New York: New Viewpoints, 1979), pp. 120–121; Alice Kessler-Harris, *Out to Work: A History of Wage-Earning Women in the United States* (New York: Oxford University Press, 1982), pp. 137–138; introduction to Butler, *Women and the Trades*, by Maurine Weiner Greenwald, p. xvii.

31. Native-born women who were teachers came into contact with immigrants as their superiors, not as their peers.

32. Only 5.1 percent of eligible children in Pittsburgh were enrolled in public high schools in 1908. U.S. Immigration Commission, *The Children of Immigrants in Schools* (Washington, 1911), p. 9.

made clothes and store-bought foodstuffs becoming increasingly available at the turn of the century. The Commercial Department, furthermore, was not merely a "high school"; it trained young women for the top of the working-class female occupational hierarchy.[33]

Office employment required not only a high level of education but also a substantial investment in appropriate attire. A woman's tailored wool suit cost ten dollars in Pittsburgh in 1901—already equaling one-eighth of the average Pennsylvania family's clothing expenditure for that year.[34] Even if a working-class clerical worker kept her entire salary for herself, thereby eliminating the need to dip into family coffers to maintain her wardrobe, she still needed something to wear when applying for jobs. Over the years many women stenographers and their advocates would discuss what came to be known as "the clothes problem."[35] The problem had two parts. On the one hand, clerical workers were urged to dress up to their place in the business world. As one writer put it, "The business girl needs good quality, well-cut clothes, because it is part of her business capital to look her best." On the other hand, office workers were encouraged to look "businesslike" and to avoid conforming to every vagary of fashion. In 1900 a *Phonographic World* column (the "Fem-Sten's Retreat") contained an article reminding readers that their dress should be neither too "mannish" nor too "gay or showy."[36] Solutions to both sides of the "clothes problem" all required substantial material resources and therefore contributed to the "conspicuous employment" qualities of clerical work.[37]

The status implied by conspicuous employment not only played a role in women's decisions to enter the labor market, but also contributed to young women's dreams of their futures. While most female clerical workers evinced little interest in advancing into middle-management positions, clerical work did hold out the promise of a different sort of "promotional opportunity." Encouraged by rumor, fiction, and sugges-

33. Susan B. Carter and Mark Prus, "The Labor Market and the American High School Girl, 1890–1928," *Journal of Economic History* 42 (March 1982), 166.

34. *How to Become a Successful Stenographer: For the Young Woman Who Wants to Make Good* (N.p.: Stenographic Efficiency Bureau, Remington Typewriter Co., 1916), pp. 62, 65–66 (hereafter cited as *Successful Steno*); Shergold, *Working-Class Life*, table 44, p. 169, and table 56, p. 199.

35. *Successful Steno*, p. 62.

36. *Successful Steno*, p. 63; *PW* 15 (June 1900), 593. Not only the clerical workplace, but also the journey to that work required appropriate dress. Two young women told Butler that they preferred work in a neighborhood factory "because then they didn't have to wear hats as they would if they rode in the [street]car." Butler, *Women and the Trades*, p. 318.

37. *Successful Steno*, p. 64.

tive jokes, young women working in offices could always hope to marry the boss—or his dashing young son.[38] While these highest of hopes were rarely fulfilled in reality, office work did provide women with employment that, even if actual tasks were segregated by sex, did not isolate them entirely from male companionship. Fellow clerical workers, company sales personnel, and visiting businessmen all became part of an expanded pool of marital possibilities.[39]

Clerical work thus occupied a special position within Pittsburgh's female job market. Given such material considerations as wages, hours, seasonality, and working conditions, office work provided numerous advantages over other nonteaching female occupations. In the case of teaching, a tight job market often outweighed that occupation's benefits, whereas the growing need for clerical workers provided constant openings for qualified young women. At the same time, clerical work offered less tangible benefits of status. The conspicuous nature of the training and apparel necessary for entry into a clerical job reinforced ethnic divisions, within both the female job market itself and the city's working-class neighborhoods. Work in Pittsburgh's offices also held a special appeal to young working-class women, as popular fiction contributed to young women's fantasies of socializing with bankers and industrial magnates in downtown streets.

The task of comparing clerical work to other job opportunities is much trickier when men are considered, for no other reason than that men, even accounting for class and ethnic limitations, had a wider range of options before them. An examination of the brothers of male Commercial Department students in 1900 illustrates this problem. Their occupations ranged from laborers to sausage makers, wire winders, glassworkers, carpenters, draftsmen, machinists, tobacco dealers, dentists, brokers, and many others. However, when these occupations are classified according to skill, industry, and status, the most common of the brothers' nonclerical occupations fall into three groups. The first group consists of sales jobs— low-level white-collar positions with a social status roughly equivalent to that of clerical work. The second group contains skilled trades, which required an equal amount of training time as that devoted to formal education for office positions. The third group consists of those jobs

38. See, for example, the *National Labor Tribune,* hereafter cited as *NLT,* 8/3/1899, 4/20/1899, and *PW* 25 (1905).
39. See chapter 6.

whose very short training period matched low returns in both social status and wages. Laborers and unskilled or semiskilled factory workers make up this group. How did these jobs compare to clerical work?

Pittsburgh's male clerical workers earned about $15.00 a week at the turn of the century. As with women, however, wages varied among different clerical job categories. Clerks earned the least, averaging about $11.00 a week, though their earnings ranged from a low of $3.00 to a high of almost $29.00. Male stenographers also earned wages below the male clerical average, with an average compensation of $12.50. The range of stenographic pay was relatively small, from $10.00 to $15.00. The predominance of women stenographers affected these male wages, as did assumptions that while a man might begin his career as a stenographer, he would soon move on to other positions. Bookkeepers earned the highest salaries, with an average of over $19.00 a week and a range of $5.00 to $40.00 a week. The wide variations in earnings within occupational categories suggest changes over the course of a career. Beginning at fairly low wages, men planned on eventually earning $30.00 to $40.00 a week. These weekly wage figures equal an average annual salary of about $750.00, with potential peak earnings of $1,500.00 to $2,000.00.[40]

Male clerical workers could expect to work, on average, 56-hour weeks. As in the case of women, however, hours varied depending on the nature of the employing business. The most dramatic example of the correlation between production and clerical workers' hours comes from the steel industry. The Jones & Laughlin steel mill payrolls for the spring of 1900 report 69-hour weeks for clerks in the company's manufacturing departments. Similarly, in 1907 the Pittsburgh Survey found clerks sharing production workers' 12-hour "turns" in the mills.[41]

40. Wage figures derived from U.S., *Work and Wages;* U.S., *Wages in Commercial Countries;* U.S. Interstate Commerce Commission, *13th Annual Report on the Statistics of the Railways in the United States for the Year Ending June 30, 1900* (Washington, 1901), p. 39; U.S., *23rd Annual Report on the Statistics of the Railways in the United States for the Year Ending June 30, 1910* (Washington, 1912), p. 35; Jones and Laughlin Steel Corporation, Pittsburgh Works, Payroll and Tabulating Department, "Earning Records, 1862–1901," in the Archives of Industrial Society, Hillman Library, University of Pittsburgh; John A. Fitch, *The Steel Workers* (New York: Charities Publication Committee, 1910), "Wage Statistics of Representative Depts in a Typical Steel Company of Allegheny County, October 1, 1907," pp. 301–305. See DeVault, "Sons and Daughters of Labor," pp. 121–123.

41. Jones & Laughlin Steel Corporation, "Earning Records, 1862–1901," "Manufacturing Hands Time for April, 1900," and Fitch, *Steel Workers*, pp. 301–305. Also see Harry Henig, *The Brotherhood of Railway Clerks* (New York: Columbia University Press, 1937), pp. 22, 273.

Unemployment figures reported for male clerical workers in 1890 and 1900 compared quite favorably to overall male unemployment. In 1890, when over 22 percent of Pittsburgh's male work force was unemployed for some portion of the year, less than 5 percent of the city's male clerical workers experienced any unemployment. The figures were comparable in 1900, when almost 25 percent of the male work force and just over 32 percent of the men employed in "manufacturing and mechanical pursuits" were unemployed at some time: in contrast, just under 7.5 percent of male clerical workers were unemployed for some part of the year.[42]

Hours, wages, and unemployment were important considerations for young men entering the job market, but the possibility of a higher wage and position in the future was also crucial. A short story in Pittsburgh's working-class press began with the following mock job advertisement: "Wanted—A bright boy to begin at the bottom of the ladder in my office and gradually work up by his own conscientious efforts until I can take him into partnership and marry him to my only daughter."[43] And it was not only fiction that promulgated such dreams of success. Journals directed toward clerical workers assured their readers that advancement was not only possible, but forthcoming. "What gentleman engaged in the position of stenographer," asked one author, "does not look forward to the day when he will be the dictator, and someone else will be occupying the position he now occupies? . . . Not one per cent. of those who enter life as stenographers . . . ever continue in that field throughout life."[44]

The encouragement thus offered actually held out two possibilities for promotion. The most widely discussed was also the least likely: the young man's meteoric rise to partnership and wealth. Arguing against the effortlessness of fiction, serious proponents of this path emphasized skill and initiative, stating repeatedly that promotion comes from individual effort, not from any intrinsic qualities of one clerical occupation over another.[45] But less sensational goals also existed. In the course of a *Phonographic World* debate over the merits of business versus railroad office work, one of the railroad proponents pointed out that, in addition to promotional opportunities, railroad work assured the clerical worker of employment unaffected by business failures.[46] Especially for working-class youths,

42. U.S. *Census,* 1890, pt. II, table 118, pp. 712–713; U.S. *Census Occupations,* 1900, table 43, pp. 682–683.

43. "An 1897 Boy's Story," *NLT,* 4/7/1898.

44. *PW* 4 (March 1889), 145.

45. *PW* 4 (March 1889), 145; 4 (May 1889), 183; 25 (April 1905), 261–267; 25 (January 1905), 67; *Accountics* 1 (April 1897), 10–13.

46. *PW* 4 (June 1889), 215. The debate in *PW* ran from May through August 1889 (4:9–10–11–12, pp. 183, 215, 237, 277).

well aware of the vagaries of the economy, this kind of bureaucratic stability might be as attractive as the more sensational success stories.

The general availability of promotional opportunities is difficult to ascertain. For example, although the majority of railway officials in the late nineteenth century began their railroad employment in clerical and sales positions, as Stuart Morris has pointed out, "The number of higher executive positions relative to the total number of employees was never very high."[47] Some railroad clerks realized this. The *Locomotive Firemen's Magazine*, commenting in 1902 on the formation of the Brotherhood of Railway Clerks two years earlier, emphasized that some clerks had finally "realized that all clerks could not hope to be 'general managers' and most of them would spend their days trying to 'figure out' how a $40-salary can be made to pay the expenses of an American family."[48] This was true for virtually all office positions; as businesses elaborated office hierarchies, they created many more clerical than managerial positions. Nonetheless, for young men making initial job choices, rumors of sensational possibilities might easily outweigh less alluring realities.

The rumors and realities of clerical employment can best be understood in the context of a young man's entire array of options. For example, over 18 percent of the aspiring clerical workers' brothers held sales positions, well over the representation of sales workers in the work force as a whole.[49] The wages of Pittsburgh's salesmen varied greatly, from just $2.00 a week to over $40.00, due in large part to the different situations in which salesmen found themselves, and particularly considering whether they found themselves in retail or wholesale positions.[50]

In the 1890s the federal study on *Work and Wages* reported retail salesmen in Pennsylvania earning between $11.00 and $15.00 a week. A decade later the Pittsburgh Survey investigators found that department store salesmen usually began at wages between $8.00 and $12.00 a week, with the possibility of eventually rising to $18.00 to $25.00 with experience.[51] Despite their relatively low wages, Pittsburgh salesmen generally

---

47. Stuart Morris, "Stalled Professionalism: The Recruitment of Railway Officials in the United States, 1885–1940," *Business History Review* 47 (1973), quote p. 324, table 2, p. 323.

48. Quoted in Henig, *Brotherhood of Railway Clerks*, p. 11.

49. Salesmen made up about 3.5 percent of Pittsburgh's male work force in 1890, 1900, and 1910. U.S. *Census*, 1890, pt. II, table 118, pp. 712–713; U.S. *Census Occupations*, 1900, table 43, pp. 682–683; U.S. *Census*, 1910, vol. IV, table VIII, pp. 591–592.

50. U.S., *Wages in Commercial Countries;* U.S., *Work and Wages;* Meyer Bloomfield, ed., *Readings in Vocational Guidance* (Boston: Ginn, 1915), p. 527.

51. John R. Commons and William M. Leiserson, "Wage-Earners of Pittsburgh," in Paul Underwood Kellogg, ed., *Wage-Earning Pittsburgh* (New York: Survey Associates, 1914), p. 132.

enjoyed better working conditions than sales clerks elsewhere in the country. From the mid-1880s until 1905, many of the employees of Pittsburgh's larger stores belonged to one of the nation's few organizations of retail clerks, Salespeople's Local Assembly No. 4907 of the Knights of Labor. At its peak in 1902–03 the union signed agreements with twenty-five of the city's stores and represented some 1,200 members. Other stores improved their working conditions in order to stave off the union. The vast number and range of workplaces made it impossible for the union to set wages, so their contracts instead controlled working conditions (e.g., hours, overtime, meals), and maintained union shops.[52]

Retail work, however, did not provide men their only opportunity for sales employment. Salesmen for manufacturing firms earned considerably higher wages than their retail counterparts. For example, the *Work and Wages* study reported that the salesmen at one Pennsylvania sewing machine "agency" earned average salaries of $33.80 per week, while traveling salesmen for the same concern earned $27.50. Even more impressive were the salaries reported in a 1900 federal study. Examining the records of fourteen of the country's major corporations, the researchers found that these companies' traveling salesmen earned on average about $2,000.00 a year, or $40.00 a week. The minimum reported was $1,079.00 ($21.58 a week) and the maximum was $5,000.00 a year, or $100.00 a week.[53] In addition to higher wages, wholesale salesmen also enjoyed very different conditions from their retail brethren. Often paid on a commission basis, these men came closer to setting their own hours, though this did not necessarily mean that their hours were shorter. Of course, for traveling salesmen the benefits accruing to them from this flexibility might have been offset by the necessity for regular absences from their families.

More subtly than variations in wages and working conditions, differences in status separated retail and wholesale salesmen. Wholesale salesmen were closely attached to the office staff of manufacturing concerns and often included in the same lines of promotion.[54] Age and marital status also contributed to these subtle differences: salesmen in stores tended to be young (about 40 percent were under twenty-four years of age in both 1890 and 1900), and a majority of them were single; wholesale

52. Commons and Leiserson, "Wage-Earners of Pittsburgh," pp. 130–131. Neither the 1894 Pennsylvania, *Industrial Statistics,* report nor Butler's *Women and the Trades* give any indication that women sales clerks participated in this union.

53. U.S., *Work and Wages,* p. 509; U.S. Department of Labor, "Trusts and Industrial Combinations," Bulletin no. 29, by Jeremiah W. Jenks (Washington, 1900), p. 684.

54. For example, see Lee Galloway, *Office Management: Its Principles and Practice* (New York: Ronald, 1919), pp. 308–375; *PW* 15 (May 1900), 529.

salesmen were generally older and more likely to be married.[55] To some extent, then, the different sales occupations represented different life stages. However, the retail sales ranks did include older, married men as well. Sheer numbers worked against movement from retail to wholesale positions, since retail workers made up at least 80 percent of all Pittsburgh's salesmen. While some of these men eventually moved from retail into wholesale positions, others remained in an occupation dominated by men less encumbered by family responsibilities, a situation that worked to lower both wages and status. The long existence of the Knights of Labor Salespeople's Assembly also reflected this distinction in status; these retail clerks allied themselves firmly with Pittsburgh's working-class union traditions.

If some of the aspiring clerical workers' brothers thus invested white-collar jobs with working-class forms, others remained firmly within the working class proper. Over 28 percent of the brothers entered skilled trades. Of these, over 40 percent became machinists, 28 percent entered the building trades, and almost 22 percent became skilled workers in the iron and steel industry. All of these trades required a period of either formal apprenticeship or informal but extended training. The young men entering these occupations began with low wages and few skills, but counted on reaching the ultimate security provided by skilled trades. Table 6 illustrates the earnings possible for three of these skilled occupations: machinists, carpenters, and plumbers. Skilled occupations in the iron and steel industry are not included in the table because comparable data is not available; however, we do know that the most highly skilled workers in iron and steel, such as rollers and heaters, earned as much as $35.00 to $45.00 a week at the turn of the century.[56] The impact of unemployment on these workers is virtually impossible to estimate. For both 1890 and 1900 the census reports lumped together all iron and steel workers, combining skilled and unskilled, primary steel production, and fabrication workers. For this combined group over 42 percent experienced some unemployment during 1900. The furnaces and rolling mills that employed these workers rarely operated all year long.[57] Theoretical

55. U.S. *Census,* 1890, pt. II, table 118, pp. 712–713; U.S. *Census Occupations,* 1900, table 43, pp. 682–683. In 1900, 55.5 percent of the salesmen in stores were unmarried, while only 34.2 percent of commercial travelers were.

56. Jones and Laughlin Steel Corporation, "Earning Records, 1862–1901," maximum for heaters $42.00, for rollers $45.50; Fitch, *Steel Workers,* maximum for heaters $37.32, for rollers $44.58, pp. 301–305.

57. David Brody, *Steelworkers in America: The Nonunion Era* (New York: Harper & Row, 1969), pp. 39–40. Charles Gulick claimed that even in the "prosperous year" of 1910 it was probably impossible to work more than 45 weeks. Charles A. Gulick, Jr., *Labor*

Table 6. Annual earnings possible for three skilled occupations, Pittsburgh, 1890–1908

	Average weekly wages	Earnings for 52-week year	Portion of occupation unemployed 1–3 months	Earnings for 39-week year (3 months unemployed)
Machinists				
1890s[a]	$12.25	$ 637.00	8.7%[b]	$ 477.75
Prior to 1904[c]			9.0[d]	
Union scale				
Minimum	16.20	842.40		631.80
Maximum	21.60	1,123.20		842.40
1906[e]	18.49	961.48		721.11
Carpenters				
1890s[a]	16.74	870.48	14.8[b]	652.86
1890s[f]	18.79	977.08		732.81
1903 (union)[g]	21.00	1,092.00	18.3[d]	819.00
1906[e]	21.02	1,093.04		819.78
1907–08[c]				
Union scale	24.00	1,248.00		936.00
Nonunion	21.00	1,092.00		819.00
Plumbers				
1890s[a]	18.53	963.56	8.9[b]	722.67
1894 (union)[c]	21.00	1,092.00		819.00
1901 (union)[c]	24.00	1,248.00	9.0[d]	936.00
1907 (union)[c]	27.00	1,404.00		1,053.00

Sources:

a. U.S. Department of Labor, *Wages in the United States and Europe, 1870 to 1898,* Bulletin no. 18 (September 1898), pp. 678, 673, 681.

b. U.S. *Census,* 1890, pt. II, table 118, pp. 712–713.

c. Commons and Leiserson, "Wage Earners of Pittsburgh," pp. 140, 154, 162.

d. U.S. *Census Occupations,* 1900, table 43, pp. 680–681.

e. Shergold, *Working-Class Life,* pp. 46, 62.

f. Pennsylvania, *Industrial Statistics* (1894), p. B.3.

g. Pennsylvania, *Industrial Statistics* (1903), p. 469, returns from United Brotherhood of Carpenters and Joiners.

fifty-two-week earnings for these men reached $2,000.00 and over, but in fact many worked only half to three-quarters of the year, stripping even their gains down to $1,000.00 to $1,500.00. By the 1890s and early 1900s, these men also worked 12-hour shifts, while the other three skilled occupations had generally gained 8- or 9-hour days.[58]

All of these skilled trades required some sort of training period, though

Policy of the United States Steel Corporation (New York: Columbia University, 1924), p. 63. *NLT* paid constant attention to which mills were open or shut, and to the general market conditions for iron and steel.

58. Commons and Leiserson, "Wage-Earners of Pittsburgh," pp. 140, 146, 162.

not always a formal apprenticeship. In the iron and steel mills, both working-class traditions and employer policies encouraged a process whereby men worked their way up from unskilled to skilled positions. This process could take years, though gaining a position through relatives working at the same mill might speed it up some.[59] The other skilled occupations had more formal apprenticeships, though their actual operation depended on union strength in the particular trade. Plumbers and steamfitters maintained the strictest apprenticeships, ranging from three to five years in length. The 1907 union scale, for example, specified four classes of workers: the steamfitters themselves, earning $24.00 a week; "second men," young men in the last years of their apprenticeships, earning $16.50 a week; "experienced helpers," apprentices after their first three months at the trade, earning $13.50 a week; and "inexperienced helpers," who earned only $9.00 a week.[60]

Those in other trades, for various reasons, found it impossible to regulate apprenticeships so carefully. Carpentry apprenticeships supposedly took three years in the mid-1890s, but even then many carpenters never served any at all. On one hand, many young men picked up carpentry skills without formal training. On the other hand, mechanization continued to minimize skills by the turn of the century, and carpenters were increasingly required to do little more than assemble pieces produced in planing mills.[61] Machinists experienced the most dire consequences of the increased division of labor. Despite their growing numbers, by 1907 only about a third of Pittsburgh's machinists were "all-round" men able to operate a wide range of machines. The rest were "specialists," operating a single machine performing a single function. The all-round men, generally members of the machinists' union in Pittsburgh, still maintained formal apprenticeships and received the highest wages.[62]

In all these occupations, then, young men could expect to earn moderate wages during several years of training before achieving the high wages that accompanied fully skilled positions. Unlike the formal education required for clerical positions, training for skilled trades combined immediate earnings with the anticipation of future advancement.

59. Commons and Leiserson, "Wage-Earners of Pittsburgh," pp. 141–142; Fitch, *Steel Workers*, pp. 13, 141–142.

60. Pennsylvania, *Industrial Statistics* (1894), sect. B; Commons and Leiserson, "Wage-Earners of Pittsburgh," pp. 145, 163–164.

61. Pennsylvania, *Industrial Statistics* (1894), p. B.4; U.S. Department of Commerce and Labor, "Conditions of Entrance to the Principal Trades," Bulletin no. 67, by Walter E. Weyl and A. M. Sakolski (Washington, 1906), pp. 690, 694.

62. Commons and Leiserson, "Wage-Earners of Pittsburgh," pp. 140–141; U.S. Department of Commerce and Labor, "Conditions of Entrance," pp. 686–689.

Of course, many young men did not have the luxury of plotting a long-term strategy. Over a quarter of the aspiring clerical workers' brothers found employment as laborers or factory operatives. These jobs usually required no experience; starting wages equaled "peak" wages. Almost 17 percent of the brothers were listed as laborers in 1900. Some of these may in fact have been working in entry-level positions for the skilled trades. But others were concerned more with immediate employment than with future opportunities. Laborers earned between $7.00 and $12.00 a week, depending on the employing industry. Easy entrance created a highly competitive situation. The Pittsburgh Survey authors noted that a knowledge of English might earn a laborer two extra cents an hour, but for most of these jobs, language skills were extraneous. Many were hired by the day or by the hour as casual laborers; even the high unemployment figures given in the 1890 and 1900 censuses probably understate the tenuous nature of this type of employment.[63]

The almost 9 percent of the brothers employed in miscellaneous factory jobs worked in positions virtually unknown to their fathers, in the new world of semiskilled factory work. Pittsburgh businesses such as the Westinghouse electrical supply plants hired these young men at weekly wages between $9.00 and $12.00 a week. Though weekly wages barely differed from those for laboring jobs, factory employment provided more job security. These jobs also represented the city's expanding industries. While skilled trades declined in such traditional industries as iron and steel, and glass, the new factory jobs expanded.[64] They provided steady work to an increasing portion of the city's work force.

Faced with these and other options, then, the young men who chose to become clerical workers did so in the context of what are now familiar considerations: material conditions and benefits, training necessary, promotional opportunities, and status. As far as wages were concerned, even an average clerical salary outstripped possible earnings in retail sales and unskilled or semiskilled manual occupations. Peak wages in the skilled

63. Shergold, *Working-Class Life*, Appendix table 2, pp. 240–241; Commons and Leiserson, "Wage-Earners of Pittsburgh," pp. 119–121. In 1890, 27.47 percent of laborers were unemployed for one to twelve months; in 1900, 37.58 percent. U.S. *Census*, 1890, pt. II, table 118, pp. 712–713; U.S. *Census Occupations*, 1900, table 43, pp. 680–681.

64. U.S. Department of Commerce, Bureau of the Census, *Thirteenth Census of the United States, 1910: Manufactures, 1909, Reports by States, with Statistics for Principal Cities* (Washington, 1912), pp. 1106–1109; Commons and Leiserson, "Wage-Earners of Pittsburgh," p. 135; Glenn E. McLaughlin, *Growth of American Manufacturing Areas: A Comparative Analysis with Special Emphasis on Trends in the Pittsburgh District* (Pittsburgh: University of Pittsburgh, Bureau of Business Research, 1938), p. 195.

trades surpassed the clerical average, as did earnings in wholesale selling positions. For clerical workers, though, there was no clear apex of wage earning, no union scale to provide a wage ceiling. Maximum clerical salaries exceeded those of most skilled trades and equaled those at the very top, such as the iron and steel rollers and heaters. Furthermore, the stability of clerical employment might outweigh any wage discrepancies; unemployment rates for clerical workers were minuscule compared to those for industrial and sales workers. Clerical workers also enjoyed the best working conditions of all these occupations. Hours were generally shorter than those for sales or industrial workers, and the work environment was both cleaner and less dangerous than an industrial environment. Killing or maiming accidents were common in the city's mills and factories, and even escaping these, the manual worker often found himself discarded in old age, worn down by the constant strain of his work. Either way, the peak earnings of the skilled trades were often cut short.

Long-term opportunities were thus greatest in clerical work, though wholesale positions, often sharing the same promotional ladder and pool, were comparable. Skilled workers might hope to be self-employed some day, but even that was a more modest aim than the clerical worker's dream of commercial or financial greatness. And as mentioned before, even without such astounding success, the bureaucratic stability of employment in banks, railroads, and other large corporations outweighed the vagaries of industrial employment—accident, age, and technological obsolescence chief among them.

Considering the more immediate future, however, young men desiring clerical employment faced a crucial obstacle. Unlike the other occupations, office jobs could be obtained only after a course of formal and nonremunerative education. Would-be clerical workers had to gain one to three years of education beyond the eighth grade, common school, level. As was the case for women, young men were unlikely to extend their schooling in this way, and the decision to do so was a momentous one. The least skilled industrial jobs required little formal education of any kind; in an immigrant-laden city such as Pittsburgh, even English language skills were unnecessary. The skilled trades more often required, both through necessity and through proud working-class tradition, some formal education: reading, writing, and mathematical skills combined with those taught through trade apprenticeships. Sales positions, except in the most humble corner stores, also required certain English language and arithmetical skills, along with the social graces encompassed in "salesmanship."

Clerical work for Pittsburgh's young men involved many of the same social considerations as it did for women, and in fact afforded a similar social status. But while the idea of "conspicuous employment" may have operated in similar ways for both sexes, considerations of status played a somewhat different role in men's decisions than in women's. The social status of clerical work may well have played an important role in some young women's decisions to enter the labor market at all. However, young men did not face the decision whether to work for wages, and conspicuous employment was far less important than more material considerations in their decisions to seek clerical work.

At the same time, ambiguous (and often contradictory) distinctions between manual and nonmanual labor contributed to society's perceptions of the social status of office employment for men. North American culture had always fostered a schizophrenic view of manual labor. One set of traditions glorified those who worked with their hands and scorned those who didn't—lawyers, politicians, financiers. Certainly Pittsburgh's workers upheld a working-class version of this tradition in the late nineteenth century, basing trade union and political power on their belief that it was their labor which created the city's—and the nation's—wealth. However, even the city's "aristocracy" of skilled labor often tried to escape from the very work they glorified, becoming full-time unionists or politicians or, in the case of clerical training, seeking something "better" for their sons. Less skilled industrial workers found less to glorify in their work and more to gain from having their sons escape it.[65]

By the turn of the century, new ethnic divisions appeared within the male labor force as well, exacerbating social distinctions between occupations. The new immigrants from southern and eastern Europe filled the unskilled and semiskilled jobs created by technological innovations and by the further subdivision of labor in the skilled trades. John Fitch found the results of this in Pittsburgh steel mills in 1908: "Many American boys fancy that they degrade themselves by entering into competition with a

65. *NLT* for 1870s–90s; Francis G. Couvares, *The Remaking of Pittsburgh: Class and Culture in an Industrializing City, 1877–1919* (Albany: SUNY Press, 1984); Leon Fink, *Workingmen's Democracy: The Knights of Labor and American Politics* (Urbana: University of Illinois Press, 1983); Gregory S. Kealey, "Labour and Working-Class History in Canada: Prospects in the 1980s," *Labour/Le Travailleur* 7 (Spring 1981), 67–94; David Montgomery, "Labor and the Republic in Industrial America: 1860–1920," *Le Mouvement Sociale* 111 (April–June 1980), 201–215; Richard J. Oestreicher, "Industrialization, Class, and Competing Cultural Systems: Detroit Workers, 1875–1900," in Hartmut Keil and John B. Jentz, eds., *German Workers in Industrial Chicago, 1850–1910: A Comparative Perspective* (DeKalb: Northern Illinois University Press, 1983), pp. 52–69. Also see this text, chapters 4 and 5.

Table 7. Nativity of Pittsburgh's male labor force: 1890, 1900, 1910

	Native-born (native parents)	Native-born (foreign parents)	Foreign-born	Nonwhite
1890				
Total male work force	24.6%	27.4%	43.5%	4.5%
Clerical workers	48.5	37.4	13.4	.8
Salesmen (stores)	43.2	36.8	19.9	.1
Carpenters	41.7	23.7	33.9	.7
Machinists	32.9	30.3	36.6	.2
Laborers	11.8	19.0	62.3	6.9
Male population	30.7	35.7	30.2	3.4
1900				
Total male work force	26.4	27.9	38.9	6.8
Bookkeepers and accountants	53.6	34.6	11.6	.2
Salesmen	43.1	36.1	20.0	.7
Carpenters	46.3	24.4	28.3	1.0
Machinists	35.5	35.6	28.6	.3
Laborers	11.2	20.0	57.3	11.5
All manufacturing occupations	23.4	30.3	42.7	3.7
Male population	32.1	35.8	27.3	4.9
1910				
Total male work force	28.0	27.3	39.1	5.6
Bookkeepers and accountants	55.4	33.9	10.4	.3
Salesmen (stores)	44.8	33.1	21.6	.5
Carpenters	38.6	23.5	36.1	1.7
Machinists	30.2	32.9	36.5	.5
Laborers (blast furnaces, rolling mills)	6.6	14.6	76.2	2.6
Male population	32.0	34.1	28.9	5.0

Sources: U.S. *Census,* 1890, pt. II, table 118, pp. 712–713.
U.S. *Census Occupations,* 1900, table 43, pp. 682–683.
U.S. *Census,* 1910, vol. IV, table VIII, pp. 591–592.

Slav for a job. Accordingly, lacking experience and hence skill, they shut themselves out of the avenues of approach to the better mill positions."[66] Already by 1900, as table 7 illustrates, foreign-born workers made up 39 percent of Pittsburgh's male work force, while clerical, sales, and many skilled manual jobs were dominated by native-born men. Thus, just as the female labor market was stratified by nativity and ethnicity, so was the male labor market.

66. Fitch, *Steel Workers,* p. 145.

Like clerical work for women, clerical work for men also occupied a unique niche in the job market. While other available jobs provided either comparable material benefits or similar social status, clerical work seemed to provide it all. For young men who could afford to defer immediate earnings in order to gain the necessary training, the long-term material benefits of clerical work proved well worth the effort. In addition, just as it did for women, the social status of office employment also appealed to young native-born men.

Clerical work and its alternatives thus provided a range of material and social benefits. All young people took these into account to varying degrees as they faced decisions concerning their employment. But what about the students in the Commercial Department? How did these job-choice factors fit into their lives? The young men and women of the Commercial Department based their decisions on their knowledge of the labor market and working conditions. Their understanding of the significance of this information, however, was filtered through their families and their other experiences.

4 /

Families and the Collar Line
"The file clerk is just as essential"

Social mobility studies begin with the assumption that movement from any blue-collar job to any white-collar job represents unmitigated betterment of an individual's or generation's social status. These studies represent this movement across the collar line in a linear fashion, following the movement from fathers' occupations to sons'.[1] This is the basic method that Jürgen Kocka suggested historians could use to illuminate "the relevant lines of distinction, tension and conflict segmenting and dividing the emerging working class internally" and the "outer boundary" of that working class, the visibility and rigidity of "the distinction between workers and those who own and control."[2] However, the linearity of traditional social mobility studies conceals diversity among siblings within a single family and ignores altogether the significance of women's changing roles in the paid labor force.

By the 1890s and the early 1900s, we are no longer looking at an "emerging working class," but at an existing class undergoing rapid transformation. At this time clerical occupations formed an increasingly large social category positioned precisely between "workers and those

---

1. See, for example, Stephan Thernstrom, *The Other Bostonians: Poverty and Progress in the American Metropolis, 1880–1970* (Cambridge: Harvard University Press, 1973); Michael B. Katz, *The People of Hamilton, Canada West: Family and Class in a Mid-Nineteenth-Century City* (Cambridge: Harvard University Press, 1975); Clyde and Sally Griffen, *Natives and Newcomers: The Ordering of Opportunity in Mid-Nineteenth-Century Poughkeepsie* (Cambridge: Harvard University Press, 1978); Seymour Martin Lipset and Reinhard Bendix, *Social Mobility in Industrial Society* (Berkeley: University of California Press, 1959).

2. Jürgen Kocka, "The Study of Social Mobility and the Formation of the Working Class in the 19th Century," *Le Mouvement Sociale* 111 (April–June 1980), 107.

who own and control." Examining the occupations of all members of the families sending children to the Pittsburgh Commercial Department provides insight into both family strategies concerning education and the role played by clerical work in the families' economic and social situations. Within the families themselves we find a microcosm of the "internal divisions" and "outer boundaries" in the society at large.

The families of the Commercial Department students do not provide a picture of a sharp cleavage between white- and blue-collar occupations; rather, the members of these families are distributed on both sides of the collar line. The existing data allows examination of five different types of families. Social mobility studies would place two of these—those families headed by clerical and sales workers and those headed by proprietors—on the white-collar side of the scale. Unskilled and skilled manual workers would appear on the blue-collar side. The fifth group, made up of families headed by widows, is more ambiguous, since the absent fathers of these families could have been employed on either side of the collar line. All five types of families tended to have about four children living at home in 1900.[3]

A number of differences among these five types of families immediately become apparent. First of all, the children played different roles in different family economies. The two types of families in the most precarious financial positions, those of unskilled workers and widows, sent more of their children into the labor market than did the other families. In fact, fully half of the widows' children were employed in 1900, as opposed to 38.5 percent of unskilled workers' children. Thirty percent of skilled workers' children and 29 percent of proprietors' children worked in the labor market; only 24.8 percent of white-collar workers' children did the same.

The children in these families also demonstrated different patterns of job choices. Figure 1 portrays graphically the apportionment across the collar line of children's occupations for these five types of families. Since these are families of Commercial Department students, it is not surprising to find that a large portion of the children in every type of family found employment in clerical or sales positions. What is more startling—and more interesting for our purposes—is that the collar line runs through this generation in each type of family. Siblings gained employment on both

3. Unskilled manual workers' families and proprietors' families were the largest, with averages of 4.4 children, while widows' families and white-collar workers' families were smallest, with 4.0 and 4.1 children, respectively. Skilled manual workers' families averaged 4.2 children.

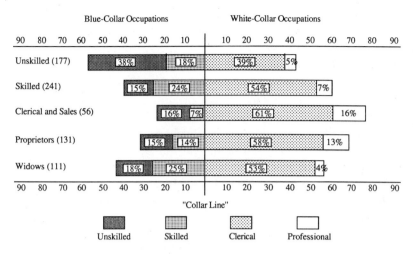

Percentage of children employed in different occupations in each type of family
Note: The number in parentheses is the number of employed children in each family type.

Figure 1. The collar line in five types of Commercial Department families, 1900

sides of the supposed social chasm between white-collar and blue-collar occupations. This suggests that the meaning of "social mobility" for the members of each of these families, families in which at least one child sought clerical training, is much more complex than simply "upward" or "downward." For these young people, the collar line began at home.

A more detailed examination of each of these five family types reveals the complex interaction between family organization around the collar line and more traditional indices of economic and social status. The following portraits explicate possible reasons individuals enrolled in Pittsburgh's Commercial Department and begin to suggest the sources of the ambiguous class position of clerical workers at the turn of the century. This ambiguity is apparent even in families whose parents were on the white-collar side of the collar line. We will begin with these families.

William A. Munson enrolled in the Commercial Department in 1900, at the age of sixteen. The oldest son of a native-born telegraph operator, he left the program in 1902 after attending for twenty months. In several ways William was typical of Commercial Department students from the families of white-collar clerical and sales workers. These families sent more boys than girls to the program, and their children of both sexes were more likely than average to leave school without graduating (see tables 8 and 9).[4] These and other characteristics suggest that white-collar parents responded to the Commercial Department's practical curriculum and at the same time tried to maintain "middle-class" standards.

These white-collar families present a more homogeneous class and ethnic identity than any other group in the program. Forty percent of these families had children employed in white-collar occupations and another 14.5 percent had children in professional positions. Only 16 percent of them had children employed in unskilled or skilled blue-collar occupations, a much lower rate of "collar-line crossing" than other occupational categories in the program. Not surprisingly, given the nativity of clerical workers in general, over 70 percent of these students were the native-born children of native-born parents (see table 10).

White-collar parents could judge the efficacy of the Commercial Department by comparing it against the realities of their own work lives. While 64 percent of the students from white-collar families never graduated from the program, that figure does not imply blanket criticism of its curriculum.[5] Understanding as they did the actual lines of promotion and opportunity within the city's offices, the business-ownership rhetoric of the program would have rung hollow for these white-collar parents and their children. They appreciated more the practical aspects of the curriculum, recognizing the importance of technical skills such as bookkeeping and accounting. Although the "self-paced" design of the program makes it difficult to determine exactly, many of the nongraduating students in this group, like William Munson, may have opted for skipping the "Actual Business" portion of the course, knowing that technical skills would serve them better in the work force than would pretending to be business partners and bank presidents. Furthermore, since their fathers already worked in office jobs, they had contacts for clerical jobs which might prove at least as useful—if not more useful—for gaining employment than a diploma from the Commercial Department.[6]

4. Young men made up 63 percent of Commercial Department students from white-collar families over the course of the 1890s, while men made up 57 percent overall. Only the small group of professionals' families had a higher percentage of men (65 percent). See table 8. Thirty-six percent of the children from white-collar families graduated from the program, 41 percent of all students. See table 9.

5. The only higher percentage of nongraduates was for children of professionals, 71.7 percent of whom did not graduate. A lot of these transferred into the Commercial Department from the Academic Department, so their failure to graduate probably means they transferred back.

6. Chapter 6 discusses this phenomenon from the vantage point of the eventual jobs these students held.

Table 8. Sex of students attending Commercial Department, 1890–1903, by parental occupation (absolute numbers and percentages)

	Unskilled		Skilled		Clerical and sales		Proprietors		Unknown*		Total**	
Male	296	58.7%	524	57.1%	222	63.1%	314	59.0%	192	46.0%	1,780	57.1%
Female	208	41.3	394	42.9	130	36.9	218	41.0	225	54.0	1,340	42.9
Total	504		918		352		532		417		3,120	

Notes: Weighted for sampling difference: women graduates = 1, others = 2. Two out of 18 (11.1 percent) of the valid cells have expected cell frequency less than 5.0. Minimum expected cell frequency = 3.006. Chi square = 32.86200 with 8 degrees of freedom. Significance = 0.0001. Cramer's V = 0.10263. Number of missing observations = 4.

*This category approximates the number of families headed by widows. Figures in text are those for families headed by the mother.

**This includes figures for categories not explicitly considered here. These include occupations as foremen ($N = 206$), in public service ($N = 92$), professional ($N = 92$), and agricultural ($N = 7$) occupations.

Table 9. Graduation status of Commercial Department students, 1890–1903, by parental occupation (absolute numbers and percentages)

	Unskilled		Skilled		Clerical and sales		Proprietors		Unknown*		Total**	
Graduate	224	44.6%	412	44.9%	128	36.2%	238	44.9%	137	32.9%	1,286	41.2%
Enrollee	278	55.4	506	55.1	226	63.8	292	55.1	280	67.1	1,832	58.8
Total	502		918		354		530		417		3,118	

Notes: Weighted for sampling difference: women graduates = 1, others = 2. Two out of 18 (11.1 percent) of the valid cells have expected cell frequency less than 5.0. Minimum expected cell frequency = 2.887. Chi square = 34.20943 with 8 degrees of freedom. Significance = 0.0000. Cramer's V = 0.10475.

*This category approximates the number of families headed by widows. Figures given in text are those for families headed by the mother.

**This includes figures for categories not explicitly considered here. These include occupations as foremen (N = 206), in public service (N = 92), professional (N = 92), and agricultural (N = 7) occupations.

Table 10. Nativity of students attending Commercial Department in 1900, by parental occupation (absolute numbers and percentages)

	Unskilled		Skilled		Clerical and sales		Proprietors		Unknown*		Total**	
Native-born, native-born parents	16	19.8%	84	51.5%	34	70.8%	51	58.0%	30	50.8%	247	48.7%
Native-born, foreign-born parents	47	58.0	75	46.0	9	18.8	27	30.7	29	49.2	214	42.4
Foreign-born	15	18.5	1	0.6	3	6.3	8	9.1	0	0.0	32	6.3
Black	3	3.7	3	1.8	2	4.2	2	2.3	0	0.0	14	2.8
Total	81		163		48		88		59		507	

Notes: Weighted for sampling difference: women graduates = 1, others = 2. Thirteen out of 32 (40.6 percent) of the valid cells have expected cell frequency less than 5.0. Minimum expected cell frequency = 0.442. Chi square = 96.76443 with 21 degrees of freedom. Significance = 0.0000. Cramer's V = 0.25223. Number of missing observations = 199.
*This category approximates the number of families headed by widows. Figures in text are those for families headed by the mother.
**Foremen (*N* = 35), public service (*N* = 17), and professional (*N* = 16) occupations not included here.

The proprietors who sent children to the Commercial Department must have had a very different reaction to the program's small-business rhetoric, though one no less bounded by their own experiences. Although the occupational group "proprietors" includes owners of a wide range of enterprises, Thomas Weist comes close to being a typical Commercial Department student from a proprietorial family. A first-generation German-American, Thomas's father, John M. Weist, owned and operated a small tobacco dealership. The shop was located on the ground floor of the multiunit building owned and inhabited by the Weist family in the city's 17th ward. Thomas enrolled in the Commercial Department in 1898 and graduated in 1901, after twenty-eight months in the program. He was the third child and second son in a family of six children. In 1900 his older brother, Edward, worked as a laborer in one of the neighborhood's iron foundries, and his older sister stayed at home without participating in wage earning of any kind. The three youngest children, ranging in age from six to fourteen, all attended school. By 1905 the Pittsburgh city directory listed John Weist as the owner of a "notions" store, rather than as a tobacconist. The image of the Weist establishment—a small storefront selling various items to the local ethnic neighbors—is representative of many other Commercial Department proprietors who owned corner groceries, saloons, tobacco shops, confectioneries, or notions or dry-goods stores.

In Pittsburgh as in other industrial cities, such small businesses had deep roots in their neighborhoods. These included economic ties with local customers and social connections based on the ethnicity and class origins of the shopkeepers.[7] The ethnic backgrounds of Commercial Department families reveal as much. Compared to other students in the program, proprietors' children were more likely to be of German (26 percent) or eastern or southern European (15 percent) heritage (see table 11). These figures reflect the established role of small businesses in serving ethnic communities, providing specialized consumer goods and service in a common language. Pittsburgh's retail shopkeepers also shared class ties with their customers. Children in proprietors' families, as the case of the Weist family demonstrates, worked at a range of occupations, depending on the variations in their financial circumstances and on their ties with different social groups. Almost 37 percent of the proprietors'

7. See, for example, Herbert G. Gutman, "Class, Status, and Community Power in Nineteenth-Century American Industrial Cities," in Gutman, *Work, Culture and Society in Industrializing America* (New York: Vintage, 1977), p. 257, on economic and social connections of shopkeepers in Paterson, New Jersey.

Table 11. Ethnic background of students attending Commercial Department in 1900, by parental occupation (absolute numbers and percentages)

	Unskilled		Skilled		Clerical and sales		Proprietors		Total*	
United States	21	22.6%	80	49.1%	29	63.0%	29	39.2%	191	42.7%
German	12	12.9	25	15.3	5	10.9	19	25.7	69	15.4
Irish	40	43.0	28	17.2	1	2.2	10	13.5	99	22.1
British	13	14.0	27	16.6	4	8.7	5	6.8	54	12.1
East and south European	6	6.5	1	0.6	4	8.7	11	14.9	28	6.3
Other	1	1.1	2	1.2	3	6.5	0	0.0	6	1.3
Total	93		163		46		74		447	

Notes: Weighted for sampling difference: women graduates = 1, others = 2. Thirty-one out of 54 (57.4 percent) of the valid cells have expected cell frequency less than 5.0. Minimum expected cell frequency = 0.013. Chi square = 125.42250 with 40 degrees of freedom. Significance = 0.0000. Cramer's V = 0.23689. Number of missing observations = 259.

*Foremen (N = 29), public service (N = 23), professional (N = 14), agricultural (N = 1), and unknown (N = 4) occupations not included here.

families had children employed in manual, working-class occupations, slightly more than did the skilled workers' families. Proprietors also had children in nonmanual occupations; 53 percent of the families had children in white-collar jobs, and 13 percent had children in professional positions. While the small businesses represented among the Commercial Department students often had close ties to working-class neighbors and customers, they also embodied petit-bourgeois notions of success through individual effort and independence.

For these families the Commercial Department's blend of practical clerical skills and small-business rhetoric spoke convincingly to their own needs. The proprietorial families sent young men and women to the school at a ratio equal to that of the program as a whole. While quite a few of the men transferred from the academic program (20 percent), not many of the women entered the Commercial Department from the Normal School (7 percent). These figures suggest that their parents were not interested in just any vocation for their children; Commercial Department skills were useful both in the wider job market and in the parents' businesses.[8] In addition, more of the proprietors' children than average remained in the program until they graduated.[9] For these students the "actual business" portion of the curriculum recreated and, for most of them, augmented their parents' experiences of buying, selling, renting, and hiring.

The students from families headed by clerical and sales workers or business proprietors, then, responded to the Commercial Department from the context of their parents' own varied experiences of the white-collar world, though other experiences surely must have come into play, including their own siblings' experiences in professions and in blue-collar jobs.

Traditional social mobility studies would place the families examined so far in the white-collar category. The next group, widows' families, would not appear in these studies at all, since most studies focus on male mobility patterns. The examination of widows' families explicitly introduces gender to the equation. Children from widows' families make up too large a group within the Commercial Department (14 percent) to ignore simply because no male head of household existed to attribute his occupational status to the family. This category includes families across

8. See chapter 6 on the different work experiences of proprietors' children.
9. Forty-five percent of these students received diplomas, compared to only 41 percent of the entire student body. See table 9.

the spectrum; some fathers had been white-collar workers, and others had been blue-collar.

Mary Ellen McCarthy's situation was typical of that of widows' children in the Commercial Department, sixty percent of whom were girls. Mary entered the program in 1899 and graduated in 1902. Her presence in the program, and the presence of other widows' daughters, suggests that young women were particularly attracted by the program's clearly vocational nature. Widows would view the training of the Commercial Department in a different light than other mothers; having experienced the transience of marriage and the economic trials of widowhood, they sought vocational skills for their daughters.

Rose McCarthy had not been a widow for long, her youngest child being only four years old in 1900. The oldest daughter, who was twenty-three, was "at home" that year, presumably having reached wage-earning age while her father was still alive. Although it is impossible to tell what role the father's death played in the decision to send Mary, the second daughter, to the Commercial Department, the program's training might have had new meaning to the recently widowed mother. While the census did not list Rose McCarthy as gainfully employed, widows generally participated in wage earning more often than other Commercial Department mothers.[10] Employed mothers worked at sewing or cleaning or kept boarders, none of which provided attractive options either in terms of wages or working conditions. The chance for one's daughter to gain office skills had dual significance for these widows. On one hand, of course, clerical daughters could eventually contribute more money to the family coffers. On the other hand, clerical training could also be a form of insurance, providing daughters with a means of self-support should they someday find themselves once again without male economic support.

Despite these concerns for their daughters' futures, the Commercial Department widows were generally not in desperate economic straits; such a situation would have required immediate employment by their daughters, not education for future employment. As with almost three-quarters of the Commercial Department widows, Mary's mother, Rose, owned the home the family lived in. Thus relieved of rent, and generally of mortgage payments as well, these widows relied on their oldest children to support the family—and to finance the education of younger sib-

10. Thirty-nine percent of the widows in the Commercial Department sample reported employment in the 1900 census, compared to 3 percent of all mothers (including the widows). In a comparative sample of families with teenagers in 1900, 21 percent of the widows and 4 percent of all mothers were employed. (See Appendix, Description of Data.)

lings.[11] Mary was the middle child of seven; two older brothers worked in 1900, one as a machinist and one as a clerical worker. Twenty-four percent of widows' families included children employed as unskilled workers, while 38 percent contained children in skilled positions, and almost 60 percent had white-collar workers in the family. In fact, reflecting their precarious financial position, widows' families were more likely to include wage-earning children than any other group.

These brief sketches of different types of families have illustrated some of the constellations of information young people brought with them to the Commercial Department. The varied economic and social backgrounds of these students affected the way they were likely to view clerical training and employment. Widows' daughters sought safeguards against sharing their mothers' precarious fates, while the sons of white-collar workers planned on following in their fathers' footsteps. The children of proprietors, both large and small, saw in their families' businesses practical applications of the Commercial Department's skills. The majority of the program's students, however, came from blue-collar working-class families. How did clerical education fit into their lives? In other words, what role did the collar line play in determining the "outer boundaries" and "internal divisions" of Pittsburgh's manual working class?

Charles Robert Hobson entered the Commercial Department in the fall of 1898. He was fifteen years old at the time and had graduated from Saint Paul's parochial school. His father, a laborer, had been born in England and emigrated to the United States in 1880 along with his wife and their three oldest sons. While Charles's grandparents had also been born in England, he had Irish great-grandparents. Charles himself was the first of the Hobson children born in the United States. By 1900 he had eight siblings: three older and two younger brothers, and three younger sisters. His maternal grandparents also lived with the family in their rented home in Pittsburgh's 6th ward. During his last year in the Commercial Department, four of Charles's brothers were employed. Of his three older brothers, one was a bookkeeper, one a railroad conductor, and one a day laborer like their father. One of Charles's younger brothers was also employed in 1900, as an office boy. His youngest siblings, ranging in age

---

11. Sixty percent of the widows owned their homes outright, whereas only 16 percent were paying off mortgages. In the comparative sample of families with teenaged children, 58 percent of the households headed by widows lived in rented homes. Almost 44 percent of the widows' Commercial Department students were the youngest children in their families.

from six to fifteen and including all three girls, were attending school. Charles left the Commercial Department without graduating at the end of the 1899–1900 school year.

Charles Hobson's classmates entering in 1898 included Mary Martha Sweeney, who also lived in a rented dwelling in one of the crowded downtown wards. Mary's father, Dennis, worked as a watchman. Though he had emigrated from Ireland in 1854 at the age of fourteen, by 1900 Dennis Sweeney was still not a U.S. citizen, though he had applied for citizenship. Mary was the only girl in the Sweeney family, though she had three older brothers and one younger brother. An aunt from Ireland also lived with the family. In 1900 Mary's father was unemployed for six months, and two of her three older brothers were also out of work for some part of the year. Her oldest brother, a theater usher, did not work for three months, while the next brother found employment as a day laborer for only one month of the year. Mary's third brother worked as a bartender throughout the year, while her younger brother, fourteen years old, neither attended school nor was employed. In 1901, at the age of eighteen, Mary Sweeney graduated from the Commercial Department.

In many ways Mary Sweeney and Charles Hobson represent the Commercial Department students from unskilled workers' families. Fifty-eight percent of these students, like Charles and Mary, were the native-born children of foreign-born parents (see table 10). Furthermore, most of those foreign-born parents were Irish or of Irish descent: over 40 percent of the students from unskilled workers' families were of Irish heritage (see table 11). Not surprisingly, then, the unskilled workers' children, like Charles Hobson, were more likely than others to enter the program after attending parochial schools. Almost 16 percent of unskilled workers' children came to the program from parochial schools, compared to just 8 percent of all students (see table 12). At least 35 percent of the Irish-American Commercial Department students had first attended the city's parochial schools.[12] The Irish fathers represented in the high school program, even those who had lived in the United States for some time, still found themselves at the turn of the century in occupations characterized by arduous labor, little skill, and low pay, as did Irishmen in Pittsburgh's work force as a whole.[13] The motivations of unskilled workers in

12. Some of these students transferred to the Commercial Department from other branches of high school. An indeterminate number of these probably attended parochial grammar schools earlier.

13. In 1890 Irish-born men made up 41.5 percent of Pittsburgh's laborers; in 1900 men of Irish parentage made up 26 percent of the city's laborers: U.S. Department of the

Table 12. Type of school previously attended by students enrolled in Commercial Department, 1890–1903, by parental occupation (absolute numbers and percentages)

	Unskilled		Skilled		Clerical and sales		Proprietors		Unknown*		Total**	
Ward grammar	341	67.9%	677	74.1%	255	72.0%	352	66.4%	265	64.2%	2,136	68.7%
South Side High School	25	5.0	33	3.6	13	3.7	14	2.6	13	3.1	116	3.7
Parochial	79	15.7	51	5.6	8	2.3	44	8.3	31	7.5	243	7.8
Normal Department	26	5.2	49	5.4	14	4.0	15	2.8	18	4.4	140	4.5
Academic Department	27	5.4	88	9.6	56	15.8	85	16.0	75	18.2	406	13.1
Other	4	0.8	16	1.8	8	2.3	20	3.8	11	2.7	67	2.2
Total	502		914		354		530		413		3,108	

Notes: Weighted for sampling difference: women graduates = 1, others = 2. Thirteen out of 54 (24.1 percent) of the valid cells have expected cell frequency less than 5.0. Minimum expected cell frequency = 0.151. Chi square = 249.10341 with 40 degrees of freedom. Significance = 0.0000. Cramer's V = 0.12661. Number of missing observations = 16.

*This category approximates the number of families headed by widows. Figures in text are those for families headed by the mother.

**Foremen (N = 206), public service (N = 90), professional (N = 92), and agricultural occupations not included here.

sending their children to the Commercial Department become clearer when considering these dynamics of ethnicity and economic status.

Unskilled workers would have viewed clerical training and ultimate office employment for their children as an avenue of escape from the narrowed choices of poverty. Economic necessity surely would have influenced their decisions. On one hand, these families often needed the immediate earnings of children for the family to survive. On the other hand, clerical work represented a leap in social status impossible for the heads of these families. With upward advancement cut off or halted for unskilled fathers, they strove to gain such upward mobility for their children.

Over half of the unskilled workers whose children attended the Commercial Department were listed in the school records as laborers. The others worked at a range of unskilled occupations, from teamsters and drivers to mill workers and unskilled factory workers. In good times unskilled workers such as these generally earned between $7.00 and $12.00 a week in Pittsburgh.[14] During the depression of the 1890s, these wages dropped and unemployment soared. The same decade also marked the first appearance of substantial numbers of southern and eastern European immigrants in the city. By the turn of the century, observers such as the investigators for the Pittsburgh Survey focused their attention on these groups.[15] The new-immigrant unskilled workers had become a "social problem" and therefore a target of investigation. While those investigations have proved crucial in understanding the dynamics of immigration and industrial change, they provide little insight into the Commercial

Interior, Census Office, *Report on Population of the United States at the Eleventh Census: 1890*, pt. II (Washington, 1897), table 118, pp. 712–713; U.S. Department of Commerce and Labor, Bureau of the Census, *Special Reports: Occupations at the Twelfth Census, 1900* (Washington, 1904), table 43, pp. 680–681. Also, see David N. Doyle, "Unestablished Irishmen: New Immigrants and Industrial America, 1870–1910," in Dirk Hoerder, ed., *American Labor and Immigration History, 1877–1920s: Recent European Research* (Urbana: University of Illinois Press, 1983), p. 195.

14. Peter R. Shergold, *Working-Class Life: The "American Standard" in Comparative Perspective, 1899–1913* (Pittsburgh: University of Pittsburgh Press, 1982), pp. 240–241.

15. See, for example, the following sections from Pittsburgh Survey volumes: Margaret Byington, *Homestead: The Households of a Mill Town* (1910; rpt. Pittsburgh: Center for International Studies, University of Pittsburgh, 1974), pp. 131–168; John A. Fitch, *The Steel Workers* (New York: Charities Publication Committee, 1910), pp. 140–149; Paul Underwood Kellogg, ed., *The Pittsburgh District: Civic Frontage* (New York: Survey Associates, 1914), pp. 3, 98–103, and throughout; Paul Underwood Kellogg, ed., *Wage-Earning Pittsburgh* (New York: Survey Associates, 1914), pp. 33–95; Elizabeth Beardsley Butler, *Women and the Trades: Pittsburgh, 1907–1908* (1909; rpt. Pittsburgh: University of Pittsburgh Press, 1984), pp. 20–26.

Department students. Only 6.5 percent of the students from unskilled workers' families came from eastern or southern European backgrounds; 23 percent had native-born parents or grandparents, and 70 percent were of Irish, German, or British (including Scotch and Welsh) heritage (see table 11). These were not the "problematic" unskilled workers upon whom settlement house workers expended their energy; rather, they were a forgotten strata of the work force, relatively privileged vis-à-vis many other unskilled workers but definitely less well-off than the city's skilled workers.[16]

Information on sibling employment bears testimony to the intermediate situation of Commercial Department students from unskilled workers' families. Even though they could afford to send one child to the high school, families like the Hobsons and the Sweeneys needed the immediate earnings of other children to finance the undertaking. Like widows' children, siblings of these students were more likely to be employed in wage-earning capacities than siblings of other students. Furthermore, as figure 1 demonstrates, more of the unskilled workers' family members worked at blue-collar jobs than at white-collar jobs, the only group in the Commercial Department sample for which this was true. Forty-two percent of these families included children working in unskilled or semi-skilled jobs, and over a quarter of the families had children in skilled trades. At least one child held a clerical or sales job in 44 percent of these families. The family members sent to the Commercial Department were unlikely to be the oldest or second-oldest children in the family. As in both the Hobson and the Sweeney families, the earnings of older siblings helped support younger children's education.

Home ownership patterns illustrate the impact of ethnicity on the economic circumstances of these unskilled workers. Stephan Thernstrom has argued that the "land hunger" of Irish immigrants often stood in the way of their children's upward occupational mobility.[17] Irish families represented in the Commercial Department, however, successfully combined both goals. While over half of the unskilled workers' families represented in the Commercial Department rented their residences, sixty-two percent of the Irish families owned their homes, and over two-fifths of them had no outstanding mortgages. In contrast, three-fourths of the Irish

16. Shergold, *Working-Class Life*, pp. 225–227; he, too, focuses on the new immigrants. The Pittsburgh Survey volumes cited in note 15 exemplify the contemporary concern with the new immigrants.

17. Stephan Thernstrom, *Poverty and Progress: Social Mobility in a Nineteenth-Century City* (New York: Atheneum, 1975), p. 156.

families in a comparative sample of households containing teenagers in 1900 rented their homes.[18] Commercial Department families, then, were a relatively elite group within their communities, both as Irish-Americans and as unskilled workers.

Mary Sweeney graduated from the Commercial Department in 1901 despite the unemployment of other family members, while Charles Hobson, enjoying a more stable family economy, failed to graduate. Mary and Charles shared a common Irish heritage, both with each other and with almost half of the other unskilled workers' children in the Commercial Department. This ethnic heritage influenced the kinds of decisions they made, but only within a context of the general economic background they shared with all the students from unskilled workers' families.

While the Commercial Department's unskilled Irish families illustrate a numerically important group, a similar confluence of ethnicity and economic characteristics shows up in one of the school's smallest groups as well. Blacks made up only 3 percent of the Commercial Department's students. Over the fourteen-year span of the enrollment records, eight students' records included the notation "Colored," but these eight individuals were not the only black students in the program. Howard Emanuel Rickmond, for example, entered the Commercial Department in the fall of 1897. He gave his father's occupation as janitor and his address as 1513 Sarah Street, South Side. Howard stayed in the program for a little over one academic year, making quite adequate grades before he left the school in the autumn of 1898. Howard's school record made no mention of his race. However, his sister, Ella, entered the department in 1901, transferring from the South Side High School, and her records listed her as "colored." Perhaps Howard's skin was exceptionally light, and he could "pass" for white, for two other black students entering the program in 1897 had their race duly noted. Ella's skin color might have been more obvious, or perhaps her race was known on the South Side and transferred downtown along with her. The 1900 census lists fifteen of the Commercial Department students in that year as black.

Just as the program's Irish students were generally better off than other Irish in Pittsburgh, so the black students came from families in better economic situations than most of the city's black population. While most (nine of the fifteen) of their fathers worked in manual occupations, and seven of these in unskilled jobs, this represented a percentage below that

18. Only 16.3 percent of the Irish families in the comparative sample owned homes without outstanding mortgages.

for Pittsburgh's black community.[19] Half of the program's black students came from families holding mortgages on their homes, a much higher rate than for the student body as a whole. The siblings of black Commercial Department students most often found employment in manual working-class occupations. Over half of the black families included children employed in unskilled jobs, while a third of them had children in skilled trades. Another third had children employed in white-collar jobs or professions, mostly as teachers.

It is not surprising to find black teenagers enrolled in high school at this time; many people—both contemporaries and later scholars—have noted an emphasis on education within black families. But the Commercial Department did not provide a general education; it gave individuals skills that were applicable to a narrow group of jobs, jobs generally not open to blacks at the time.[20] Considering the limited number of job opportunities for young blacks, their presence in the Commercial Department, like that of unskilled workers in general, highlights the program's role in the city as a provider of employment opportunities to those otherwise unable to attain them.

Whether they were black, Irish, or of some other ethnicity, the children of unskilled workers in the Commercial Department brought their own characteristic aspirations to the program. Better off economically than the majority of the city's unskilled laborers, the members of these families still sought to improve their situations. They compared themselves not only to downtown office workers, but also with the skilled workers who ideologically dominated Pittsburgh's working-class community just as their offspring numerically dominated the Commercial Department.

Skilled workers' children made up the largest single category within the Commercial Department. Social mobility studies place the collar line between the "low-level white-collar" and "skilled manual" groups. Some of these studies found that individuals from the skilled manual group tended to remain in that group, a tendency Stephan Thernstrom attributed

19. John Bodnar, Roger Simon, and Michael P. Weber, *Lives of Their Own: Blacks, Italians, and Poles in Pittsburgh, 1900–1960* (Urbana: University of Illinois Press, 1982), p. 64.

20. Bodnar, Simon, and Weber, *Lives of Their Own,* pp. 35–36; Leon Litwack, *Been in the Storm So Long: The Aftermath of Slavery* (New York: Vintage, 1980), pp. 472–476; August Meier and Elliott Rudwick, *From Plantation to Ghetto,* 3d ed. (New York: Hill & Wang, 1976), pp. 173–181. Bodnar, Simon, and Weber say clerical positions closed almost entirely to blacks by 1930, and that there were few earlier (p. 242). In addition, they found that the number of black-owned businesses in Pittsburgh actually declined between 1900 and 1920 (p. 133). But, of course, no one knew beforehand that this would happen.

to "the downward pull exerted by the working-class family."[21] An examination of this group, then, gets to the heart of the social meaning of the collar line—the social organization of class—at the turn of the century.

For skilled workers clerical training and employment for their children represented an affirmation of their social standing. Enjoying a relatively privileged place within the working class as a whole, these workers more than others could express choice in investing in their children's commercial education. They made their decisions from a position of greater strength, both economically and socially. Children's contributions to the family economy were less likely to be crucial. Daughters felt little economic pressure to enter the waged labor force. Sons faced a real dilemma in deciding between the status and benefits of their fathers'. skilled crafts and those of clerical work. Both economic and social factors must be considered in order to understand the presence of so many skilled workers' children in the high school's program.

In the fall of 1900 Harry Williamson Redman entered the Commercial Department. Two years later his sister, Florence, would do the same. Their father was Jacob Thomas Redman, a Pennsylvania-born railroad conductor. A widower, he headed a family of six children. When Harry, his second and youngest son, entered the high school program, his two oldest daughters stayed at home, probably taking care of their younger siblings as well as a maternal uncle living with the family. The oldest Redman son, Jacob, Jr., worked as a clerk. The family rented a home in the comfortable, working-class 23rd ward. Harry attended the Commercial Department for almost two full years before dropping out; his sister remained only five months, leaving the program after receiving an exam grade of only 65 percent.

Garfield Evans enrolled in the Commercial Department in January 1901, and his time there overlapped with both of the Redmans. He remained in the program for three school years until his graduation in 1904. Garfield, who lived across the Monongahela River, attended the South Side High School before transferring to the main Fifth Avenue program. His father, James Evans, worked as a sheet roller in one of the South Side steel mills—perhaps the huge Jones & Laughlin complex just a few blocks from the home he owned in the 25th ward. James had been born in Wales and immigrated to the United States in 1866, at the age of twenty-two. In 1900 all four of his children, three boys and a girl ranging in age from ten to twenty-seven, were attending school.

21. Thernstrom, *Other Bostonians*, p. 97.

Garfield Evans and the two Redman children were only 3 of over 900 children of skilled workers who passed through the Commercial Department between 1890 and 1903. These young people came from the most privileged families of Pittsburgh's working class. In fact, these workers constituted a "labor aristocracy" in Pittsburgh in the late nineteenth century. Following Eric Hobsbawm's schema, historians of the British working class have delineated a labor aristocracy in that country based on its steady work and high wages, its autonomy and authority at the workplace, its role in organizing the working class economically and politically, its ability to improve its situation, and its position within the larger community as a link between unskilled workers and the lower middle class.[22] The examples of Jacob Redman and James Evans demonstrate these same qualifications in Pittsburgh's skilled workers.

As a railroad conductor Jacob Redman received at least $3.00 a day in wages, a respectable amount that maintained his family at a standard of living above that of the average worker. Like many others in his line of work, Redman worked steadily in 1900. He was virtually guaranteed employment by the railroad, having worked his way up through the seniority system from brakeman to conductor. He probably belonged to one of the Railway Brotherhoods, which protected his seniority rights and provided him with insurance in case of accident or ill health. At one of the top rungs of the trainmen's promotional ladders, a conductor commanded respect from those beneath him on the train and in the yards and from his superiors. As the most visible railroad employee, he also occupied a privileged position in the public eye.[23] This public perception reinforced

22. Eric Hobsbawm, "The Labour Aristocracy in Nineteenth-Century Britain," in *Labouring Men* (New York: Basic Books, 1965), pp. 272–315. See Geoffrey Crossick, *An Artisan Elite in Victorian Society: Kentish London, 1840–1880* (London: Croom Helm, 1978); John Foster, *Class Struggle and the Industrial Revolution* (London: Weidenfeld & Nicolson, 1974); Robert Q. Gray, *The Labour Aristocracy in Victorian Edinburgh* (Oxford: Clarendon Press, 1976); as well as the essays in Eric Hobsbawm, *Workers: Worlds of Labor* (New York: Pantheon, 1984), pp. 214–272. In recent years more attention has been paid to the application of the category to the U.S. working class as well. See Andrew Dawson, "The Paradox of Dynamic Technological Change and the Labor Aristocracy in the United States, 1880–1914," *Labor History* 20 (1979), 325–351, and Dawson, "The Parameters of Craft Consciousness: The Social Outlook of the Skilled Worker, 1890–1920," in Hoerder, ed., *American Labor and Immigration History*, pp. 135–155.

23. An average daily compensation of $2.97 is listed for conductors in the region including Pittsburgh in U.S. Interstate Commerce Commission, *13th Annual Report on the Statistics of Railways in the United States for the Year Ending June 30, 1900* (Washington, 1901), p. 41; see Shergold, *Working-Class Life*, for information on the standard of living supported by these wages. There were two competing Railway Brotherhoods in Pittsburgh,

his desire to present a "respectable" image, while his economic status gave him the wherewithal to do so.

But the skilled iron and steel workers, like James Evans, stood at the pinnacle of Pittsburgh's working class. As a sheet roller Evans might have earned as much as $8.50 a day for 12 hours of work, the highest possible for skilled work. Work was steady only as long as the iron and steel trade prospered, but the wages were also high enough to sustain a family through intermittent unemployment. In 1900 Evans enjoyed full employment. At the workplace itself he oversaw the work of helpers and laborers; his was the responsibility to control both men and machines in attaining the proper thickness for the resultant sheet metal. Rollers had organized unions since the 1860s, and though the debacle of the Homestead strike on the eve of the 1890s depression had seriously damaged their union, it was making a mild comeback by the turn of the century. To a large degree the staying power of the union was dependent on the skilled workers' shared ethnic bonds as well as on their workplace experiences. Thus union reports included updates on its members' participation in such activities as Welsh *eisteddfods,* or singing competitions.[24] The union provided men like Evans not only with job security and insurance measures, but also with vehicles through which they expressed their own sense of dignity and worth.

Few skilled workers experienced the economic and social status of iron rollers like Evans, and not all exhibited the social characteristics of the labor aristocracy as clearly as did railroad conductors like Redman. But they did enjoy a standard of living and a level of control over their work which far exceeded that experienced by Pittsburgh's unskilled workers. And by sending their sons and daughters to the high school's Commercial Department, all these skilled workers lived out what Hobsbawm called the labor aristocracy's "prospects of advancement" for their children.[25] Enrolling their children in the Commercial Department reflected both the privileges of their elite status within the working class and their recogni-

---

both of which included conductors: the Switchmen's Union and the Brotherhood of Railway Trainmen (Kellogg, *Wage-Earning Pittsburgh,* p. 125). Contemporary novels and other literature provide insight into the social status of conductors: for example, see Frank Beers, *The Green Signal or Life on the Rail* (Kansas City: Franklin Hudson, 1904).

24. Fitch, *Steel Workers,* p. 53; David Montgomery, *The Fall of the House of Labor: The Workplace, the State and American Labor Activism, 1865–1925* (Cambridge: Cambridge University Press, 1987), pp. 22–23, 34. See the *National Labor Tribune,* 12/29/1898, for example (hereafter cited as *NLT*).

25. Hobsbawm, "Labour Aristocracy," p. 273.

tion of the limits of that status. Through the 1890s these limits became increasingly clear, as the labor aristocracy underwent changes of crisis proportion.[26] Economic downturn, union defeats, technological changes and increased division of labor, and an influx of new-immigrant groups all played a part in the decisions these workers' families made about their children's futures.

The sons and daughters of skilled workers attended the Commercial Department in about the same proportions as the program's entire student body, 57 percent boys and 43 percent girls (see table 8). Like the children of unskilled workers, they were more likely to graduate from the program than were other students.[27] Young men and young women from the families of skilled workers had almost identical graduation rates.

Almost three-quarters of these students entered the Commercial Department after attending the city's public grammar schools, more than any other occupational group. To a large extent this reflects the identification with and support of the public schools by Pittsburgh's skilled workers, a connection explored in more detail in the next chapter. Skilled workers' children were less likely than average to have attended parochial schools, especially when compared to unskilled workers' children. Only 6 percent of skilled workers' children first attended parochial schools, compared to 8 percent of all Commercial Department students and 16 percent of students from unskilled workers' families (see table 12).

The ethnic backgrounds and nativity of the skilled workers help explain these differences. While almost half of all unskilled workers' children were of Irish descent, only 17 percent of skilled workers' children were. In fact, some 52 percent of all skilled workers' children were the native-born children of native-born workers (see tables 10 and 11). However, 67 percent of the boys' parents were native-born, compared to only 47 percent of the girls' parents. Of those with foreign-born parents or grandparents, girls were more likely to be of British (including Scotch and Welsh) or Irish stock. These ethnic differences are discussed again later in this chapter with the analysis of different family strategies that lay behind decisions to enroll a son or a daughter in the Commercial Department.

Family employment patterns provide insight into the economic situation of the families of these skilled workers. While children in these families were less likely than unskilled workers' children to be gainfully employed, they came closer to balancing white-collar and blue-collar employment. Almost 40 percent of these families had children employed

26. Hobsbawm, *Workers*, pp. 266–268.
27. Forty-five percent of skilled workers' children graduated, compared to 41 percent of the entire student body and 45 percent of unskilled workers' children. See table 9.

as white-collar workers in clerical or sales positions. Another 22 percent included children working in skilled trades, while only 15 percent had unskilled or semiskilled workers in the family. The relatively low incidence of children's employment suggests that immediate economic concerns were not prime motivating forces in educational decisions for these families; investing in white-collar education or training in a skilled trade was more important than immediate earnings, particularly with the low unemployment rates in these families. Only 10 percent of the skilled workers found in the 1900 census experienced any unemployment that year, compared to 23 percent of the unskilled workers.

Why did these skilled workers send their children to the Commercial Department in the first place? Traditional social mobility studies provide a quick and easy answer: they were searching for a way to boost their children out of blue-collar employment and into "superior" white-collar occupations. But did these workers share the assumption that white-collar occupations were indeed superior? Authors of social mobility studies often gloss over this question, ignoring evidence that for skilled workers the line between all blue-collar manual occupations and all white-collar nonmanual occupations was not a crucial one.[28]

What values lay behind the self-perception of skilled workers and their views of other social groups and occupations? I chose to call these workers a labor aristocracy not only because the term aptly describes their material circumstances, but also because it implies a world view conditioned by both their identification with the working class and their own elite position within that class. Skilled workers displayed their distinctive ideology in their publications, the actions of their organizations, and in this case, the efforts they made to ensure that their children enjoyed secure futures. Pittsburgh's labor aristocrats were proud of their skills and saw those skills as the productive basis for the city's economic strength. They were also aware that their personal success depended on group solidarities. Their unions and trade councils provided them with even greater economic security and the means to regularize their workplace control. At the same time, acting and speaking through such organizations, they saw themselves as spokesmen for the entire working class; their unions, cooperatives, and political organizations were meant to be models for the formation of a more truly democratic republic.[29]

28. For example, see Thernstrom, *Other Bostonians*, pp. 93–97.

29. This capsule of skilled workers' ideology comes from reading publications such as the *NLT* and *The Carpenter*, as well as from secondary works such as David Montgomery, "Workers' Control of Machine Production in the Nineteenth Century," in Montgomery, *Workers' Control in America: Studies in the History of Work, Technology, and Labor*

In their rhetoric and actions, then, labor aristocrats reveal a level of class consciousness traditionally thought to be negligible in the United States.[30] But did the fathers of Commercial Department students share these values? Or did they embody the antithesis of class consciousness, seeking to remove their families from the working class by assuring their children's upward mobility into clerical positions? A survey of Pittsburgh's labor movement in the 1890s reveals the activities of a number of the parents of Commercial Department students. These men played active roles in union affairs and working-class politics. For example, Frank Bonsall, a painter whose daughter Irene attended the Commercial Department between 1897 and 1899, was elected secretary of the Pittsburgh Building Trades Council in February of 1898 and later that year ran for the third district legislative seat on the United Labor ticket.[31] John Pierce, a rougher for Jones & Laughlin, sent his son to the Commercial Department in the mid-1890s. He had served as a school director for Pittsburgh's 24th ward in the 1880s and ran for the ward's select council seat in 1898, at which time he was a trustee of the Amalgamated Association of Iron, Steel and Tin Workers (AAISW), which later employed him as a full-time organizer.[32] Also in 1898, four years after his son graduated from the Commercial Department, glassblower John Schlicker, treasurer of the Knights of Labor Local Assembly 300, was involved in an intricate dispute over control of the Window Glass Workers' Association.[33] Other fathers played similar roles in Pittsburgh's union life. Many more partici-

---

Struggles (Cambridge: Cambridge University Press, 1979), pp. 9–31; Montgomery, "Labor and the Republic in Industrial America: 1860–1920," *Le Mouvement Sociale* 111 (April–June 1980), 201–215; Shergold, *Working-Class Life;* Francis G. Couvares, *The Remaking of Pittsburgh: Class and Culture in an Industrializing City, 1877–1919* (Albany: SUNY Press, 1984); Leon Fink, *Workingmen's Democracy: The Knights of Labor and American Politics* (Urbana: University of Illinois Press, 1983); and Dawson, "Parameters of Craft Consciousness."

30. This is not to say that their class consciousness was unproblematic. As we will see, here and in chapter 5, the labor aristocrats' self-perception as the moral, cultural, and political leaders of the working class often led to actions belying their supposed sense of class solidarity. This issue is a common one in studies of labor aristocracies. For the mixed messages of British skilled workers' actions, for example, see James Hinton, *The First Shop Stewards' Movement* (London: Allen & Unwin, 1973).

31. *NLT,* 2/3/1898; 9/15/1898.

32. *NLT,* 1/27/1898. Pierce appears in some capacity in the *Proceedings* of the AAISW's national conventions every year from 1889 to 1906. The 1900 city directory listed him as an "organizer."

33. *NLT,* 9/15/1898, 12/15/1898; "Official Records of Window Glass Workers' L.A. 300, K. of L.," pp. 503, 580, Joseph Slight Papers Microfilm Edition, Ohio Historical Society (roll 7).

pated as rank-and-file members, such as William Hughes, a roller at Republic Iron Works, whose daughter Minnie recited a poem at a district meeting of the AAISW, or Henry Briggs, who made it a practice to visit the *National Labor Tribune* offices every December with a Christmas gift.[34] These men represent the tip of the proverbial iceberg; the high rates of unionization among Pittsburgh's skilled workers suggest that most of these parents participated at some level in the city's union movement and its related associational life.

Why, then, did these workers choose to send their sons and daughters to the Commercial Department to prepare them for employment as clerical workers? The relatively high income of skilled workers meant that there was usually no overwhelming need for the economic contributions of working daughters. Pride in their trades and in their privileged position within the working class suggests that sons would more likely follow their father's trades before crossing the collar line into the office. The answer lies in the rapid economic changes of the 1890s, changes that not only created the burgeoning number of office occupations but also transformed many of Pittsburgh's skilled trades. This transformation led to a crisis within the labor aristocracy, a crisis in which skilled workers' privileges within the workplace were eroded and their social status appeared threatened as well.

This crisis had four main components, all integral to the development of monopoly capitalism. First, entire industries declined in importance in Pittsburgh's economy. In the glass industry, for example, the formation of the U.S. Glass Company in 1891 put family-owned companies out of business in the city. In addition, the consolidated company could afford to take advantage of new technologies that were not dependent on the Pittsburgh region's original natural advantages for glass manufacturing. Other artisan industries, such as tailoring, were simply pushed out of business by large-scale, ready-made production and sales. Second, in Pittsburgh as elsewhere, corporate emphasis on smoother production and higher profits led to numerous attempts to break the shop-floor power of skilled workers through combinations of new automated technologies and a more intense division of labor. This dual process affected virtually every skilled trade. Glassblowers and many iron and steel workers faced technological innovations that dampened or even eliminated the power of

34. Another Hughes daughter, Gladys, was in the Commercial Department, *NLT,* 7/28/1898, 11/24/1898, 12/8/1898; Briggs's son was in the Commercial Department, *NLT,* 12/29/1898.

their skills; tailors saw their craft divided into minute steps done by the piece in factories filled with young women and recent immigrants; machinists faced the increasing use of specialized machine tools to divide the skills of the former "all-round" craftsmen; even carpenters found portions of their work transferred to planing mills, leaving them simply to assemble prefabricated pieces.[35]

Third, employers pressed their new advantages in order to destroy the power of the skilled craft unions where they could. While workers struggled to maintain their shop-floor control over the work process, the new corporations used their immense economic power to crush workers' organizations. In Pittsburgh this was vividly demonstrated by the 1892 Homestead Strike, when the Carnegie company wiped out union power in steel, leaving some union men blacklisted and many more working under conditions strictly and totally determined by the company. Finally, these skilled workers, faced with economic threats at the workplace, found themselves addressing a related issue in their communities. Increasingly the workers filling the new unskilled and semiskilled positions created by automation and division of labor were the new immigrants from southern and eastern Europe. Skilled workers saw these immigrants used by the corporations to undermine their economic power in the workplace; at the same time the new immigrants were also changing the complexion of community life in many of Pittsburgh's working-class neighborhoods. Fearing a real decline in their privileged economic status, these skilled workers sought to bolster their social status by distinguishing themselves from the new immigrants.[36]

35. Josephine McIlvain, "Twelve Blocks: A Study of One Segment of Pittsburgh's South Side, 1880–1915," *Western Pennsylvania Historical Magazine* 60 (1977), 364; Glenn E. McLaughlin, *Growth of American Manufacturing Areas: A Comparative Analysis with Special Emphasis on Trends in the Pittsburgh District* (Pittsburgh: University of Pittsburgh, Bureau of Business Research, 1938), p. 315; George E. Barnett, *Chapters on Machinery and Labor* (Cambridge: Harvard University Press, 1926); Pearce Davis, *The Development of the American Glass Industry* (Cambridge: Harvard University Press, 1949); John William Larner, Jr., "The Glass House Boys: Child Labor Conditions in Pittsburgh's Glass Factories, 1890–1917," *Western Pennsylvania Historical Magazine* 48 (1965), 355–364; U.S. Department of Commerce and Labor, "Conditions of Entrance to the Principal Trades," Bulletin no. 67, by Walter E. Weyl and A. M. Sakolski (Washington, 1906), pp. 681–780; Dawson, "The Paradox of Technological Change"; Montgomery, "Workers' Control of Machine Production"; Bob Reckman, "Carpentry: The Craft and Trade," in Andrew Zimbalist, ed., *Case Studies on the Labor Process* (New York: Monthly Review Press, 1979), pp. 85–92; David M. Gordon, Richard Edwards, and Michael Reich, *Segmented Work, Divided Workers: The Historical Transformation of Labor in the United States* (Cambridge: Cambridge University Press, 1982), pp. 128–135; Montgomery, *Fall of the House of Labor*, pp. 9–57.

36. David Brody, *Steelworkers in America: The Nonunion Era* (New York: Harper & Row, 1969); James Livingston, "The Social Analysis of Economic History and Theory:

These dramatic changes in their economic and social position led skilled workers to develop new strategies for their sons' and daughters' futures. For while the late-nineteenth-century corporations eroded much of the material basis for their privileged position within the working class, these same corporations also created the new office occupations. Clerical jobs, in flux through the 1890s and early 1900s as much as were the skilled manual trades, occupied a similar economic and social position. For the sons of Pittsburgh's skilled workers, clerical work was an alternative to the newly problematic conditions in their fathers' trades. For daughters, office positions provided remunerative work with a social status that could reinforce their families' otherwise declining position within the working class. A close look at a few of the students in the Commercial Department illustrates these strategies.

Charles Auth entered the Commercial Department in 1900. His father, Conrad, was a Pennsylvania-born glassblower of mixed German and English heritage and national treasurer of the Glass Bottle Blowers' Association (GBBA).[37] Glassblowers like Auth made up almost 3 percent of the skilled workers represented in the Commercial Department. Conrad Auth, his English-born wife, five sons, and one daughter lived in a house with a fully paid mortgage near the glasshouses on Pittsburgh's South Side. Charles was the youngest son. His two oldest brothers held manual jobs; one was a glassblower like his father, and the other was an unspecified "steelworker." During the year ending with the federal census taking of June 1900, Conrad Auth and his glassblowing son had both been unemployed for twelve full months. Even as treasurer of his national union, Auth, Sr., did not receive a salary, although he did sometimes

---

Conjectures on Late Nineteenth-Century American Development," *American Historical Review* 92 (1987), 69–95; A. T. Lane, "The British and American Labour Movements and the Problem of Immigration, 1890–1914," in Kenneth Lunn, ed., *Hosts, Immigrants and Minorities: Historical Responses to Newcomers in British Society 1870–1914* (New York: St. Martin's Press, 1980), pp. 343–367; David Montgomery, "Immigrant Workers and Managerial Reform," in Montgomery, *Workers' Control,* pp. 32–47; Bruce Laurie, Theodore Hershberg, and George Alter, "Immigrants and Industry: The Philadelphia Experience, 1850–1880," *Journal of Social History* 9 (1975), 219–267; James R. Green, *The World of the Worker: Labor in Twentieth-Century America* (New York: Hill & Wang, 1980), pp. 3–31; Gordon, Edwards, and Reich, *Segmented Work,* pp. 141–144.

37. In the 1890s Conrad Auth had been president of the Pittsburgh branch of the GBBA (J. C. Lucey, ed., *The Trade Unions of Pittsburg and Allegheny, Their History and Biographical Sketches of Prominent Union Officers and Friends of Labor* [Pittsburgh: Duncan, 1895], p. 8). Auth served as national treasurer of the GBBA from at least 1900 until his death in 1911 (Glass Bottle Blowers Association, *Proceedings of the Glass Bottle Blowers Association of the United States and Canada, Composed of Glass Bottle Blowers,* 1900, 1902, 1903, 1904, 1906, 1908, 1909, 1910, 1911 [Obituary on p. 119]).

receive per diem payment and costs for time spent on union business.[38] Auth's steelworker son had been unemployed for seven months of 1900. Faced with this dramatic experience of the precariousness of the skilled trades, the Auth family switched to a new plan for their three younger sons. When fifteen-year-old Charles entered the high school's program, his other two brothers worked as clerks, one for a plumbing business and the other as a grocery clerk. Unlike their older brothers, neither of these young men employed in white-collar jobs had any periods of unemployment in 1900. Since the family had paid off the mortgage on their home, their economic situation had not always been so bleak as it was in 1900. Nonetheless, the pattern of employment in the family demonstrates a change in strategy for the sons' futures over the course of the 1890s.

But fathers did not have to be in such dire personal straits to follow the same path. James Evans, the Welsh sheet roller introduced earlier, experienced no such catastrophic unemployment. Even as late as 1907 his job in the mill would not be affected by new automated technology. All around him, however, other skilled workers faced increasing automation, and Evans had witnessed in his own working life the return of the 12-hour workday and the 7-day week in the Pittsburgh mills. He probably agreed with the furnace boss who told Pittsburgh Survey investigator John Fitch in 1907, "I'm gettin' along, but I don't want the kids ever to work this way. I'm goin' to educate them so they won't have to work twelve hours."[39] And while Evans most likely participated in the AAISW's economic and social activities, he had witnessed the dissolution of much of the union's strength in the 1890s and might not have wanted his sons to be dependent on it. Twenty-five iron or steel rollers sent children to the Commercial Department between 1890 and 1903, mostly sons undoubtedly hoping to find more secure employment than did their fathers.

Tailors also sent disproportionate numbers of sons to the Commercial Department. One of these was Joseph Zinsmeister, a first-generation German-American, whose son Theodore attended the program in 1900. As an officer of the Pittsburgh local of the Journeymen Tailors' Union (JTU) during the 1890s, Zinsmeister would have been very aware of the havoc wreaked by the subdivision of the work process in his trade. Factory work had begun to replace custom tailoring in the 1870s, and by the 1890s the trend had accelerated. At the national level Zinsmeister's union would later engage in a jurisdictional dispute with the United

38. See, for example, GBBA, *Proceedings . . . , 1900*, p. 277.
39. Fitch, *Steel Workers*, p. 52; David Brody, *Steelworkers in America*, pp. 35–38; quotation in Fitch, *Steel Workers*, p. 12.

Garment Workers over the distinction between custom-made and factory-made products. The JTU attempted to keep its apprenticeship system intact, but fought a losing battle against the encroachment of factories and piecework.[40] In these circumstances even a loyal union man like Zinsmeister looked elsewhere for his son's future.

Machinists have provided the textbook case of "deskilling" through technological change and the subdivision of the labor process ever since the trade was first studied at the turn of the century. A 1906 federal study found that "probably no craft has undergone such rapid disintegration within recent years as that of the machinist." Around the same time, investigators for the Pittsburgh Survey found that only about a third of the city's machinists still worked as "all-round mechanics," while the rest were simply specialized "machine hands." And though the International Association of Machinists had been strong in the city through the 1880s, specialization of the craft had weakened it considerably by the opening of the twentieth century.[41] These developments in the machine trades probably explain why Michael Hefferman, an Irish machinist, sent his son, John, to the Commercial Department in 1895. But he also sent his daughter, Margaret, and the implications of that decision are somewhat different.

Pittsburgh's labor aristocrats did not generally expect their daughters to work for wages. From at least the 1870s on, being a truly "worthy workingman" meant being able to support one's family on a single male wage. The ideal union man had a wife at home maintaining the household, and healthy children attending public schools, or if they were older sons, apprenticed to honorable trades. In fact, as Alice Kessler-Harris has pointed out, these workers developed a working-class version of the idea of "separate spheres" for men and women. According to this view wives stayed home as good housekeepers, and daughters stayed home in order to become good housekeepers. Thus, after posing the question, "What Shall Be Done With Daughters?" Pittsburgh's working-class press recommended: "Teach them to make bread. Teach them to make shirts. . . . Teach them how to wash and iron clothes. . . . Teach them all the mysteries of the kitchen, the dining-room and the parlor."[42]

40. Lucey, *Trade Unions of Pittsburg and Allegheny,* p. 26; *NLT,* 12/29/1898; U.S. Department of Commerce and Labor, "Conditions of Entrance," pp. 691, 704.

41. U.S. Department of Commerce and Labor, "Conditions of Entrance," p. 686; John R. Commons and William M. Leiserson, "Wage-Earners of Pittsburgh," in Kellogg, *Wage-Earning Pittsburgh,* p. 140.

42. Alice Kessler-Harris, *Out to Work: A History of Wage-Earning Women in the United States* (New York: Oxford University Press, 1982), p. 84; *NLT,* 10/11/1879.

Skilled workers often invoked this vision of the working-class nuclear family as a collective goal, an argument for unionization and higher pay for male workers. But they also presented it as a goal for which individuals should strive. Articles and editorials in the *National Labor Tribune* raged against female and child labor: "Women and children are not made to drudge in shops and factories."[43] Organized skilled workers had two main complaints against such drudgery. On one hand, female labor was often used in combination with automation and piecework systems to undermine skilled male labor. On the other hand, such employment was in fact "drudgery." Long hours of numbing, poorly paid work in Pittsburgh's factories, or servile dependence on the city's upper class in domestic positions, hardly seemed consonant with the social status of the labor aristocracy.

The increase in clerical positions open to women at the end of the nineteenth century invited a new and different outlook on daughters' employment. Clerical work embodied the values of this privileged stratum of Pittsburgh's working class. The characteristics of "conspicuous employment"—education, clothing, ascribed prestige—reinforced the labor aristocracy's social status, relative both to other, less fortunate, members of the working class, and to the upper classes. Two of the largest groups of skilled workers in the Commercial Department illustrate this fact: carpenters, and those men at the apex of the railroading hierarchy, conductors and engineers.

Carpenters made up 13 percent of the Commercial Department skilled fathers, conductors and engineers another 12 percent. Both groups sent disproportionate numbers of daughters to the program. Seth Rogers, a native-born railroad engineer, sent his daughter, Lila, to the Commercial Department in 1898; another of his daughters worked as a clerk in the courthouse in 1900. Florence Bolton, daughter of a native-born carpenter and occasional building inspector, attended the high school's program in the two years before Lila Rogers. Two of Florence's older sisters worked as schoolteachers. Both of these fathers worked in trades overwhelmingly dominated by native-born men like themselves.[44] As clerical workers

---

43. *NLT*, 2/3/1877.

44. In 1900 46 percent of both carpenters and "steam railway employees" were native born of native-born parents. In 1910 61 percent of locomotive engineers were native born of native-born parents (figures for Pittsburgh). U.S. Department of Commerce and Labor, Bureau of the Census, *Occupations at the Twelfth Census* (Washington, 1904), pp. 678–683; U.S. Department of Commerce, Bureau of the Census, *Thirteenth Census of the United States Taken in the Year 1910: Population: Occupation Statistics*, vol. IV (Washington, 1914), pp. 590–591.

their daughters would be employed in settings similarly dominated by women of the same background.

The Commercial Department, however, also enrolled many native-born daughters of Irish and British skilled workers. These families would have had views similar to those of native-born workers. The family of the English carpenter, Henry E. Charles, and his Irish wife, Catherine, sent at least three of their six daughters to the high school program. Still renting an apartment as late as 1910, the Charles family would have considered clerical employment or teaching their only options for bringing in additional wages and at the same time maintaining or possibly even boosting their social standing. Daughters' clerical employment can thus be seen as one of many attempts by native-born and old-immigrant group workers to define themselves in opposition to the city's new immigrants from southern and eastern Europe. When Elizabeth (Bessie) Mooney, for example, attended the Commercial Department, her Irish-born father, a steel mill heater, headed a family that included his sister-in-law, who worked as a servant. For the Mooney family, as for many others, clerical training for a daughter represented a chance for family members to move further away from the unskilled occupations filled by recent immigrants.

For both daughters and sons clerical employment fit into skilled workers' views of their own importance to the economy. Despite erosions in position and power, skilled workers at the turn of the century still would have argued that it was their labor that created the industrial wealth of the nation. But they also understood that the wealth they produced and distributed was now controlled in the corporate offices downtown. These workers paid careful attention to developments in the corporate world, hoping to gain insight into their own economic futures. For example, throughout the spring and early summer of 1901, the *National Labor Tribune* detailed the moves into Pittsburgh of U.S. Steel's component offices and staffs upon the creation of the giant corporation.[45] Though clerical workers obviously wielded little power in those offices, they nonetheless worked at the very center of the economic developments of the day. The fathers of these young people might well have agreed with the writer who proclaimed that "the file clerk is just as essential to the steel business, under modern conditions, as the puddler."[46] A child

---

45. *NLT,* 4/25/1901, 5/9/1901, 7/11/1901. Just a year earlier the *NLT* had bemoaned the move to New York City of the offices of the American Steel Hoop Company as a loss to Pittsburgh's financial importance (*NLT,* 6/28/1900).

46. Lee Galloway, *Office Management: Its Principles and Practice* (New York: Ronald, 1919), p. ix.

working as a file clerk, then, might be an extension of the economic, as well as social, position of a puddler—or other skilled worker—as a father.

The examples in this chapter demonstrate the most vivid cases of the late-nineteenth-century crisis of the labor aristocracy and the ways in which the public high school's Commercial Department provided one avenue of response to that crisis. Other skilled workers experienced the 1890s in different ways: not all started at the same heights of skill and remuneration; few saw their crafts undergo the same intense division of labor as did machinists, or the complete mechanization of tasks that affected glassblowers; only a handful experienced as brutal a crushing of their union as did the steelworkers after Homestead. However, they all shared at least some of the characteristics described here—characteristics that earn them the descriptive title "labor aristocracy" and that reflect the transformation of their working and living conditions. Furthermore, these skilled workers, whether of native-born, British, German, or Irish stock, lived in close-knit working-class communities in which their shared social status brought them together in class, ethnic, and civic organizations.

5 /

Skilled Workers, Office Workers

"Aristocracy in the crafts"

The families of the Commercial Department students illustrate relations across the collar line in microcosm, with the children of almost every family pursuing a range of options. These varied familial experiences provided young people one source of information about clerical work and the values associated with it. More than just the family imparted the significance of these experiences, however. The community within which these families lived supplied an even wider constellation of meanings.

The students of the Commercial Department came from all of Pittsburgh's neighborhoods: the residential East End, the congested business district, the mill and glass wards of the South Side. Focusing on the dynamics of two working-class communities can help to further elucidate the predominance of skilled workers' children in the Commercial Department. Lawrenceville, located along the Allegheny River (15th, 16th, and 17th wards), and the Hill Top district (31st, 32nd, and 35th wards), overlooking the factories of Pittsburgh's South Side, both sent proportionately more working-class students, particularly skilled workers' children, to the program than did other areas (see map of Pittsburgh, figure 2). While 54 percent of all the Commercial Department students came from working-class families, and 35 percent from the families of skilled workers, working-class students made up almost two-thirds of those who entered the program from Lawrenceville and the Hill Top. In both neighborhoods almost half of the students were skilled workers' children.[1]

1. Of students from the Lawrenceville public schools, 69 percent were from working-class families and 46 percent from skilled workers' families; the Hill Top students included 64 percent from the working class and 46 percent from skilled workers' families (figures

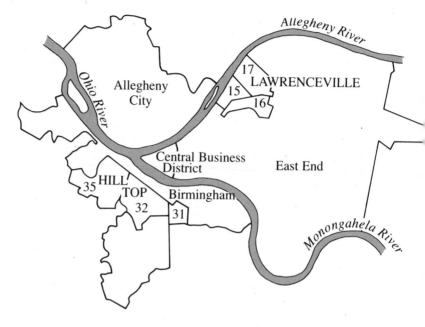

Figure 2. Map of Pittsburgh, 1910

On the streets of neighborhoods such as Lawrenceville and the Hill Top, Pittsburgh's skilled workers daily worked out the content and implications of the mutualistic ethic by which they measured their self-worth. Shaped by their workplace experiences and grounded in their ethnic backgrounds, this ethic informed their interactions with other social groups.[2] As one author wrote in the city's labor paper, "Aristoc-

derived from the Commercial Department enrollment records). Data on the students from the 1900 manuscript census indicate that 75 percent of those from the Lawrenceville wards were from working-class families and 53 percent from skilled workers' families; those from Hill Top wards were 67 percent from working-class and 56 percent from skilled workers' families. Unlike the earlier figures, these numbers include those students who entered the Commercial Department from parochial as well as from public schools, though they exclude widows' children.

2. See David Montgomery, *The Fall of the House of Labor: The Workplace, the State, and American Labor Activism, 1865–1925* (Cambridge: Cambridge University Press, 1987), pp. 9–57, as well as works cited in chapter 4.

racy . . . is composed of people so conceited that they fancy themselves better than other people. There may be aristocracy in the trades and in commerce as easily as in society, and we may add with the emphasis of fact . . . that there is aristocracy in the crafts only less clearly defined than in society."[3] The local social relations that had thereby developed over the decades following the Civil War faced new obstacles at the turn of the century. Neighborhood studies of Lawrenceville and the Hill Top reveal how skilled workers attempted to respond to these obstacles and develop new modes of social interaction, as well as how their attempts were sometimes thwarted by forces too strong or too misunderstood for these workers to combat. These skilled workers made up Pittsburgh's labor aristocracy.

Children's training for and employment in clerical positions took place in this context. The Hill Top's Peter Stoerkel, a planing mill sawyer and a German-born resident of the 31st ward, served as a director of his ward's grammar school from the mid-1890s through 1906. His daughter, Katy, attended that school before going on to the Commercial Department in 1897. Stoerkel exhibited his commitment to the public schools through both his civic activities and his daughter's preparation for entering the new office work force. Other parents had less explicit connections to the city's educational system. John A. Snyder, a native-born railroad engineer from Lawrenceville's 15th ward, sent all of his children to public schools; the three oldest (two boys and a girl) all attended the Commercial Department between 1890 and 1903. Examining the social dynamics of Lawrenceville helps to explain why workers like Snyder viewed the Commercial Department, and clerical work, so favorably. Since skilled workers like Stoerkel and Snyder left no written commentaries on their families' decisions, we need to consider their actions and their particular circumstances in order to understand how they regarded their own social position relative to that of the new clerical workers.

Despite similarities between the two neighborhoods, Lawrenceville and the Hill Top present two rather different situations in which clerical work became a viable option for the children of skilled workers. The skilled workers of both neighborhoods held similar views of public education, evident not only in their use of the high school's programs, but also in their active participation in running the local grammar schools. In

3. *National Labor Tribune,* hereafter cited as *NLT,* 11/5/1892.

addition, workers in both neighborhoods took part in a wide range of associational activities, including trade union organization. Beyond these similarities, however, the two communities differed in important ways.

Lawrenceville, an old industrial area of the city, mirrored the social divisions and economic developments of Pittsburgh as a whole. The iron mills and other metal factories that dominated the area insured that its residents occupied the entire range of the social scale, from day laborers to the owners of manufacturing concerns. By the beginning of the twentieth century, the neighborhood also housed increasing numbers of the new immigrants from southern and eastern Europe. The Hill Top, on the other hand, displayed more of a suburban complexion. Though its residents included members of all social strata, the area was dominated by a mix of skilled manual workers and white-collar clerical and sales workers. These differences in the history and development of the two neighborhoods illustrate two different routes to clerical employment for skilled workers' children, one predicated on a desire to distinguish themselves from the new immigrants, and one based on social identification with low-level white-collar workers.

From its village beginnings in the 1810s, Lawrenceville played an important role in Pittsburgh's industrial development. Throughout the nineteenth and into the twentieth centuries, the area boasted a combination of industrial and commercial development along with largely working-class housing. In this setting skilled workers of German, Irish, and Anglo-American backgrounds created their own culture and community through an interweaving of labor, fraternal, and civic organizations. At the turn of the century these old-immigrant-group skilled workers felt increasingly threatened—economically and socially—by the new immigrants from southern and eastern Europe moving into the area. During the same years they also had to find new ways to deal with Pittsburgh's upper classes. Not only did the new corporations seek to destroy trade union power, but a new professional elite simultaneously sought changes in the city's social conditions. Lawrenceville's skilled workers responded to both of these groups out of their long-standing perceptions of their own role within the community. For both sons and daughters clerical education and employment reaffirmed the labor aristocracy's social status while distinguishing them from recent immigrants and providing new job opportunities.

The Hill Top region shared many of Lawrenceville's cultural characteristics, most notably a large German population and an overlapping but not entirely synonymous skilled workers' community. The area's geographical characteristics and therefore its economic development, however, also made it quite different. Pittsburgh's Hill Top existed as a world apart from the central city through much of the nineteenth century. Located across the Monongahela River on the city's South Side, the hills rose suddenly from the congested industrial plain along the riverbanks. The history of the Hill Top's integration into the city's life is dominated by the area's geography and by residents' attempts to conquer that geography. Until the turn of the century the area's community clusters developed at their own pace, more closely tied to the lower South Side (Birmingham) economy than to that of the peninsular city. However, with new transportation links between the Hill Top and the rest of the city at the end of the century, the area's social complexion began to change as white-collar workers moved into new housing developments. These connections between the Hill Top neighborhoods and the city's central business district introduced skilled workers to new options for their children's futures.

These two neighborhoods, then, exemplify the concerns and values of Pittsburgh's labor aristocracy and thus provide further insight into the way these workers perceived the collar line at the turn of the century.

Lawrenceville

Emanuel Schillo, a German-born iron heater residing and working in Lawrenceville's 15th ward, served as corresponding secretary of the Amalgamated Association of Iron and Steel Workers' (AAISW) William Martin Lodge No. 86 in the early 1890s. In that capacity he became a leader of his local union's strike in support of the locked-out steelworkers of Andrew Carnegie's Homestead plant in July of 1892. Despite the lack of support from the national leaders of the AAISW, the sympathy strikers held high hopes for their actions. As Schillo explained to the press on July 13, "We are going on our own hook in this matter. The Amalgamated Association has nothing to do with our action to day, and we are acting independently of them. We will stick by our fellow workmen, and if they are not granted another conference all of the Carnegie works will be closed, as the men are determined to have a fair deal."[4] Schillo and his compatriots soon would be disappointed. One other sympathy strike collapsed almost immediately, and strikers at a third location voted to

4. *NLT*, 7/16/1892.

return to work on November 19, the day before the strike at Homestead officially ended.[5]

The Lawrenceville strikers were more obstinate. Even after Homestead workers called off their strike, the union men at the Carnegie company's Upper and Lower Union Mills remained on strike. As "A Striker" (perhaps corresponding secretary Schillo?) wrote to the *National Labor Tribune* in January 1893,

> We came out for the purpose of upholding the principles of the Association. . . . Homesteaders were locked out; we came out voluntary. . . . The boys here made the noblest fight that was ever made by any class of men that is spoken of in history. . . . In our effort to bring one of the most unscrupulous money-makers in the land to some reasonable terms we must admit that perhaps we have made a mistake, but we have some consolation that in our defeat others will benefit in the long run, and we know that wage-workers must at times suffer for one another or else there will be no wages paid by the anarchist capitalist.[6]

When the Union Mills strikers finally called off their strike on August 14, 1893, their unions were in disarray, and virtually all of the strike leaders discovered that not only had they lost their old jobs with the Carnegie Steel Company, they were blacklisted throughout the iron and steel industry.[7]

After almost two years without work, then, in 1894 Emanuel Schillo finally gained employment as a messenger in the Pittsburgh post office.[8] A few months later Schillo's daughter Elizabeth entered the Pittsburgh High School's Commercial Department in order to gain training as an office worker. While Schillo's participation in the renowned Homestead strike makes him one of the more famous of the Commercial Department fathers, he was still like other skilled workers: he and his family viewed office training and work as appropriate employment for Elizabeth. This view grew out of the realities of life in Lawrenceville, life dominated but not completely circumscribed by the mills lining the Allegheny River.

Lawrenceville, located along the south shore of the Allegheny River

5. Arthur G. Burgoyne, *The Homestead Strike of 1892* (1893; rpt. Pittsburgh: University of Pittsburgh Press, 1979), pp. 137, 176, 224; John A. Fitch, *The Steel Workers* (New York: Charities Publication Committee, 1910), p. 132; Pennsylvania Secretary of Internal Affairs, Annual Report of the Secretary of Internal Affairs of the Commonwealth of Pennsylvania, pt. III, *Industrial Statistics*, 1892, pp. D9–D10, hereafter cited as Pennsylvania, *Industrial Statistics* (year).

6. *NLT*, 1/5/1893.

7. *NLT*, 8/17/1893.

8. *NLT*, 1/27/1898.

7. 3600 block of Charlotte Street, Lawrenceville, Pittsburgh. Third door from the right is 3621 Charlotte, home of Emanuel Schillo in the 1890s. Photo by Ileen A. DeVault, 1988

just two miles east of downtown Pittsburgh, was first settled in the 1810s. After the federal government built an arsenal there in 1814, a small but bustling town began to grow. By the 1850s horse-drawn omnibuses and streetcars carried passengers between Pittsburgh and Lawrenceville. Although the arsenal stopped producing munitions after an explosion in 1862, it had already attracted other manufacturing to the area. The town's core of shopkeepers and skilled workers found economic sustenance in a variety of concerns established along the flat plain adjacent to the river. Andrew Carnegie opened his Lucy Furnace in Lawrenceville in 1865, and other iron mills soon appeared as well. In 1868 Lawrenceville, along with five other townships east of Pittsburgh, was annexed to the city of Pittsburgh. The town's annexation coincided with the beginning of a population boom for the area. In 1860 Lawrenceville had a population of just over three thousand. A decade later the three wards into which the borough had been divided boasted over eleven thousand residents.[9]

By the 1890s Lawrenceville's economy provided a range of jobs for workers and their children. White-collar employment was fairly limited within the boundaries of the neighborhood's three wards. Small shops of various sorts—grocers, confectioners, tobacconists, and so on—furnished jobs for only a few salespeople. Though clerical positions were somewhat more common, most of them were the types of jobs open principally to men. Small neighborhood banks employed handfuls of tellers, clerks, and bookkeepers, while a few railroad clerks worked in Lawrenceville's four railroad stations. Each of the area's iron or steel plants might hire a dozen clerks and timekeepers, as did the other industrial establishments in the area.[10] For other office employment Lawrence-

9. G. T. Fleming, ed., *History of Pittsburgh and Environs* (New York: American Historical Society, 1922), 2:59, 62; Sr. M. Martina Abbott, S.C., *A City Parish Grows and Changes* (Washington, D.C.: Catholic University of America Press, 1953), pp. 29–30; Joel A. Tarr, *Transportation Innovation and Changing Spatial Patterns: Pittsburgh, 1850–1910* (Pittsburgh: Carnegie-Mellon University Transportation Research Institute, 1972), pp. 5, 9; Bion J. Arnold, *Report on the Pittsburgh Transportation Problem* (Pittsburgh: N.p., 1910), p. 35; Abbott, *City Parish*, p. 32; Fleming, *History of Pittsburgh and Environs*, 2:93. Abbott, *City Parish*, pp. 32, 36, 40; U.S. Department of Interior, *Population of the United States at the 8th Census: 1860* (Washington, 1864), table 3, p. 413; Pittsburgh Central Board of Education, *5th Annual Report of the Superintendent of Public Schools for the School Year Ending June 1, 1873* (Pittsburgh: N.p., 1873), p. 17 (hereafter cited as Pittsburgh Board of Education, *–th Annual Report* [year]).

10. This description is based on establishments appearing on the plat maps for the 15th, 16th, and 17th wards: *[Pittsburgh] Real Estate Plat-book*, vol. 3, plates 22–31 (1900), in the holdings of the Carnegie Library of Pittsburgh. Estimates of clerks working in iron and steel plants are from Fitch, *Steel Workers*, appendix IV, table II: "Wage Statistics of Representative Departments in a Typical Steel Company of Allegheny County, October 1, 1907," pp. 301–305.

ville residents had to travel two or three miles by streetcar to Pittsburgh's central business district (see map of Lawrenceville, figure 3).

Blue-collar employment, on the other hand, existed within the boundaries of Lawrenceville in abundance. Women in the neighborhood who sought wage-earning faced a condensed version of the opportunities available to them throughout the city. Elizabeth Butler believed in 1909 that most of Lawrenceville's wage-earning women worked in the Warde-Mackey Bakery in the 16th ward or the Armstrong Cork Company along the river just below the 15th-ward boundaries.[11] Smaller factories hired other women in the manufacture of various metal items and cigars. Several commercial laundries in the area also offered employment to women.[12] Young women could also find work as domestic servants, either in Lawrenceville's wealthier households or in the residences of the nearby East End.

Industrial employment for Lawrenceville's men also resembled city-wide opportunities. Primary iron and steel mills, such as the Carnegie Company's Union Mills, as well as large fabricating plants like the Keystone Bridge Works of the American Bridge Company, lined the Allegheny River plain. These concerns hired hundreds, ranging from highly skilled workers of native and old-immigrant origins to unskilled laborers from Eastern Europe and the American South. Similarly, an array of foundries and machine shops also employed workers of varying skills. A number of Lawrenceville's German men worked in the area's breweries, which included two of the city's largest (Wainwrights' and Iron City) and one of its oldest, Straub's. Four railroad stations, and the headquarters and yards of the Pittsburgh Junction Railroad Company at the foot of Thirty-eighth and Thirty-ninth Streets, employed railway workers in the neighborhood, while building-trades workers found work in the continuing development of the contiguous East End residential areas.[13]

11. Elizabeth Beardsley Butler, *Women and the Trades: Pittsburgh, 1907–1908* (1909; rpt. Pittsburgh: University of Pittsburgh Press, 1984), pp. 267, 319.

12. *[Pittsburgh] Real Estate Plat-book*, vol. 3, plates 22–31 (1900), holdings of the Carnegie Library of Pittsburgh; Lake Erie and Ohio River Ship Canal Co., "Industrial Map of Manufacturing Works Pittsburg District Showing Their Proximity to Rivers" (May 1907); Pennsylvania Secretary of Internal Affairs, *Eleventh Annual Report of the Factory Inspector of the Commonwealth of Pennsylvania, for the year 1900* (Harrisburg: Wm Stanley Ray, 1901), pp. 1166–1301. The occupations described here were those engaged in by teenagers located in a comparative sample of Lawrenceville and Hill Top families. See Appendix, Description of Data.

13. *[Pittsburgh] Real Estate Plat-book*, vol. 3, plates 22–31 (1900), holdings of the Carnegie Library of Pittsburgh; Lake Erie and Ohio River Ship Canal Co., "Industrial Map of Manufacturing Works Pittsburg District Showing Their Proximity to Rivers" (May

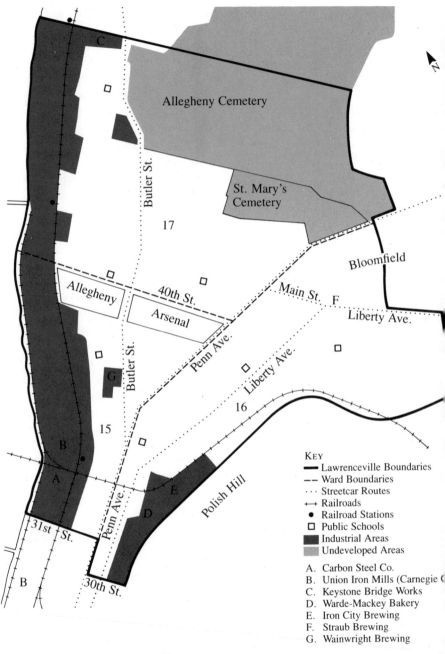

Figure 3. Map of Lawrenceville, c. 1900

The industries located in and around Lawrenceville were among the city's most highly unionized. Skilled workers in the iron and steel works along the Allegheny River plain belonged to trades-based locals of the AAISW. Moving inland from the river, small to midsized machine shops hosted lodges of the International Association of Machinists (IAM). The neighborhood's breweries employed only union labor in one of the few industrially organized unions of the time.[14] Both railroad workers and building-trades workers might also have belonged to the unions of their trades.[15] Except for its lack of glassworkers, then, Lawrenceville reflected the industrial mix that characterized Pittsburgh's union-based working-class culture.[16]

Lawrenceville also resembled the rest of Pittsburgh in its wide, interconnecting web of fraternal organizations. In 1895 the city directory listed Lawrenceville lodges of almost thirty different organizations. Some of these, like the Junior Order of United American Mechanics (JOUAM), justified their existence in nativist terms.[17] Others, such as the North American Sangerbund and the Loyal Orange Lodges, were based in the

---

1907); Pennsylvania Secretary of Internal Affairs, *Eleventh Annual Report of the Factory Inspector of the Commonwealth of Pennsylvania, for the year 1900* (Harrisburg: Wm Stanley Ray, 1901), pp. 1166–1301; John Bodnar, Roger Simon, and Michael P. Weber, *Lives of Their Own: Blacks, Italians, and Poles in Pittsburgh, 1900–1960* (Urbana: University of Illinois Press, 1982), p. 72. Bodnar, Simon, and Weber cite East End building as a major reason for Italians moving into the 16th ward.

14. [Pittsburgh] *Dispatch*, 4/7/1894, listing assessments on businesses in city; *[Pittsburgh] Real Estate Plat-book*, vol. 3, plates 22–31 (1900), in the holdings of the Carnegie Library of Pittsburgh; Lake Erie and Ohio River Ship Canal Co., "Industrial Map of Manufacturing Works Pittsburg District Showing Their Proximity to Rivers" (May 1907). On brewery workers' union, see John R. Commons and William M. Leiserson, "Wage-Earners of Pittsburgh," in Paul Underwood Kellogg, ed., *Wage-Earning Pittsburgh* (New York: Survey Associates, 1914), pp. 136–138. The brewery workers were affiliated with the Knights of Labor until 1900. See *NLT*, 2/22/1900 and 3/8/1900.

15. Pennsylvania, Secretary of Internal Affairs, Annual Report of the Secretary of Internal Affairs of the Commonwealth of Pennsylvania, Part III, *Industrial Statistics* (1903), lists about one thousand members of the Bricklayers' Union in Pittsburgh (p. 465) and over four thousand members in twenty-one locals of the Carpenters' Union, which is listed separately from the United Brotherhood of Carpenters and Joiners, which had only about fifty members in 1903 (pp. 469–470) (hereafter cited as Pennsylvania, *Industrial Statistics* [year]).

16. In both his book and his dissertation, Francis Couvares describes this culture for the 1870s and 1880s, but does not follow it into the 1890s. Francis G. Couvares, *The Remaking of Pittsburgh: Class and Culture in an Industrializing City, 1877–1919* (Albany: SUNY Press, 1984), and "Work, Leisure, and Reform in Pittsburgh: The Transformation of an Urban Culture, 1860–1920," diss., University of Michigan, 1980.

17. See 1895 city directory. Nativist organizations listed were the JOUAM, the American Protestant Association, and the Daughters of Liberty.

old-immigrant ethnic communities. Not surprisingly in a working-class neighborhood, most existed mainly as beneficial societies, providing members with death benefits or life insurance as well as recreation and camaraderie. The Ancient Order of United Workmen (AOUW), the oldest mutual-assessment insurance society in the United States, topped the list of these groups.[18] Two posts of the Grand Army of the Republic (GAR) met in Lawrenceville each week, and there was also a "Camp" of the Sons of Veterans.[19] The 16th ward also boasted a lodge of the Independent Order of Good Templars, a "total abstinence" organization.[20] Finally, Lawrenceville also supported four lodges of the Independent Sovereigns of Industry, a group interested in "discussing economic questions and . . . experimenting with cooperation."[21]

The Sovereigns of Industry's interest in "economic questions" and "cooperation" suggests one of the links between Lawrenceville's fraternal organizations and its unions. The Noble and Holy Order of the Knights of Labor, with its origins as a secret society, its rites and rituals, and its very name, invites instant comparison with the fraternal societies. But other unions also had parallels to the nonoccupational orders, in their local lodge structure, their beneficial aspects, their rituals, and in the sense of fraternal community that they fostered.[22]

18. Noel P. Gist, *Secret Societies: A Cultural Study of Fraternalism in the United States*, University of Missouri Studies, vol. XV, no. 4 (Columbia: University of Missouri, 1940), p. 39. Assessment societies in Lawrenceville also included Royal Arcanum, Improved Order of Heptasophs, Knights of the Golden Eagle, Knights and Ladies of Honor, Order of United Friends, Protected Home Circle, Ancient Order Knights of the Mystic Chain, and the Fraternal Legion. Nonassessment beneficial societies included Knights of Malta, Knights of Pythias (and "uniformed ranks"), Order of the World, and the Odd Fellows, including one Encampment of the Independent Order of Odd Fellows.

19. The GAR often held encampments at the Lawrenceville Arsenal grounds. Pittsburgh, Howard (16th-ward) Sub-District School Board, Minute Book, 7/3/1894, 9/5/1894; Pittsburgh, Washington (17th-ward) Sub-District School Board, Minute Book, 6/7/1894.

20. Albert C. Stevens, comp. and ed., *The Cyclopaedia of Fraternities* (New York: Hamilton, 1899), p. 403. The existence of this organization is ironic, since several of Pittsburgh's largest breweries were located in the 16th ward.

21. Stevens, *Cyclopaedia of Fraternities*, p. 399. Stevens lists "Sovereigns of Industry" as "extinct" (1898). Edwin M. Chamberlin, *The Sovereigns of Industry* (Boston: Lee & Shepard, 1875) describes the early formation of the group.

22. Stevens, *Cyclopaedia of Fraternities*, chap. 10, "Labor and Railway Brotherhoods and Cooperative Fraternities," pp. 378–401. See also David Montgomery, "Workers' Control of Machine Production in the Nineteenth Century," in Montgomery, *Workers' Control in America: Studies in the History of Work, Technology, and Labor Struggles* (Cambridge: Cambridge University Press, 1979), pp. 9–31; James B. Kennedy, *Beneficiary Features of American Trade Unions*, Johns Hopkins University Studies in Historical and Political Science, series 26, nos. 11–12 (November–December 1908) (Baltimore: Johns Hopkins University, 1908), pp. 11–15.

Lawrenceville's trade unions and fraternal orders formed both parallel and interconnecting webs of organizations. The unions, most of which adhered to narrow craft definitions, and the fraternal groups, often with ethnic but cross-class membership requirements, were not mutually exclusive. A skilled worker on his way to work in the morning might greet a shopkeeper as a brother from an ethnic organization, a day laborer as a beneficial lodge brother, and a fellow craftsman as a union brother. Late-nineteenth-century working people used both fraternal orders and labor unions in their attempts to shape collectively the circumstances of their lives. Seeking to respond to the problems they faced and to build their own versions of a just republic, they created beneficial societies to minimize the effects of illness, accident, and death; ethnic fraternal orders to create (or recreate) a sense of community; and trade unions to gain control of, and compensation for, their labor.[23] At times the objectives of these organizations conflicted. Membership in one group often led to divisiveness in another, most clearly seen in ethnic hostilities. Nevertheless, their common roots in a culture of democratic voluntarism meant that they often supported each other as well.[24]

By the late nineteenth century disagreements between German, Irish, British, and native-born workers rarely disrupted community harmony. However, a new nativism on the part of the skilled workers from these ethnic groups grew out of their complex responses to changes in both personnel and technology at their workplaces. Sounding as if it could have been lifted from a JOUAM tract, the *National Labor Tribune* headlined a front-page story in 1900: "Hordes of Europe Expected Here to Work in American Sweatshops. Mostly Italians and Hebrews."[25] Lawrenceville's industries attracted many southern and eastern European immigrants. In the Carnegie Steel Company plants, for example, Slavs made up almost three-quarters of the unskilled workers by 1907. Italians filled the ranks of day laborers in Lawrenceville's railroad yards and in construction work.[26] These unskilled workers did not compete directly

23. Though he does not talk about fraternal orders in quite this way, Gist, in *Secret Societies*, provided an important catalyst for my thinking on this topic.

24. See Mary Ann Clawson, "Fraternal Orders and Class Formation in the Nineteenth-Century United States," *Comparative Studies in Society and History* 27 (1985), 672–695, for a more detailed discussion of these and other issues.

25. *NLT*, 7/26/1900.

26. Robert Asher, "Union Nativism and the Immigrant Response," *Labor History* 23 (1982), 338; A. T. Lane, "The British and American Labour Movements and the Problem of Immigration, 1890–1914," in Kenneth Lunn, ed., *Hosts, Immigrants and Minorities: Historical Responses to Newcomers in British Society 1870–1914* (New York: St. Martin's Press, 1980); Fitch, *Steel Workers*, Appendix X, table A, p. 349; Bodnar, Simon, and Weber, *Lives of Their Own*, pp. 57–58.

for jobs with the native-born and old-immigrant workers. However, as they entered the new unskilled and semiskilled jobs created by new technologies and the subdivision of labor, they became symbols of the myriad changes that were destroying skilled workers' control over their working lives.

Moving into Lawrenceville's industries, the newcomers also moved into the neighborhood's residences. Poles employed in the metal shops along the river found little affordable housing in the 15th ward itself and so moved onto the steep hillsides that rose up beyond the Pennsylvania Railroad tracks, just behind the ward. This area, previously unsettled, soon became known as "Polish Hill." By 1900 the 15th ward, which in 1880 had contained no southern or eastern European immigrants, was 5.5 percent Eastern European. Italian immigrants entered Lawrenceville from another direction, moving into the Bloomfield area at the southeast corner of the 16th ward. Some streets quickly became entirely Italian, as that group came to make up over 6 percent of the ward's population by 1900.[27] Even the 17th ward, with a higher native-born population to begin with, found some streets, especially the alleyways close to the railroad tracks and mills, given over almost entirely to the new immigrants. Lawrenceville's skilled workers, then, began to feel hemmed in by the new immigrants both at work and at home (see map of Lawrenceville, figure 3).

In the context of this social and economic world, then, skilled workers like Emanuel Schillo decided to enroll their children in the high school's Commercial Department. The ways in which this world formed their ideas about public education can be seen in the roles such skilled workers played in the local schools. Before 1911 ward or "subdistrict" school boards ran the grammar schools that were the city population's main contact with public education. Each subdistrict board consisted of six directors, two elected each year, who were legally empowered to choose teachers for their local schools and to levy the local property tax that paid for the erection and maintenance of school buildings and equipment, janitors' salaries, and supplies. The subdistrict board also chose a representative to Pittsburgh's Central Board of Education, which dealt with citywide functions.[28] In the civic arena provided by the ward school boards, different interest groups within the community sought both physi-

27. Bodnar, Simon, and Weber, *Lives of Their Own*, pp. 69, 71, 76; Abbott, *A City Parish*, pp. 45–46; Bodnar, Simon, and Weber, *Lives of Their Own*, pp. 69, 72. Bodnar, Simon, and Weber, *Lives of Their Own*, cite one six-block area, previously entirely German, as half-German and half-Italian in 1900, entirely Italian by 1920 (p. 72).

28. Pittsburgh Board of Education, *35th and 36th Annual Reports* (1904), pp. 1–2.

cal and political space. The roles played by the area's skilled workers reveal not only their attitudes toward education, but also the place of those attitudes in their wider self-perceptions.

From the 1870s through the early twentieth century, the three Lawrenceville school boards attempted to balance educational concerns and other demands of the citizenry. Lawrenceville's industrial and residential mix meant that the schools had always served a wide range of social groups, a constituency divided by both ethnicity and class. This task was further complicated in the first decade of the twentieth century, however, when the arrival of southern and eastern European immigrants upset the modus vivendi established by the native-born and old-immigrant residents. At the same time the system of ward control of the grammar schools faced external threats. Losing control of the local schools had special significance for the area's native-born and old-immigrant skilled workers. For them the decline of their power in educational matters replicated the decline of their power in the workplace as well.

The men that Lawrenceville residents elected as their school directors were not precisely representative of the neighborhood. From all three of the subdistricts for the years between 1890 and 1910, about one-fourth of the school directors came from the working class, while another quarter were proprietors of small retail or service establishments. Nineteen percent of the directors were clerical or sales workers. Only 9 percent were professional men, and less than 3 percent were the proprietors of wholesale or manufacturing concerns (see table 13).[29]

The composition of the school boards illustrates the potential leadership role of skilled workers within the working class. The 15th ward contained the lowest proportion of skilled workers among its population in 1900 and the highest number of members of the nonmanual classes. In this, historically the most polarized, ward in Lawrenceville, the upper end of the class scale maintained effective control of the school boards, while in the other wards a middle range running from skilled workers through clerical and sales workers dominated the boards. In these wards, where skilled workers either outnumbered unskilled workers (17th ward) or had relatively few "middle-class" groups contending for power (16th ward), the skilled workers gained an important measure of control over the

29. The sample of subdistrict directors for 1890, 1895, 1900, 1905, and 1910 was traced in the Pittsburgh city directories for those years. It was impossible to trace the occupations of almost 12 percent of the directors, either because they were not listed in the appropriate city directories, or because they were listed without any occupation, suggesting that they may have been retired.

Table 13. Occupations of general population (1900) compared with occupations of school directors (1890–1910) in Lawrenceville

	15th ward		16th ward		17th ward		All three wards	
	General population	School directors	General population	School directors	General population	School directors	General population	School directors
Unskilled*	51.8%	4.3%	51.1%	9.1%	33.2%	0	44.0%	4.3%
Skilled**	21.8	8.7	33.2	27.2	44.0	29.1%	35.6	21.7
Service proprietors	0	8.7	1.7	18.2	3.3	12.5	2.1	13.0
Public employees	1.8	0	0.7	9.1	0.7	12.5	0.9	7.2
Clerical and sales	3.6	21.7	1.4	18.2	7.4	16.7	4.2	18.8
Retail proprietors	14.6	17.4	6.8	4.5	5.9	12.5	7.7	11.6
Professionals	0.9	13.0	1.4	4.5	2.9	8.3	1.9	8.7
Wholesale proprietors	0	4.3	0	0	0.4	0	0.1	1.4
Manufacturing proprietors	0	0	0	0	0.4	4.2	0.1	1.4
Unknown	5.5	21.7	3.8	9.1	1.8	4.2	3.3	11.6
N	110	23	292	22	271	24	673	69

Sources: 1900 population from sample of every tenth male head of household in 1900 manuscript census. School directors from linkage of school directors' names (1890, 1895, 1900, 1905, 1910) with Pittsburgh City Directory listings in those years.
Note: This table follows the second occupational schema described in the appendix.
*Including semiskilled.
**Including foremen.

schools. In the 15th ward, on the other hand, where unskilled workers far outnumbered skilled workers, the upper end of the social scale controlled the board.

On the school boards, then, skilled workers, given a critical mass, could provide a working-class presence in local politics. Several actions by the different boards suggest the impact of working-class representation among the school directors. From the 1870s onward, for example, Pittsburgh's grammar schools began to establish evening classes to serve children who worked during regular school hours. The 15th-ward school board, with its relatively low working-class representation, offered evening courses for only four years between 1878 and 1882. The 16th ward schools, on the other hand, offered evening courses throughout the 1880s. Although evening schools were suspended in the early 1890s, they resumed again in 1897. The 17th-ward school board offered evening classes in at least one of its two buildings almost continuously from 1871 through the 1890s, even though enrollments were relatively small.[30] By offering evening classes the school boards demonstrated their sensitivity to the needs of their working-class constituencies.

The Lawrenceville school boards also evinced varying degrees of interest in other educational schemes that historians have traditionally identified with "progressive" and "middle-class" control of the schools. By the early twentieth century groups dominated by middle-class women and social workers sought to establish two innovative educational programs in the local schools: summer schools and playgrounds, and kindergartens.[31] The 15th-ward subdistrict board once again had minimal dealings with the two schemes. In June of 1908 the board allowed the Pittsburgh Kindergarten Association to establish a kindergarten in the local school. The Pittsburgh Playground Association, working through

30. Pittsburgh Board of Education, *11th Annual Report* (1879), pp. 42–43; Pittsburgh, Howard (16th-ward) Sub-District School Board, Minute Book, 1/6/1897; Pittsburgh, Washington (17th-ward) Sub-District School Board, Minute Book, 9/18/1871. Pittsburgh Board of Education, *Annual Reports*, 1878–94, give district-by-district evening school enrollment figures.

31. Couvares, *Remaking of Pittsburgh*, pp. 113–115. The Pittsburgh Playground Association was incorporated in 1906, composed of a joint committee of members of the Civic Club (involved in playground work since 1896) and the city's women's clubs (involved since 1900). Paul Underwood Kellogg, ed., *The Pittsburgh District: Civic Frontage* (New York: Survey Associates, 1914), pp. 306–324. The Kindergarten Association was established in 1892. It supplied teachers for local kindergartens, but the subdistrict school boards had to provide equipment. This arrangement often led to conflict and confusion over the kindergartens. Kellogg, *Pittsburgh District*, pp. 289–291. See also Paul Violas, *The Training of the Urban Working Class* (Chicago: Rand McNally, 1978).

the Lawrenceville Board of Trade, approached the board in 1910. The subdistrict board then granted the group's request "for various departments Social centers for sewing and cooking school etc."[32]

The 16th-ward school board had more extensive relations with these organizations. In the spring of 1905, when fully half of the board members were manual workers, the board agreed to let a "Joint Com. of Women's Clubs for Playgrounds and Vacation Schools" use two of their buildings for a four-week summer school, a project repeated every summer thereafter. In the fall of 1909 the Pittsburgh Playground Association approached the board once again with a plan for lectures, a library and reading room, playrooms, a gymnasium, courses in domestic science, and more, in the district's third school building. At an extended meeting the board discussed the proposal, ultimately suggesting that the project begin with a more limited range of activities, including an elementary-level night school run by the school district rather than by the Playground Association. On taking this proposal back to the Playground Association, however, the board members discovered that the subdistrict would have to fund nearly the entire project themselves, a revelation that ended the plans. In the case of the Kindergarten Association, the board approached the Association rather than vice versa. In April 1911 the 16th-ward school board asked the group to open a kindergarten in one of its buildings, a request with which the association gladly complied.[33]

Paul Violas has argued that progressive educational reformers saw the "play movement" as a way to inculcate the working class with values and habits deemed proper by these professional educators and their supporters. As such it was part of the general Progressive movement that removed education from the purview of its consumers and placed it under the control of "experts." This connection certainly existed in Pittsburgh, where the president of the Playground Association, Beulah Kennard, was also one of the main proponents of abolishing local control of the schools altogether. In a 1910 article Kennard wrote that the playground movement was directed toward the immigrant children of the cities' slums, those children "who fail to 'measure up' to our standard of American childhood and who seem likely to fall still farther from the standard of American manhood and womanhood."[34] In the context of progressive education,

32. Pittsburgh, Lawrence (15th-ward) Sub-District School Board, Minute Book, 7/9/1908, 7/1/1908, 6/3/1908, 3/2/1910.

33. Pittsburgh, Howard (16th-ward) Sub-District School Board, Minute Book, 3/8/1905, 10/19/1909, 11/3/1909, 12/10/1909, 4/5/1911, 6/7/1911.

34. Violas, *Training of the Urban Working Class*, chap. 4, "The Play Movement," pp. 67–92; Beulah Kennard, "The Playground for Children at Home," *The Annals of the*

this is a clear statement of the imposition of upper-class standards upon the working class. But some members of Lawrenceville's working class would have seen it quite differently. While the area's skilled workers did not think their neighborhood was a "slum," they had their own ideas and fears about a "standard of American childhood." The actions of the 17th-ward school board indicate skilled workers' own interpretations of "Progressive" educational reforms.

In 1901 "the Ladies of the 'Summer School' Association" asked the 17th-ward school board for permission to conduct a six-week playground and kindergarten program "for the children of the poor." The board allowed them the use of a ward school for that purpose, but only for a four-week session. At the same meeting the board tabled a request from the Kindergarten Association to set up a kindergarten in another of the school buildings, citing the cost of the project to the local school board.[35] After these initial dealings with the "ladies" of the official organizations, however, the 17th-ward school board took a novel approach to the issue. The next year, and for several years thereafter, the board bypassed the citywide organizations and instead instituted programs run by the wife of Lawrenceville's original central board representative, a druggist. Mrs. Anna Covert established a program that initially included "a cooking school, sewing school, and Manual training school" and was soon expanded to include a kindergarten as well.[36] In this case the local school board accepted the Progressive concept of summer schools, but ensured its own control of the project. By investing a trusted neighbor with the program, the board had more influence over values imparted and methods used.

In 1906 the 17th-ward school board went even further in appropriating progressive education for its own ends when it took the first steps toward establishing an industrial training school in the ward. When they first considered the idea, board members included a steel roller serving as president and central board representative, a railroad dispatcher, an "inspector," a physician, the owner of a local sand and gravel company, and

---

American Academy of Political and Social Science 35 (1910), 380. Also see her article, "The Playgrounds of Pittsburgh," in Kellogg, *Pittsburgh District,* pp. 306–324. Kennard was a member of Pittsburgh's first appointed school board.

35. Pittsburgh, Washington (17th-ward) Sub-District School Board, Minute Book, 6/6/1901.

36. Pittsburgh, Washington (17th-ward) Sub-District School Board, Minute Book, 3/6/1902, 7/2/1902. Anna Covert's husband, J. J. Covert, was one of the original committee members to set up the high school's commercial and normal departments (see chapter 2).

8. Domestic Science room in Washington Industrial School, Pittsburgh. From Pittsburgh School Board, *41st and 42nd Annual Report* (1909 and 1910), opp. p. 72.

one unemployed member notorious for his inattendance at board meetings. By December of 1906 they had decided to go ahead with the project. As one of the relatively few wards in the city whose schools supported no bonded indebtedness, the board felt obliged to place before the electorate the question of raising sixty thousand dollars in bonds to fund the project. In January 1907 17th-ward residents voted almost three to one for the industrial school.[37] In July 1908 the school board granted permission to a local Council of the Junior Order of United American Mechanics to lay the cornerstone for the new building. When completed, the "Washington

37. Pittsburgh City Directory, 1905; Pittsburgh, Washington (17th-ward) Sub-District School Board, Minute Book, 6/7/1905, 5/1/1906, 12/4/1906, 3/27/1907. Pittsburgh, Washington (17th-ward) Sub-District School Board, Minute Book, 2/7/1907. Three hundred fifty-six voted for it (72 percent), and 141 against it (28 percent). This is a fairly low voter turnout; in the November 1906 gubernatorial election, the 17th ward cast 1,888 ballots. Thomas B. Cochran, comp., *Smull's Legislative Handbook, and Manual of the State of Pennsylvania 1907* (Harrisburg: State Printer of Pennsylvania, 1907), p. 369. No figures were available on other primary election turnouts.

Industrial School" not only housed "industrial equipment" (including facilities for cooking classes for women), but also a gymnasium and swimming pool.[38]

Even more than the playground movement, historians have viewed the establishment of industrial schools as the pinnacle of educational reformers' efforts to incorporate working-class youth into the existing capitalist system. In this case, however, a major industrial school was established, not by Progressive reformers, but by the kind of local school board the city's reformers ultimately worked to abolish. What did the men of the 17th-ward board—working class and non–working class alike—think the industrial school would do for the working-class children of Lawrenceville? A newspaper article at the time claimed that "there is urgent need for such a school in Lawrenceville," and the school directors obviously agreed.[39] But the school directors saw that need arising not from their own social ranks, but from those below them—and especially from the new-immigrant residents of the area. The establishment of the 17th-ward industrial school demonstrates skilled workers' perceptions of a stratified educational system. Participating in the administration of the local grammar schools, skilled workers still viewed them as the source of the basic education necessary for all members of a democratic republic. They treated the high school's programs, such as the Commercial Department, as extensions of the grammar schools. The "People's College" would provide further education and specific vocational training to the children of those workers who wished to partake of it. Their conceptions of the industrial school's clientele were quite different.

By the early 1900s the new immigrants had begun to make requests of the ward school systems. The 17th-ward board, which had sponsored summer German-language classes as late as 1901, by 1910 granted the YMCA permission to use school rooms "to teach Foreigners in that district, Civic Instruction and Hygiene."[40] For the 17th ward's skilled workers, as for Progressive professional educators, the industrial school

38. Pittsburgh, Washington (17th-ward) Sub-District School Board, Minute Book, 7/2/1908; Pittsburgh Board of Education, *41st and 42nd Annual Reports* (1909–10), p. 54, and picture of school opposite p. 72.

39. See Violas, *Training of the Urban Working Class;* Samuel Bowles and Herbert Gintis, *Schooling in Capitalist America* (New York: Basic Books, 1976); David John Hogan, "Capitalism and Schooling: A History of the Political Economy of Education in Chicago, 1880–1930," diss., University of Illinois at Urbana-Champaign, 1978; newspaper quotation from loose (and unidentified) newspaper clipping in vol. 3 of Pittsburgh, Washington (17th-ward) Sub-District School Board, Minute Book.

40. Pittsburgh, Washington (17th-ward) Sub-District School Board, Minute Book, 11/3/1910, 6/20/1901.

would serve the new immigrants pressing into their neighborhood. Organized workers at the turn of the century generally opposed industrial schools, viewing them as destructive of trade-union apprenticeships. When the Pennsylvania Department of Industrial Statistics asked construction workers in 1894 whether they preferred industrial schools or apprenticeship programs, virtually all the respondents supported apprenticeships.[41] But these questions were asked in terms of the skilled workers' own trades. Preferring union-controlled apprenticeships over educational programs without such control differed from creating educational programs for trades without apprenticeships and workers with little other chance of gaining skills. Organized workers saw little hope that the new immigrants would ever contribute to the established labor movement. As one author explained it, "The Hun of Braddock, the Italian of the street contractors in the cities, are the rawest of the raw; the citizen workmen of the older and firmly established and judiciously managed labor organizations are at the other extreme from them."[42] Just as the high school's Commercial Department provided training for the clerical occupations that had no organized apprenticeships, so an industrial school would impart skills to one sector of the working class without undermining the organized workers' apprenticeship programs. The fact that the JOUAM laid the cornerstone of the Washington Industrial School illustrates local conceptions of whom the school would serve.

The JOUAM, a nativist fraternal organization dating from the 1840s, espoused immigration restriction and Bible readings in "nonsectarian" public schools. In the 1890s they called for "a flag on every public school in the land, the Holy Bible within, and love of country instilled into the heart of every child." Hitting its peak during the decade that historian John Higham called "the Nationalist Nineties," the JOUAM was particularly strong in Pennsylvania.[43] The 1895 Pittsburgh city directory listed sixty-six councils of the organization, seven of them in Lawrence-

41. Philip R. V. Curoe, *Educational Attitudes and Policies of Organized Labor in the United States* (New York: Teachers College, Columbia University, 1926), pp. 163–164. When the American Federation of Labor established a Committee on Industrial Education in 1908, its main concern was to make sure that students would not be "exploited." Damning the increasing specialization of trades, the committee's 1912 report called for industrial schools to replicate the all-round training of the best apprenticeships. U.S. Congress, Senate, *Report of Committee on Industrial Education of the American Federation of Labor*, 62d Cong., 2d sess., 1912, Sen. Doc. No. 936, pp. 7, 20; Pennsylvania, *Industrial Statistics* (1894), pp. B.419–420.

42. *NLT*, 1/10/1891.

43. "A flag on every . . . ," Stevens, *Cyclopaedia of Fraternities*, p. 302; JOUAM on public schools, Edward S. Deemer, ed., *History of the Junior Order United American Mechanics* (Boston: Fraternity Publishing Co., 1896), p. 43, JOUAM in Pennsylvania,

ville. There, as elsewhere in the city and country, the order vociferously supported public education, most often through ceremonial presentations of American flags that were to fly over school buildings.[44]

The Junior Order's eagerness to lay the cornerstone for the 17th-ward industrial school lays bare the working-class version of Progressive fears about urban immigrant slums. Calling turn-of-the-century immigration "the Republic's Peril," the JOUAM blamed post–Civil War industrialization for calling forth immigration damaging in both its quantity and quality. Unlike earlier immigrants, the order's spokesmen explained, the post-1870s influx was "clannish" and uncommitted to American standards and institutions. While they accepted the need for some level of immigration, they argued that only a small number at a time could be properly "Americanized," while too large an influx would "foreignize us." Public education played a crucial role, both in the process of Americanization and in the battle against "foreignization." Claiming that insular ethnic customs led to a neglect of children's education, the JOUAM maintained that this was unacceptable in a republic dependent on the informed participation of its citizens.[45] For the JOUAM, then, support for the Washington Industrial School represented yet another way to coax the poor and immigrant into public schools, providing them simultaneously with "proper" work habits and with the uplifting influence of "the little red schoolhouse."

The 17th-ward industrial school represents the ways in which skilled workers and Progressive reformers could share common goals rising out of different perceptions of the problems they faced. It also represents the culmination of skilled workers' participation in the management of Lawrenceville schools. At the same time that the school directors of the 17th ward were planning their industrial school, Pittsburgh reformers were plotting the overthrow of the subdistrict school boards themselves.

During the 1907–08 school year, the Pittsburgh Voters' League undertook a study of the city's school system and its administration. The Voters' League, a middle-class reform organization, was shocked by the results of its inquiry into the city's ward school boards:

---

p. 83; John Higham, *Strangers in the Land: Patterns of American Nativism, 1860–1925* (New York: Atheneum, 1973), chap. 4, "The Nationalist Nineties," pp. 68–105. The JOUAM was the second-largest fraternal order in Pennsylvania in 1898—see map in Stevens, *Cyclopaedia of Fraternities,* p. 119.

44. Pittsburgh City Directory, 1895, pp. 68–69. Pittsburgh, Howard (16th-ward) Sub-District School Board, Minute Book, 5/6/1892.

45. Deemer, *History of the JOUAM,* "The Republic's Peril," pp. 88–101, "The Public Schools," pp. 102–114.

Pittsburgh has a few school boards made up of educated and competent directors, and their schools are good. It has other districts where the boards are controlled by men who are honest, but without education or business experience, and their schools are inefficient. It has a third class where the boards are either entirely corrupt, or are controlled by those who are, and their schools are bad. The second and third classes are in the majority.

Arguing that "a man's occupation ought to give strong indication of his qualifications for membership on a school board," the Voters' League proceeded to label as unfit not only saloon keepers, bartenders, and "gamblers," but also laborers and unskilled mill workers, government employees of all types, contractors and sales agents, "small storekeepers, clerks, [and] workmen at many trades."[46] In 1910 these guidelines would have unseated all the members of the 15th- and 16th-ward boards, and all but one member (a physician) of the 17th-ward board.

Lawrenceville's subdistrict school directors understood this threat immediately, joining with directors throughout the city to oppose wholesale reform of the school system. Though the Commonwealth's House of Representatives defeated proposed school code changes in 1909, the changes were merely delayed. In 1911 the legislature enacted a new school code for Pittsburgh which established a Board of Public Education made up of fifteen members appointed by city judges. The establishment of a "board of visitors" for each ward, consisting of seven members with purely "advisory" functions, left only a feeble remnant of local school control.[47]

In the view of Lawrenceville's workers and small shopkeepers alike, the 1911 school code stripped them of their democratic right to self-governance. When the Chicago school system had undergone a similar transformation ten years earlier, Pittsburgh's *National Labor Tribune* had condemned the change. Declaring that "nothing touches the heart and soul of our great republic so much as our public schools," the paper's editor had argued that elected school boards were less "political" than appointed ones. One advocate of Pittsburgh's new code argued that subdistrict

46. 1907/08 study, Lila Ver Planck North, "Pittsburgh Schools," in Kellogg, ed., *Pittsburgh District,* p. 218; "Pittsburgh has a few . . . ," "Bulletin of the Voters' League Concerning the Public School System of Pittsburgh" (2/15/1911), p. 1, "a man's occupation . . . ," p. 2, "small storekeepers . . . ," p. 3. On the movement generally, see Samuel P. Hays, "The Politics of Reform in Municipal Government in the Progressive Era," *Pacific Northwest Quarterly* 55 (October 1964), 160–163.

47. Pittsburgh, Lawrence (15th-ward) Sub-District School Board, Minute Book, 4/7/1909; Kellogg, *Pittsburgh District,* p. 469.

schools had worked well in the early nineteenth century, when the homogeneity of the population had assured common standards for all the ward schools. "By the opening of the twentieth century," she continued, ". . . there was no longer homogeneousness of any kind; instead there was conflict in the aims and conduct of life. Nor was this the world-old individual variance; it was a group variance, made persistent through the maintenance of distinct racial or class habits and thoughts."[48] The Lawrenceville school directors, used to working together to serve their diverse constituencies, might have agreed with this statement. They might even have agreed that the situation had worsened since the turn of the century. They did not, however, think that they were incapable of dealing with the changes. Through the 1890s and early 1900s, the local school officials had tried to deal with the changing circumstances in their neighborhoods. They did so using their knowledge of and contact with the established working-class leaders—skilled workers from the old-immigrant groups— to inform their decisions about education for all of the community's residents.

In the late nineteenth century skilled workers such as those in Lawrenceville played a central role in shaping a world around their activities in trade unions, fraternal organizations, politics, and education. By the mid-1890s and into the early 1900s, these skilled workers faced a new situation. In many spheres of life they were losing their central position and control over events. At the workplace new technologies and the subdivision of labor increasingly limited their ability to regulate shop-floor relations. The depression of the 1890s and the ensuing corporate merger movement also changed skilled workers' positions, as the new corporations moved to halt the spread of union power. At the same time the timbre of social life also changed. New immigrants moved into Lawrenceville and disrupted the pattern of interaction between skilled and unskilled workers, which had been based largely on ethnic ties. The same immigration also brought Progressive reformers to Lawrenceville. Their actions and programs ultimately weakened the influence of skilled workers over neighborhood issues such as the schools. Unable (and often unwilling) to bridge the gap between new and old immigrants, and cut off from access to local elites, members of Lawrenceville's labor aristocracy had to find new ways to reinforce their status and to understand their world. In this context, the Commercial Department both trained their children for an expanding sector of the workforce and helped them distinguish themselves from the new immigrants.

48. *NLT*, 4/11/1901; North, in Kellogg, *Pittsburgh District*, pp. 244–245.

The Hill Top

The first houses appeared on the Hill Top in the late 1840s. Some of the early residents were farmers, while others came as miners to what was then known as Coal Hill. Many were from Germany, and they would impress upon the area both their culture and their skills. These Germans brought with them the crucial transportation concept for that locale: the inclined plane or, as it was known in Germany, the *steilbahn* (steep railway). The first inclines in the region served the coal industry and appeared in the 1850s, used simply to move the coal cars and tracks from the mines' interiors to the exterior face of the hill. After the Civil War, Hill Top residents collaborated with central-city businessmen to incorporate the Monongahela Inclined Plane Company. Granted a charter for a passenger-carrying incline in 1867, the Monongahela Incline finally opened in late May 1870. By the end of 1870 the incline had carried 218,732 passengers up and down Mount Washington.[49] Inclines brought the Hill Top into closer contact with Birmingham (the borough along the southern banks of the Monongahela) and with Pittsburgh proper. In 1872 the South Side, including Birmingham as well as the Hill Top boroughs of Mount Washington, Union, and Allentown, was absorbed into the city of Pittsburgh (see map of Hill Top, figure 4).

From the 1870s through the 1890s, the continued improvement of transportation services reinforced the Hill Top's political and economic ties to the rest of Pittsburgh. The Duquesne Incline began operation in 1873, and in 1884 the Monongahela Incline Company opened a second plane, parallel to their first, to carry freight and vehicles. By decreasing hauling costs to the Hill Top, this incline reduced the cost of food and other necessities for the area's residents and instigated something of a housing boom by cutting building costs as well. In the early 1890s two more Hill Top inclines opened, the Knoxville Incline to the 31st ward and the Castle Shannon Incline, which climbed both sides of Mount Washington and included a coal track as well.[50]

By the 1890s the Hill Top wards occupied a fairly stable niche in Pittsburgh's social and economic spectrum. The 31st ward (Allentown), faced with the least daunting geographic barriers, was heavily built up and boasted its own small business district along Washington Avenue. Skilled workers of German heritage still dominated the ward's population. The

49. Fleming, *History of Pittsburgh and Environs,* 2:86; Samuel R. Ohler, ed., *Pittsburgh's Inclines* (n.p., n.d. [1972?]), pp. 22, 10, 24, 2, 22–23.
50. Ohler, *Pittsburgh's Inclines,* pp. 23, 10.

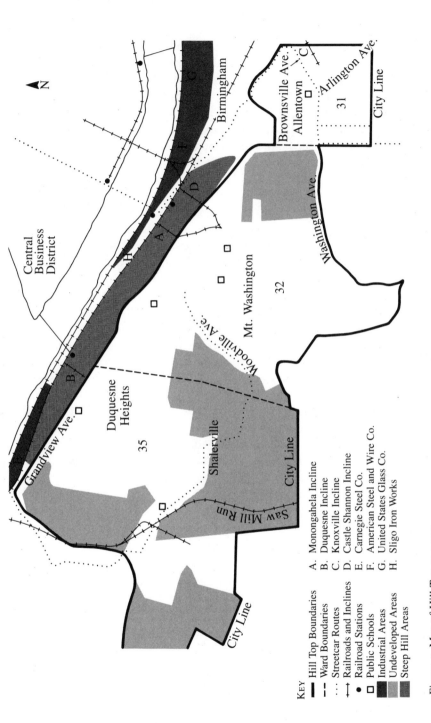

KEY

▰ Hill Top Boundaries	A. Monongahela Incline
┤├ Ward Boundaries	B. Duquesne Incline
⋯ Streetcar Routes	C. Knoxville Incline
┼┼ Railroads and Inclines	D. Castle Shannon Incline
• Railroad Stations	E. Carnegie Steel Co.
□ Public Schools	F. American Steel and Wire Co.
▰ Industrial Areas	G. United States Glass Co.
▰ Undeveloped Areas	H. Sligo Iron Works
▰ Steep Hill Areas	

Figure 4. Map of Hill Top, c. 1900

32nd and 35th wards had grown rapidly through the 1880s as suburban-style housing developments had sprung up. In 1880 the *National Labor Tribune* had commented on the beginning of a three-hundred-house project in the 35th ward, praising it as "a practical way to acquire a home." As late as 1900, however, both wards still encompassed large undeveloped spaces, especially in the outer reaches of the 35th ward. In 1902 a real estate company divided one hundred acres of 32nd-ward land into building lots and put it on the market. Their advertisements proclaimed it as "the last property within a mile of the skyscraper district." By the turn of the century, the combined population of the three wards exceeded twenty thousand, an increase of over five times its 1870 level.[51]

While the inclines solved the Hill Top's most pressing problem, that of simply getting up and down the steep slopes, they did not resolve all the residents' transportation difficulties. In fact, the presence of the inclines probably increased residents' calls for expanded services. What good was getting up and down the hill easily if you still had to walk half a mile or more between your home and the incline station? In the 1890s Pittsburgh businessmen and speculators had purchased the franchises for cable and electric trolley lines in the Hill Top region. However, the depression of the mid-nineties combined with city machine politics to create a maze of franchises and regulations, but few streetcar lines. As one promoter stated the desires of 32nd- and 35th-ward citizens, "Here we are, half a mile from the business center, as the crow flies, and no way of reaching the city."[52] Streetcars finally made it to the Hill Top in the early 1900s, creating yet another boom in residential development. At last the Hill Top had the possibility of becoming a true "streetcar suburb," with the central business district directly and easily accessible.

These transportation problems and their solutions clearly affected the employment situation for residents on the Hill Top. The options facing Hill Toppers were both similar to and different from those in Lawrence-

---

51. See George T. Fleming, ed., *Pittsburgh: How to See It* (Pittsburgh: William G. Johnston Co., 1916), p. 53, and *[Pittsburgh] Real Estate Plat-book*, vol. 4, plates 17–21, 27–28 (1901); *NLT*, 7/24/1880; Kellogg, *Pittsburgh District*, pp. 170–171; U.S. Department of the Interior, Bureau of the Census, *A Compendium of the Ninth Census (June 1, 1870)* (Washington, 1872), table IX, pp. 308–309; U.S. Department of the Interior, Census Office, *Twelfth Census of the United States, Taken in the Year 1900: Population*, vol. II, pt. II (Washington, 1902), table 24, pp. 677–678; Kellogg, *Pittsburgh District*, map on p. 99, showing population densities of wards: the 32nd and 35th wards had under 15 people per acre, and the 31st had 32 to 42.9 people per acre; in Lawrenceville the 16th and 17th wards had 43 to 53.9 people per acre, and the 15th ward had 54 to 63.9 people per acre.

52. Arnold, *Report on the Pittsburgh Transportation Problem*, p. 41; "A Row Over Franchises," [Pittsburgh] *Dispatch*, 2/24/1894.

ville. On one hand, fewer establishments of all kinds existed within the Hill Top ward boundaries. On the other hand, far more employment opportunities lay just beyond the Hill Top, down the steep hills in Birmingham or in downtown Pittsburgh less than a mile away. While only a few streets wound their tortuous ways down from Mount Washington and Allentown (and none at all from Duquesne Heights), by the 1890s residents could either ride the inclines to work or simply walk (or slide!) down the steep slopes. While the Hill Top itself therefore maintained an almost purely residential character, the economic and industrial variety of the entire city lay within reach of its residents.

Clerical and sales workers could ride the inclines down the hills and then walk or take a streetcar across the river into downtown Pittsburgh. They might also, after descending the hill, head east into the Birmingham district, where smaller banks and stores afforded white-collar employment. As in Lawrenceville two railroad stations and the offices of various manufacturing concerns also hired clerks of various sorts.

Hill Top women who sought wage-earning opportunities found many in nearby Birmingham. They might work in small department stores such as Bernardi and Company on Carson Street, which hired thirty-eight women in 1900. In addition, all sorts of small- to medium-sized concerns, ranging from paper box and brush factories to the bolt works of the Oliver Iron and Steel Company, also employed women. Birmingham's uniqueness in Pittsburgh, however, came from its glass factories. While these hired many more men than women, some employed women as glass packers or decorators. The Oriental Glass Company, for example, located directly below the 31st ward, employed over fifty women at the turn of the century.[53] Although Birmingham's stores and factories thus made sales and industrial employment for women more common than in Lawrenceville, domestic service was less of an option. Few wealthy Pittsburghers lived on the South Side of the Monongahela during these years; Birmingham streets were too cramped and polluted, and a continuing lack of public services on the Hill Top made that area less than an attractive option.

At the turn of the century, many of the qualities that made the South Side unattractive to upper-class Pittsburghers were a result of the major factories along the Monongahela river plain. Virtually all of Pittsburgh's

---

53. These examples of individual companies are taken from Pennsylvania Department of the Factory Inspector, *11th Annual Report* (1900), pp. 1237–1301. The occupations described here were those engaged in by teenagers located in a comparative sample of Lawrenceville and Hill Top families. See Appendix, Description of Data.

glass factories were located in Birmingham. These usually hired between one hundred and two hundred men, though some employed over four hundred. The glass factories coexisted with the ubiquitous iron and steel mills and related metal shops along the river below the Hill Top.

With this industrial mix, then, the South Side boasted its own version of Pittsburgh's vibrant union culture. As in Lawrenceville, skilled workers in the iron and steel mills belonged to lodges of the AAISW, while machinists in small workshops joined the IAM. Glassblowers and other glassworkers belonged to one of the three glass-trades unions, the Window Glass Workers' Association (Knights of Labor Local Assembly 300), the Glass Bottle Blowers' Association (GBBA), or the American Flint Glass Workers' Union (AFGWU).[54] Along with the puddlers, rollers, and other skilled workers of the AAISW, these skilled glassworkers formed the core of Pittsburgh's labor movement from the 1870s to the turn of the century. These labor aristocrats, paid the highest wages in the region, formed the stable base for the city's labor movement. While some skilled workers lived in the cramped alleyways of Birmingham, many rented or purchased homes on the Hill Top.

German-born Charles Herbster, a widow-glass flattener and council member of Local Assembly 300 in 1895, owned his home in the 31st ward at the turn of the century. Just three blocks away lived his brother union member, John B. Ensell, who had bought two lots for his home on his wages as a glassblower. Yet another member of LA 300, Edward Phillips, had lived in Birmingham in 1890, but had moved to the 31st ward by 1895, where he rented a home several blocks from Herbster and Ensell. All three men had sons who attended Pittsburgh's Commercial Department in the early 1890s.[55]

Skilled men such as these glassworkers shared more than union membership and a common educational program for their children. Like Lawrenceville residents, Hill Toppers joined a variety of organizations that suggest their competing cultural identities. Fraternal organizations served a wide range of interests, from the active nativism of the JOUAM, through the nostalgic patriotism of the Grand Army of the Republic

54. Lake Erie and Ohio River Ship Canal Co., *Industrial Map* (1907); Pearce Davis, *The Development of the American Glass Industry* (Cambridge: Harvard University Press, 1949), pp. 127, 145, 156.

55. Home ownership information from plat map of 31st ward; union membership information from *Convention Proceedings of L.A. 300, Knights of Labor*, 1883, 1886, 1895, Joseph Slight Papers Microfilm Edition, Ohio Historical Society (roll 8, frames 19, 52, 115–118).

(GAR), the financial security of beneficial societies, and the ethnic identity of German groups.[56] The local schools and their directors interacted with many of these organizations. The JOUAM presented flags to the schools and at one point gave medals to the 32nd-ward students with the highest high school examination scores. The 31st-ward schools maintained particularly close relationships with various German groups in the area, often holding their commencement exercises in the local Turner Hall. They also worked closely with a German Lutheran school, inviting its staff and students to the public school's annual picnic.[57] The Hill Top school boards also understood the union sentiments of their constituency; all three agreed to hire only union labor for school projects in the early twentieth century.[58]

While skilled workers' lives on the Hill Top therefore included many of the same organizational features of Lawrenceville, the social complexions of the two areas still differed significantly, due at least in part to the geography of the Hill Top. The hills' steep rise from the river plain not only isolated the area from the rest of the city, but also impeded comfortable residential life. The city provided few services to the area; the extension of sewers and gas lines lagged behind other parts of the city, and as school records reflect, some streets remained unpaved in the early twentieth century. The two school buildings in the 35th ward, almost a mile apart, were connected by a single road that was impassable for at least three months of every year. All three of the subdistrict boards frequently dealt with school plumbing problems, and the lack of sanitary

56. Eight councils of nativist societies met regularly on the Hill Top in 1895, and the "Grand Vice Grand Master" of the American Protestant Association, a carpenter by trade, lived in the 32nd ward (City Directory, 1895, p. 69; JOUAM, APA, Daughters of Liberty). The GAR and its subsidiaries were also represented (GAR, Ladies of the GAR, and Sons of Veterans), as were the current beneficial societies of different kinds (AOUW, Royal Arcanum, Improved Order of Heptasophs, Knights and Ladies of Honor, Order of United Friends, Ancient Order Knights of the Mystic Chain, Odd Fellows, Knights of Pythias, Order of the World, Protected Home Circle, Improved Order of Red Men). The Independent Sovereigns of Industry also had Hill Top meetings. Councils of the North American Sangerbund met in the Hill Top Turner and Maennerchor Halls, and two sections of the Catholic Mutual Benefit Association met in local Catholic churches. There was also an order of the German Beneficial Union.

57. Pittsburgh, Mount Washington (32nd-ward) Sub-District School Board, Minute Book, 12/5/1905, 8/3/1910; Pittsburgh, Luckey (35th-ward) Sub-District School Board, Minute Book, 10/6/1908, 4/5/1909; Pittsburgh, Allen (31st-ward) Sub-District School Board, Minute Book, 10/2/1901, 7/3/1907, 9/6/1911, 6/8/1904, 7/5/1905, 5/2/1906.

58. Pittsburgh, Mount Washington (32nd-ward) Sub-District School Board, Minute Book, 7/25/1907; Pittsburgh, Luckey (35th-ward) Sub-District School Board, Minute Book, 6/6/1910; Pittsburgh, Allen (31st-ward) Sub-District School Board, Minute Book, 8/14/1906.

9. Wyoming Street and Virginia Avenue looking toward Boggs Avenue, 32nd ward, Pittsburgh, 1910. From Archives of Industrial Society, Hillman Library, University of Pittsburgh.

services boosted the rate of illnesses on the Hill Top. As late as 1907 the 32nd-ward board signed a petition of local citizens asking for the Bureau of Health's aid in getting a sufficient water supply to the ward.[59] Given the difficulties in providing city services to the area, few wealthy Pittsburghers chose to build in the hills, preferring the flat plains of the East End instead.[60] These problems kept housing prices down even in the new

59. See description of sewage problems around Saw Mill Run in Kellogg, *Pittsburgh District*, p. 93; Pittsburgh Board of Education, 19th Annual Report (1887), p. 58; school directors request paving: Pittsburgh, Luckey (35th-ward) Sub-District School Board, Minute Book, 9/3/1906; Pittsburgh, Allen (31st-ward) Sub-District School Board, Minute Book, 7/30/1902, 2/16/1905; Pittsburgh, Mount Washington (32nd-ward) Sub-District School Board, Minute Book, 4/4/1901, 1/7/1908. Allen school board kept close track of illnesses in its school: Pittsburgh, Allen (31st-ward) Sub-District School Board, Minute Book, 1/7/1903, 12/7/1904, 10/4/1905, 3/4/1908, 2/3/1909, 10/6/1909. Kellogg, *Pittsburgh District,* p. 67, shows a high rate of typhoid in the 32nd ward. Pittsburgh, Mount Washington (32nd-ward) Sub-District School Board, Minute Book, 8/6/1907.

60. In 1900 only 0.2 percent of Hill Top residents owned manufacturing or wholesale businesses (from my 10 percent sample of wards). Susan J. Kleinberg ("Technology's Stepdaughters: The Impact of Industrialization upon Working Class Women, Pittsburgh,

developments of the early twentieth century. More skilled workers lived in these wards than did unskilled workers, who usually could not afford even the modest Hill Top housing prices. As transportation to the central business district improved, these manual workers were joined by white-collar clerical and sales workers. The owners of the small businesses that served their neighbors complete the picture of Hill Top's social strata.

The occupations represented in the Hill Top's subdistrict school boards reflected the social composition of the wards, as table 14 illustrates. Over a third of all the school directors came from the manual working class. The differences between the three wards once again indicate the role of skilled workers in working-class politics. Even more clearly than Lawrenceville's 15th ward, the Hill Top's 32nd ward demonstrates the importance of skilled workers in providing the working class with a political presence. As the table indicates, the 32nd ward had the fewest working-class residents. This translated into a weak working-class presence on the local school board, which was dominated by clerical and sales workers and retail proprietors. In the 31st ward (and to some extent in the 35th as well), the predominance of skilled workers in the neighborhood gave them an important role on the school board. In both of these wards skilled workers' representation on the subdistrict boards actually outstripped their proportion of the ward's population. In 1890, for example, all of the 31st ward's school directors were skilled workers, including four iron and steel workers, one glassblower, and one pattern maker.

The high level of skilled workers' participation on the Hill Top subdistrict boards prior to the 1911 school-code changes underscores the importance of education to these leaders of the working class. The 1890 31st-ward board included as its president Mahlon M. Garland, soon to be elected national president of the AAISW, one of the largest unions in the American Federation of Labor (AFL) at the time.[61] The AFL listed compulsory education first among its principles. For skilled workers education served two purposes. The first, and most important since it applied to everyone, came from their idea of what a democratic republic should be. As one proponent of working-class education put it:

> Is not a good citizen one that can vote intelligently, represent the people honestly and wisely, write and enact wise and just laws? Is not a good citizen

---

1865–1890," diss., University of Pittsburgh, 1973) gives percentage rates of "upper-class" residents for the Hill Top wards well below the average for the entire city in 1880 as well. Kleinberg talks about the differing distribution of city services to East End and Hill Top wards, pp. 91–92, 96, 105–106.

61. Fitch, *Steel Workers*, p. 107; *Report of the Proceedings of the 10th Annual Convention of the American Federation of Labor*, Delegate List, pp. 7–9.

Table 14. Occupations of general population (1900) compared with occupations of school directors (1890–1910) on Hill Top

	31st ward		32nd ward		35th ward		All three wards	
	General population	School directors	General population	School directors	General population	School directors	General population	School directors
Unskilled*	34.8%	4.4%	25.8%	0	39.7%	12.0%	31.3%	5.7%
Skilled**	42.2	47.8	35.5	13.6%	32.9	36.0	37.2	32.9
Service proprietors	2.2	8.7	4.6	4.5	2.7	8.0	3.5	7.1
Public employees	3.0	0	4.1	4.5	6.8	4.0	4.2	2.9
Clerical and sales	8.9	8.7	18.8	27.3	13.7	16.0	14.6	17.1
Retail proprietors	4.4	21.7	5.1	31.8	0	4.0	4.0	18.6
Professionals	3.0	4.4	3.0	9.1	1.4	4.0	2.7	5.7
Wholesale proprietors	0	0	0.5	9.1	0	4.0	0.2	4.3
Manufacturing proprietors	0	4.4	0	0	0	4.0	0	2.9
Unknown	1.5	0	2.5	0	2.7	8.0	2.2	2.9
N	135	23	197	22	73	25	405	70

Sources: 1900 population from sample of every tenth male head of household in 1900 manuscript census. School directors from linkage of school directors' names (1890, 1895, 1900, 1905, 1910) with Pittsburgh City Directory listings in those years.
Note: This table follows the second occupational schema described in the appendix.
*Including semiskilled.
**Including foremen.

one that can be called upon to fill positions of trust under the government, in the community, as Congressmen, Senators, and bring honor to the position, and defend the rights of the people? . . . I say that you cannot educate a man too much; to make a good citizen he cannot know too much.[62]

Only secondarily did skilled workers support education for future employment. As discussed earlier, the AFL and other unions remained suspicious of educational plans that either undermined apprenticeship systems or seemed to funnel workers' children into narrow or dead-end educational endeavors.[63] As long as skilled workers played a central role in the local schools, though, they trusted the entire system's programs. Peter Stoerkel, the sawyer who joined the 31st-ward board after Garland had left, is an example of this. While his children all attended the local grammar school, his daughter Katy went on to the high school's Commercial Department in 1897. Her father would know about that program not only from its public reputation, but also through inside information from the 31st ward's central-board representative.

Not surprisingly, the Hill Top school directors protested the proposed changes in the school code in 1909. All three boards joined the School Directors' Association in opposing the changes, and when the legislature voted in the new code, the 31st-ward board denounced it "as un-american in disfranchising the Voters." With the new administration approaching in the summer of 1911, the 35th ward's teachers expressed their appreciation of the old school directors: "Had all the schools in our city been under control of men as honest as yourselves, of men who had the Interest of the schools rather than the advancement of self at heart there would have been little, if any, cause for a change." As elsewhere, the new school code abolished local and thus working-class control of the schools. The secretary of the 32nd-ward board, John G. Reis, a confectioner, must have felt quite helpless when he read a letter of October 1911, laying out new plans for the schools, calling for afternoon and evening classes in cooking, sewing, and "carpentering." The author of the letter had already discussed the plans with Beulah Kennard, one of the members of the newly appointed citywide school board. Reis was simply notified of the discussion, not given an active role in it.[64]

---

62. *NLT,* 4/19/1879.
63. See *NLT,* 8/11/1898; also, Curoe, *Educational Attitudes of Organized Labor,* pp. 107, 157, 163–173.
64. Votes opposing school code: Pittsburgh, Allen (31st-ward) Sub-District School Board, Minute Book, 2/16/1909; Pittsburgh, Luckey (35th-ward) Sub-District School Board, Minute Book, 2/23/1909; Pittsburgh, Mount Washington (32nd-ward) Sub-District

Unlike the Lawrenceville school boards, those on the Hill Top had little interaction with Pittsburgh's Progressive school reformers before the school-code changes. This state of affairs reflected both the area's relative isolation and its image, which was shared by residents and outsiders alike. By the early 1900s Lawrenceville's crowded streets, shadowed by the nearby factories, had drawn the attention of settlement-house workers and other Progressives. In contrast, the Hill Top's new housing developments, populated by native-born and old-immigrant workers, gave that area a clean and "safe" image.[65] Southern and eastern European immigrants to the South Side crowded into the cramped housing immediately adjacent to the Monongahela's factories, drawing reformers' attention to the foot of the hills. The Hill Top, both reformers and residents would have agreed, did not approach "slum" conditions. The 32nd-ward school directors asked Beulah Kennard and the Civic Club for a "vacation school" and playground in 1909 and 1910, but that was the extent of their contact. When the Kindergarten Association asked subdistrict boards to have their central-board representatives vote for an increase in the kindergarten program's budget, the 35th-ward school directors flatly turned down the request.[66]

The lack of interest evinced by Progressive reformers in Hill Top schools exemplifies the difference between changes on the Hill Top in the early twentieth century and changes in Lawrenceville. Virtually none of the new immigrants moved into the three Hill Top wards; instead, this area's newest residents were downtown office workers, continuing the trend begun in the 1880s. In 1880 between 76 percent and 88 percent of the Hill Top's population worked in manual occupations; by 1900 only 69 percent of the area's residents belonged to the manual working class. While the 31st ward remained largely working class, with clerical and sales workers making up only 9 percent of it, almost 19 percent of the

---

School Board, Minute Book, 4/6/1909. "As un-american . . . ," Pittsburgh, Allen (31st-ward) Sub-District School Board, Minute Book, 4/7/1909; letter from teachers and principal to directors, Pittsburgh, Luckey (35th-ward) Sub-District School Board, Minute Book, 6/5/1911; letter from Annie Shaffer to Mr. John G. Reis, Secretary of School Board, Mount Washington schools, 10/16/1911, in Mount Washington Sub-District School Board, Miscellaneous Documents.

65. In 1900 Hill Top wards contained only 2.2 percent new immigrants, but 26.2 percent native-born and 41.0 percent German residents.

66. Pittsburgh, Mount Washington (32nd-ward) Sub-District School Board, Minute Book, 1/5/1909, 12/13/1909, 4/11/1910, 3/1/1911; Pittsburgh, Luckey (35th-ward) Sub-District School Board, Minute Book, 1/7/1907.

32nd ward's residents and 14 percent of the 35th ward's worked in clerical or sales positions in 1900.[67]

These white-collar workers moved to the Hill Top as transportation and housing improved. By 1910 the inclines were connected to streetcar lines that crisscrossed the 31st ward and cut across the 32nd and 35th wards as well. Sharing the same ethnic backgrounds as the skilled workers, the influx of clerical and sales workers into the area created no social disruption. Several urban historians and sociologists have noted that well into the twentieth century there seemed to be no such thing as a clerical white-collar neighborhood. Of all social groups clerical workers lived in the least segregated circumstances.[68] The Hill Top, therefore, was not unusual in its combination of skilled manual and clerical workers.

The connections between the two groups were noted as well by the organized labor movement and its organs, albeit indirectly. The *National Labor Tribune,* for example, carried an increasing number of stories played out in office settings. One Pittsburgh bank even advertised in the paper in 1900: "Stenographers Wanted. To deposit a certain percentage of their earnings every week in the Pittsburgh Bank for Savings." M. M. Garland, speaking to a Chicago "trust conference" in 1899, talked about the way that trusts had changed not only manual workers' jobs, but white-collar jobs as well, leading white-collar workers such as sales representatives to identify with waged workers.[69]

On the Hill Top, then, there was not a wide social gap between skilled manual workers and clerical and sales workers. For the area's skilled workers, sending children to the Commercial Department required no change in their outlook on the world. As one Chicago author wrote: "It would be foolish and dogmatic to regard such parents, able and willing to provide their children with the chances for a better future, as traitors to the working class. Why should someone who has gained a better position in life inevitably lose his consciousness of class?"[70] Joining together with

67. In 1880 Kleinberg found that "middle-class" residents made up 17.6 percent of the 31st ward, 15.9 percent of the 32nd ward, and 11.9 percent of the 35th ward. Kleinberg, "Technology's Stepdaughters," table II-5, p. 43.

68. See figure 5; Arnold, *Report on the Pittsburgh Transportation Problem,* pp. 38, 42; Amos H. Hawley, *Urban Society: An Ecological Approach* (New York: Ronald, 1971), discusses a number of these studies, p. 187.

69. Bank ad, *NLT,* 3/22/1900; M. M. Garland speech, *NLT,* 9/21/1899.

70. From a Chicago German paper (1910), quoted in Klaus Ensslen and Heinz Ickstadt, "German Working-Class Culture in Chicago: Continuity and Change in the Decade from 1900 to 1910," in Hartmut Keil and John B. Jentz, eds., *German Workers in Industrial*

their white-collar neighbors in the local Turner or Maennerchor Hall for fraternal meetings or grammar school graduation exercises, the Hill Top's skilled workers would have agreed.

Skilled Workers and the Commercial Department

Lawrenceville and the Hill Top illustrate the social context of Pittsburgh's labor aristocracy at the turn of the century. As we have seen, three different sets of circumstances during this period influenced the decisions of the skilled workers who sent sons and daughters to the public high school's Commercial Department. First of all, various changes in these workers' conditions of labor made them look approvingly on clerical work for their children. Corporations and their competitors not only introduced new production methods to break the shop-floor power of the skilled craftsmen, but also made blatant attempts to destroy workers' unions. Such developments seemed to minimize the benefits of skilled manual employment.

Second, Pittsburgh's skilled workers enjoyed a special relationship with the city's schools that went beyond the craftsman's traditional belief that a democracy required educated citizens. Workers helped define the content of their children's grammar school education through local school boards and saw the high school as an extension of the education they controlled—not as an unwanted imposition of values belonging to another social class.[71] Despite some earlier difficulties, only in the years immediately preceding the 1911 school-code reform did skilled workers have to confront a school system over which they did not exert considerable influence.

Third, skilled workers were motivated by the changing social composition of their neighborhoods, of which Lawrenceville and the Hill Top were examples. In Lawrenceville the new-immigrant groups became symbols of the changes destroying the power of skilled workers in the workplace. Increasingly deprived of control over any number of situations central to their lives, the old-immigrant labor aristocrats attempted to distinguish themselves from the unskilled southern and eastern Europeans entering their neighborhoods. In this context the Commercial De-

Chicago, 1850–1910: A Comparative Perspective (DeKalb: Northern Illinois University Press, 1983), pp. 247–248.

71. See Hogan, "Capitalism and Schooling," pp. 352–355, for a discussion of the relationship of the Chicago working class to public education.

partment not only represented the public education of which these workers were so proud, but also held the promise of employment separate from
that of the new immigrants—office work. Hill Top workers, though
facing the new immigrants (at least figuratively) at work, found few of
them in their neighborhoods. Contact with white-collar neighbors provided them with a positive rather than a negative reference group. Clerical
workers' life-styles and values appeared increasingly similar to their own,
and office work therefore seemed a "natural" and acceptable avenue of
employment for their children.

From Lawrenceville and the Hill Top, then, as from other working-
class communities in Pittsburgh, skilled workers found good reason to
send children to the public high school's Commercial Department. Not
only did Katy Stoerkel attend from the 31st ward, but the two oldest
children of Michael Hefferman, a 32nd-ward machinist, also enrolled in
the Commercial Department. From Lawrenceville came the two Calhoon
brothers, George and Jackman, whose father worked as a carpenter and
small contractor. Joseph Litschge, a cooper in one of the 16th-ward
breweries, sent his daughter, Lena, to the program. These and other
skilled workers' families who sent children to the Commercial Department through the 1890s made their decisions to do so out of the common
experiences of their lives. The eventual employment of the Commercial
Department students indicates the practicality of such decisions, and the
ways in which those decisions ultimately transformed the social horizon.

6 /

Clerical Workers' Careers
"Not a Pittsburgh man"

The former students of the Commercial Department brought with them into the work force the aspirations and expectations of their families and their communities. Their original decisions to enroll in the high school program involved weighing their needs and the benefits of various job opportunities. These young people entered the Commercial Department with their own understanding of the collar line, molded by their practical knowledge gained from both family and community experiences. The Commercial Department added a more formal veneer to those perceptions. To some extent the students' work experiences reinforced these expectations; in other ways, they did not. This interaction of expectations and experiences played itself out in the context of Pittsburgh's rapidly changing offices.

By the turn of the century, Pittsburgh's central business district showed all the hallmarks of a modern city, expanding out from "The Point" where the Allegheny and Monongahela rivers join to form the Ohio. Slowly the older manufacturing concerns along the rivers were replaced by office buildings and stores. By 1903 ten skyscrapers graced the city's skyline. These buildings' names reflected the power of Pittsburgh's iron and steel industry: the Carnegie, Frick, and Oliver buildings named after the industry's magnates, the Bessemer building named after a production process itself. Fourth Avenue became known as "the Wall Street of Pittsburgh," while Wood Street also began to resemble Manhattan's concrete canyons.[1] Every year new buildings multiplied the city's office space. Within

1. William Fell Smith, comp., *Pittsburg Real Estate Reference Book* (Pittsburgh: Davis & Warde, 1903), p. 15; typescript bibliography of Pittsburgh buildings, collection of the Western Pennsylvania Historical Society; *Greater Pittsburgh and Allegheny County Illustrated: Past, Present, Future* (Pittsburgh: American Manufacturer and Iron World, 1901).

10. A view of Wood Street, Pittsburgh. From Edward White, ed., *Pittsburgh the Powerful* (Pittsburgh: Industry Publishing Co., 1907), p. 15.

these offices worked the new clerical employees of the growing corporations.

The former students of the Commercial Department joined this new work force, riding the city's streetcars into the central business district for employment. As figure 5 illustrates, by the early twentieth century a network of streetcar lines linked almost every part of the city with its downtown. In 1900, 70 percent of the former students employed in office jobs worked in the central business district, and in 1905 that percentage grew to 81 percent. This trend continued through 1915, as fewer of the students found clerical employment in outlying districts. These related developments represented the continued concentration and centralization of corporate headquarters and business activities in the central business district.[2] In their daily streetcar rides to work, these young people traversed a social distance as well as a geographical distance from their families and neighborhoods. The journey itself was a new experience, since most of their parents had walked to local workplaces; once downtown, they found that office employment, too, differed from their parents' manual jobs or small businesses, and that it also differed from the experiences of previous office workers.

Through the 1890s and early 1900s, business schools advertised the benefits of clerical work for both men and women. Pitches aimed at male students stressed career opportunities. "Promotions come through the private office, where the stenographers and bookkeepers are invariably employed," claimed one school in 1905. This school provided prospective students with a booklet containing the stories of sixty-five "businessmen" who began their careers as stenographers and typists.[3] Such short vignettes were popular advertising gimmicks. Ironically, they also unwittingly described the limitations of clerical opportunities: the "Success Shorthand School" told of clerical workers who, with shorthand training, advanced to other clerical positions.

2. In 1910, 80 percent of the clerical workers worked downtown, and in 1915, 82.5 percent of them did. The next-most popular wards of employment were those encompassing the industrial plains along the edges of the two rivers. While 12 percent of the students worked in these wards in 1900, that percentage dropped to only 5 percent by 1905. See Appendix, Description of Data, for the sources of this information on former students' workplaces. Joel A. Tarr, *Transportation Innovation and Changing Spatial Patterns: Pittsburgh, 1850–1910* (Pittsburgh: Carnegie-Mellon University Transportation Research Institute, 1972), pp. 1, 15–16, 22–24; David Ward, *Cities and Immigrants* (New York: Oxford University Press, 1971), pp. 94–102; Amos H. Hawley, *Urban Society: An Ecological Approach* (New York: Ronald, 1971), pp. 91–95.

3. *Phonographic World* (hereafter cited as *PW*) 25 (April 1905), 284.

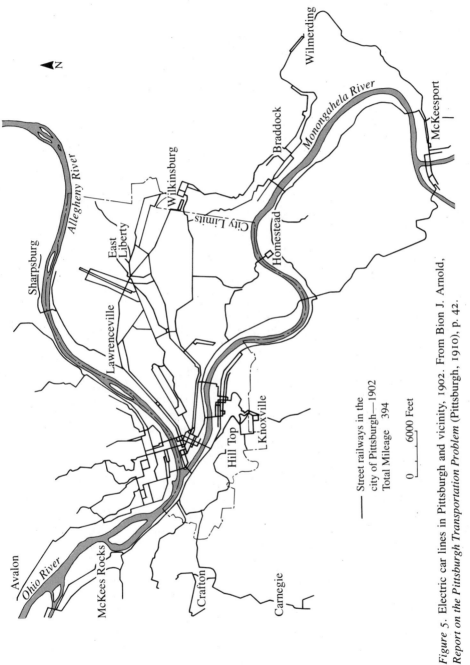

N

Avalon
Ohio River
McKees Rocks
Crafton
Carnegie
Hill Top
Knoxville
Sharpsburg
Allegheny River
Lawrenceville
East
Liberty
Wilkinsburg
City Limits
Homestead
Braddock
Monongahela River
Wilmerding
McKeesport

Street railways in the
city of Pittsburgh—1902
Total Mileage   394

0   6000 Feet

Figure 5. Electric car lines in Pittsburgh and vicinity, 1902. From Bion J. Arnold,
Report on the Pittsburgh Transportation Problem (Pittsburgh, 1910), p. 42.

In contrast, although some "businesswomen" urged female clerical workers to regard their jobs as careers, business schools focused instead on the immediate financial gains of clerical work for women and on women office workers' futures as wives.[4] A 1905 circular for Pittsburgh's private Iron City Commercial College declared that:

> A Girl's Problem—Today is to know how best to fit herself for such a position as will enable her to not only support herself, but also make her free and independent of the caprices of fortune which usually fall to the lot of the average woman.
>
> No avenue opens such splendid opportunities as the study of Shorthand.[5]

Despite this practical pitch, the ad's illustration suggested what many claimed was a more alluring aspect of office work. The drawing showed a handsome man hovering over the woman typist. Some business schools even used marriage announcements of female clerical workers as part of their advertising. Jokes and short stories encouraged the idea that women clerical workers would gain not only short-term financial benefits, but also marital bliss, usually with rich husbands.[6]

The Pittsburgh public high school's Commercial Department did not take part in elaborate advertising campaigns. Instead it relied on public perceptions influenced by others' ads, by popular culture, and by general information about the job market. The program stressed the specific skills that it imparted, such as bookkeeping, stenography, and typewriting. Although, for male students at least, the program supplemented these more mundane skills with the proprietorial rhetoric of the Department of Practice, students found their practical skills most in demand by Pittsburgh's businesses.

The paid employment that awaited the Commercial Department students reveals the reality behind popular conceptions of clerical work and demonstrates the success of the school in attaining its goals. Occupations were identified for 60 percent of the 1,844 students in the 1890–1903 Commercial Department sample.[7] The first positions held by the students

---

4. *PW* 25 (January 1905), 89–90; see *PW* 5 (February 1890), 166–167, for a discussion of "careers" for "businesswomen."

5. Iron City Commercial College, "Circular" (1905), p. 4, in box of memorabilia in the possession of Duff's Business Institute, Pittsburgh.

6. See *PW* complaint about the misleading nature of ads based on marriage announcements, 7 (December 1891), 171. Examples of stories and jokes can be found throughout *PW*, especially in the early twentieth century.

7. See Appendix, Description of Data; 1,109 students were found.

Table 15. First occupation of Commercial Department students

	All		Men		Women	
	%	N	%	N	%	N
Unskilled	5.7	63	7.3	51	3.0	12
Semiskilled	0.5	5	0.4	3	0.5	2
Skilled	3.3	37	5.3	37	0	0
Foremen	0.5	5	0.7	5	0	0
Service proprietors	0.7	8	1.0	7	0.2	1
Public employees	0.6	7	1.0	7	0	0
CLERICAL OR SALES	73.0	810	76.1	535	67.7	275
Retail proprietors	1.9	21	2.6	18	0.7	3
Professionals	4.3	48	3.0	21	6.7	27
Wholesale proprietors	0.4	4	0.6	4	0	0
Manufacturing proprietors	0.2	2	0.3	2	0	0
"At home"	8.9	99	1.9	13	21.2	86
Totals	100.0	1,109	100.2	703	100.0	406

Notes: Chi square = 178.43 with 12 degrees of freedom. Significance = 0.0000. Cramer's V = 0.40112.

illustrate the immediate applications of the skills taught in the Commercial Department's curriculum. But the more fragmentary evidence available on students' "career" patterns, including the marriages of women students, provides even deeper insight into both the nature of the clerical job market and the developing role of the collar line in the class structure.

The Commercial Department provided most of its students with what they were looking for; almost three-quarters of them found employment as clerical or sales workers (see table 15). Furthermore, their specific job titles attest to the program's successful transmittal of basic skills. Charles Hobson, the laborer's son described in chapter 4, became a "clerk" in a downtown office. John Hefferman, the 32nd-ward machinist's son, also found a position as a clerk. A third of the former students were listed in city directories or in the census as some sort of clerk. Hefferman's sister, Margaret, worked as a bookkeeper, as did 16 percent of their fellow alumni. Thomas Weist, the German tobacconist's son, was also a bookkeeper, though the telegraph operator's son, William Munson, listed himself in the city directory as an accountant. Another 14 percent of the students, mostly women, worked as stenographers, like the 31st ward's Katy Stoerkle, and Florence Bolton, the carpenter's daughter. Nine percent of all the former students who could be traced in some further record did not work for wages at all. Lila Rogers, the railroad engineer's daughter mentioned in chapter 4, was listed in the 1900 census with no gainful employment, though she had left the Commercial Department a year before. Just over one-fifth of the female students were listed with no occupation or as "at home," the phrase that several of the census enumerators chose to use.[8]

A 1914 study of women clerical workers in Boston found that "education seems to be the most important influence in office service, determining the occupation a girl can enter."[9] The employment of the Commercial Department students, both male and female, indicates that this conclusion was correct. In keeping with the proliferation of private "short courses" for clerical training, even nongraduates from the Commercial Department were likely to gain clerical positions. However, receiving a diploma from the program increased a young person's chances of clerical employment. Only 65 percent of the Commercial Department dropouts worked in office positions, while 81 percent of the graduates did. Furthermore, regardless of whether a student received the school's formal diploma, the length of time he or she remained in the program also affected chances for employment. Sixty-one percent of those who stayed in the program for a single academic year or less found clerical or sales employment, compared to three-quarters of those remaining for two years, and about eighty percent of those continuing for three or four years.

The range of occupations followed by nongraduates suggests that students had varying reasons for not completing the full commercial course. Sixteen percent of the nongraduates found employment at manual work, two-thirds of them in unskilled or semiskilled jobs. For this group immediate economic necessity probably led to their dropping out of the high school program in the first place. Other nongraduates ended up in proprietorships or professional positions, suggesting very different motivations for leaving the Commercial Department. Leo Spuhler, for example, took over the family tobacco shop after his father's death. Over a quarter

8. City directories, and to a large extent the census as well, reflect the individual's status only at a single point in time. Early twentieth-century authors all agreed that female clerical workers had a fairly rapid turnover rate, staying only a few years in any one job (see, for example, Women's Educational and Industrial Union (WEIU), *The Public Schools and Women in Office Service* [Boston: WEIU, 1914]). Women listed in one source or another as being "at home" may in fact have been employed (as clerical workers or otherwise) before the date of the source or may have found employment later. To say, then, that a fifth of the Commercial Department women did not participate in waged work is probably an overstatement. It is perhaps more representative of the situation to state that, at any given time, some 20 percent of these young women were currently, and perhaps temporarily, out of the labor market.

9. WEIU, *Public Schools,* p. 176.

of the young women students (28 percent) dropped out to stay "at home"; presumably their families had decided to forgo the daughter's wages, clerical or otherwise, making further education unnecessary.

Still other students left the program to pursue other educational endeavors. The circumstances surrounding a student's entrance into the Commercial Department is often a good predictor of this particular outcome. Although students entering the program directly from grammar school—either public or parochial—were likely to leave the Commercial Department for economic reasons (18 percent of this group ended up in manual jobs), dropouts who had transferred from other high school programs were more likely to end up in nonmanual positions. William Lange, for example, transferred from the Academic Department and then left the Commercial Department after only a few months, presumably to gain the education that eventually led to his medical practice. Annie Kinley transferred to the Commercial Department from the Normal Department. After staying in the program for only three months, she probably transferred back, since she eventually became a public school teacher.

A student's economic class background was clearly related to the likelihood of his or her graduating from the Commercial Department. Economic necessity, however, was not the only, or even the primary, reason for students leaving the program. If it had been, working-class students (and particularly the children of unskilled workers) would have had the lowest graduation rates. The possible effect of economic need is demonstrated in the case of widows' children, who were more likely than others to drop out of the program. [10] The highest graduation rates could be found among the children of unskilled and skilled manual workers and among proprietors' children. For these students and their families, the chances of graduating from the Commercial Department apparently had less to do with immediate financial need than with the power and usefulness of the program's diploma. Forty-five percent of the manual working-class students stayed in the program long enough to get a diploma. In contrast, only 36 percent of the clerical and sales workers' children actually graduated from the program. [11] These graduation rates remained generally constant whether the student was male or female.

The importance for different students of a Commercial Department

10. Only 32 percent of widows' children graduated.
11. The children of professionals were least likely to graduate—only 28 percent did so. There was not much difference between the children of skilled and unskilled manual workers; 44.6 percent of the unskilled workers' children and 44.9 percent of the skilled workers' children graduated (see table 9).

Table 16. First occupation of Commercial Department students by graduation status and parental occupation

	N	Unskilled*	Skilled	Clerical/ sales	Other**	None	Total
All students	1,109	6.2%	3.3%	73.0%	8.9%	8.6%	100.0%
Enrollees	543	10.5	5.2	64.6	10.7	9.0	100.0
Graduates	566	1.9	1.6	81.1	7.2	8.1	99.9
Unskilled workers' children	185	13.0	3.2	67.6	4.8	11.4	100.0
Enrollees	77	27.3	5.2	49.4	5.2	13.0	100.1
Graduates	108	2.8	1.9	80.5	4.7	10.2	100.1
Skilled workers' children	331	6.0	6.0	70.7	7.2	10.0	99.9
Enrollees	148	10.9	10.8	61.5	7.4	9.5	100.1
Graduates	183	2.2	2.2	78.1	7.1	10.4	100.0
Clerical and sales workers' children	130	0.8	0	89.2	6.2	3.8	100.0
Enrollees	78	1.3	0	84.6	9.0	5.1	100.0
Graduates	52	0	0	96.2	1.9	1.9	100.0
Proprietors' children	204	3.4	2.0	71.6	16.7	6.4	100.1
Enrollees	97	4.1	2.1	64.9	20.6	8.2	99.9
Graduates	107	2.8	1.9	77.6	13.0	4.7	100.0
Widows' children	105	7.6	2.9	74.3	5.8	9.5	100.1
Enrollees	56	14.3	3.6	58.9	9.0	14.3	100.1
Graduates	49	0	2.0	91.8	2.0	4.1	99.9

*Includes semiskilled occupations.
**Includes proprietorships and supervisory, public, and professional occupations.

diploma is revealed in the students' employment record (see table 16). While almost two-thirds of all the program's dropouts found clerical employment, fewer of the nongraduates from working-class families did. Unskilled workers' children had the smallest chances of working in an office without first obtaining a diploma. Just under half (49 percent) of these individuals found clerical or sales jobs. On the other hand, for clerical and sales workers' children, receiving the high school program's official diploma had little impact on their chances of gaining clerical employment. In fact, dropouts among these families had a greater chance of finding clerical work than did the average students with diplomas. Almost 85 percent of these families' dropouts worked in clerical or sales jobs. Their parents' knowledge of the skills required by businesses and their contacts in the clerical job market apparently obviated the need for these students to receive institutional endorsement of their abilities. Children from proprietors' families experienced a slightly different version of advantage in gaining employment. As the example of the tobacconist, Leo Spuhler, illustrates, proprietors' children often took over family businesses—with or without Commercial Department diplomas. Proprietorships could also provide clerical work for children. The Rosenthal family, owners of a furniture store, sent five children, four of their daughters and a son, to the Commercial Department. Their son, Benjamin, took over the family business, while at least two of the daughters, one a graduate and one not, worked as bookkeepers for that business.

Young men and women from the families of manual workers had a harder time gaining clerical employment, with or without diplomas. These students' parents could not offer their children any sort of advantage in gaining office employment beyond urging them to enter and complete the public school's program. Dropouts from skilled workers' families, for example, had somewhat greater than usual chances of going into manual jobs. In fact, the skilled worker's version of passing employment advantages on to his children might be seen only in his relative success at gaining a skilled manual job for a son who had dropped out of the program. John Gearing's case is one example. The son of a 35th-ward iron and steel roller, Gearing attended the Commercial Department for only one year, after which he followed his father's trade, becoming a roller himself. By doing so, Gearing gained a well-paying job at the top of the iron and steel industry's hierarchy of manual jobs. Following a father's footsteps could often provide a sort of employment *dis*advantage for unskilled workers' children. Katherine O'Donnell, daughter of an Irish laborer, dropped out of the Commercial Department and eventually worked as a servant; over a quarter of the dropouts from unskilled workers' families worked in unskilled manual occupations themselves. Without the informal employment contacts of either clerical and sales workers' children or proprietors' children, the children of manual workers found that receiving the Commercial Department's diploma took on greater significance for them. The impact of a diploma is clearest in the case of the children of unskilled workers. Without receiving a diploma, not even half of these students gained clerical employment. If they persevered and graduated from the program, however, over 80 percent of them achieved clerical or sales jobs. The children of skilled workers experienced a less dramatic version of the same phenomenon.

Chapter 4 described the ways in which different families' economic circumstances affected decisions to enroll in the Commercial Department.

Students' postschool employment patterns suggest that those economic circumstances continued to reverberate throughout the students' lives. In some ways similar to the situations of manual workers' children, the jobs gained by widows' children reflected their families' precarious financial positions. Eighteen percent of the widows' children who dropped out of the Commercial Department ended up in manual jobs, more often unskilled than skilled. At the same time, the relatively high chances of widows' children attaining clerical employment attests to the importance of the program's training for these families. Ninety-two percent of the widows' children who graduated from the program worked as clerical workers, while almost sixty percent of the nongraduates did. Widows' daughters were also less likely than women from male-headed households to forgo wage earning altogether; only 15 percent of these women stayed "at home," compared to 22 percent of those from male-headed households.

This interaction of the students' class backgrounds, education, and employment expresses both the potential and the limitation of programs like the Commercial Department for opening up the labor market, providing young people with new job opportunities and businesses with needed workers. The limitations of this type of "upward mobility," then, become apparent. Programs like the Commercial Department, particularly those in public institutions, did provide an important way for working-class youngsters to move out of manual occupations. At the same time, this opportunity was limited in several ways. Families of the manual working class needed considerable financial security to be able to take advantage of this education, and their children needed to obtain more education than others to achieve their employment aspirations. In addition, some of the manual workers' children may have felt uncomfortable with the social conventions of office employment, despite having chosen to enroll in the Commercial Department.[12] The opportunity provided, then, was a qualified one; some people had to work harder than others to gain the same employment ends, a situation many might have found discouraging.

Although the relationship between students' economic backgrounds and their formal educational achievements is complex, sex differences complicate the picture even further. As table 15 indicated, women and men from the Commercial Department had different postschool experi-

12. See, for example, Richard Sennett and Jonathan Cobb, *The Hidden Injuries of Class* (New York: Alfred A. Knopf, 1972), pp. 27, 182–188. For a sophisticated British version of the argument, see Paul Willis, *Learning to Labor: How Working Class Kids Get Working Class Jobs* (New York: Columbia University Press, 1977).

ences. The wider range of men's occupations represents both differing cultural expectations for men and for women and the dissimilar job markets that each faced. While skilled trades and proprietorships were open to men, women had fewer choices. Despite their limited job options, however, women, supported by the prevailing ideology, did not necessarily have to earn wages. The occupations of the former Commercial Department students, then, reflect both the sexual segregation of the work force and the societal norms and expectations that lay behind it.

Male dropouts pursued a variety of occupations, ranging from John Gearing's skilled trade to Leo Spuhler's small business, or William Lange's medical practice. While men who graduated from the program might seek nonclerical employment, those who never received a diploma were more likely to do so. For example, 19 percent of the men who had left the program without graduating worked in unskilled or skilled manual occupations, while only 5.5 percent of the male graduates did. While these examples illustrate the ways in which education, opportunities, and financial necessity determined men's interactions with the sexually-segregated labor market, a young woman's decision not to enter or to withdraw from the workforce highlights the role of ideologies in job market decisions. Women nongraduates were more likely to be "at home" than graduates; 28 percent of the nongraduates and 17 percent of the graduates were so designated. While some of the women dropouts might decide, as Annie Kinley did, to pursue another career such as teaching, for many young women dropping out of the Commercial Department meant forgoing participation in the paid work force. That so many female graduates of the program also remained "at home" suggests the ways in which both family needs and social expectations conditioned women's labor-force participation.

The same pattern of cause and effect becomes even more obvious when economic backgrounds are again considered. Table 17 allows comparison of the labor-force participation of women from different family backgrounds. Here the benefits of clerical work as conspicuous employment battle with economic necessity for the allegiance of these young women with clerical training. If only economic considerations influenced a woman's employment choice, then those families with the greatest economic need would have the lowest proportion of women remaining out of the work force. In the case of widows' families, for example, only 15 percent of the young women stayed "at home." However, fully a quarter of the daughters from manual workers' families remained out of the paid work force at least temporarily. These families, having chosen clerical educa-

Table 17. First occupation of Commercial Department students by sex and parental occupation

	N	Unskilled*	Skilled	Clerical/ sales	Other**	None	Total
All students	1,109	6.2%	3.3%	73.0%	8.9%	8.6%	100.0%
Unskilled workers' children							
Men	110	18.2	5.5	70.0	4.5	1.8	100.0
Women	75	5.3	0	64.0	5.3	25.3	99.9
Skilled workers' children							
Men	211	6.7	9.5	72.0	10.4	1.4	100.0
Women	120	5.0	0	68.3	1.7	25.0	100.0
Clerical and sales workers' children							
Men	93	0	0	93.5	5.4	1.1	100.0
Women	37	2.7	0	78.4	8.1	10.8	100.0
Proprietors' children							
Men	129	4.7	3.1	73.6	17.9	0.8	100.1
Women	75	1.3	0	68.0	14.7	16.0	100.0
Widows' children							
Men	46	13.1	6.5	73.9	4.3	2.2	100.0
Women	59	3.4	0	74.6	6.8	15.3	100.0

*Includes semiskilled occupations.
**Includes proprietorships and supervisory, public, and professional occupations.

tion for their daughters, now found themselves torn between the social as well as economic benefits of clerical employment and the social status implied by a daughter's abstention from waged work. The daughters of clerical and sales workers, by contrast, generally did not remain outside the work force. With fathers working in the heterosocial world of offices and shops, the employment of these daughters would be regarded as more socially acceptable, both in itself and as a way to supplement the family income. Proprietors' families would have wavered between acceptance of women's wage earning and concern with social appearances.

Most of the Commercial Department students—from all backgrounds, both graduates and dropouts, women and men—ultimately gained office employment. Within the clerical category itself, more specific job titles reveal both the immediate application of skills taught in the Commercial Department and the sexual division of labor in offices. Clerks (44 percent), stenographers (18 percent), and bookkeepers (22 percent) were the most common occupations. Both men and women worked in these occupations, but not in equal proportions.[13] While 62 percent of the male clerical workers worked as some sort of "clerk," only 8 percent of the women did. For stenographers the balance was reversed: 45 percent of the women were listed as stenographers or typists, while only 5 percent of the men were. Sixteen percent of the men worked as bookkeepers, while a third of the women did. These last figures suggest that the bookkeepers turned out by the Commercial Department did not inhabit that realm of the office world which encroached on the territory of the professional accountants, but rather took their places in the lower ranks of the bookkeeping staffs.[14] The Commercial Department training also did nothing to break down the barriers that excluded women from some kinds of workplaces; none of the women worked in banks, while nine of the men did, and at least three of the men worked as railroad clerks, while only one woman was employed by the railroads—as a stenographer.[15]

Beyond men's and women's initial occupations, of course, lay their very different prospects for the future. These expectations framed the sexual stratification of the clerical work force. Businesses used the differential turnover rates and ultimate goals of male and female workers to control both pay and promotions. Prevailing ideas about marriage opportunities for females and promotional opportunities for males obscured workplace dynamics for both groups. A study of the long-term careers of Commercial Department students reveals the ways in which their actual experiences conformed to these expectations.

> A bookkeeper said to me the other day: "I made the mistake of my life when I learned to keep books. I was a good bookkeeper at 25 and was proud of it. I am a good bookkeeper now at 50 and am ashamed to tell anybody that I am a bookkeeper." Draftsmen talk the same way, and stenographers; and yet the railroad presidents and corporation presidents and the great captains of industry today were almost without exceptions bookkeepers or draftsmen or stenographers at some time in their careers.[16]

The author of this parable used it to argue that "you can't keep a good man down"; individual effort would determine whether a clerical worker

13. Only three other clerical occupations were filled by both men and women: cashier (three men, five women), store clerk (one man, two women), insurance clerk (two men, one woman).

14. Only two of the men were listed as "accountants" in their first jobs.

15. Some of the other men were probably railroad clerks, too, though the city directories recorded them only as "clerks."

16. R. R. Shuman, "The Malcontent in Office Organization," *The Iron Trade Review,* 8/15/1901, 19.

moved up in the ranks or not. The proponents of commercial education encouraged such a view, arguing, for example, that shorthand and typewriting opened "the gateways to every profession and to every kind of business."[17] The male students of Pittsburgh's Commercial Department began their working careers as clerks, bookkeepers, and stenographers; they were "good bookkeeper[s] at 25," but how open were "the gateways"? Although tracing these men's occupations over a long period of time proved difficult, some assertions can still be made about the chances for the kind of upward mobility promised by business school advertisements and clerical workers' journals.[18]

Harry Donnally, Charles Fuhr, John Flood, Joseph Crowley, and Jacob Baschkopf all worked as bookkeepers when they were twenty-five years old. Ten years later, none of them listed their occupation as "bookkeeper," though none were quite captains of industry, either. Jacob Baschkopf worked as an insurance inspector. Joseph Crowley, after working for over fifteen years as a bookkeeper, had become an undertaker. John Flood worked as an office manager in the central business district, and Charles Fuhr had become an auditor in the bank in which he had started his employment. Harry Donnally was one of the only true "success" stories of the Commercial Department, though ironically he attended the program for only a few months. First employed as a bookkeeper in the South Side's Iron and Glass Dollar Savings Bank, he had become a teller in that bank by 1905. He continued to move up through the bank's hierarchy, finally becoming its president in 1933.[19] These examples reflect the range of promotional possibilities open to the Commercial Department students. Most of their upward progression came through bureaucratic promotions. Banks provided the clearest examples of this. By the turn of the century, few expected to enter banking employment as a clerk, teller, or bookkeeper and end up owning a bank. While stories such as that of Donnally kept this dream alive to some extent, banks were best known for their job security; once employed by a bank, logical steps through its departments could be expected. The other side of the bank-employment coin, however, was that job security and bureaucratic promotions were often guaranteed only within a single bank.[20] If

17. *PW* 5 (October 1889), 56.

18. See Appendix, Description of Data.

19. In addition to the data described in the appendix, Donnally's obituary in the Pittsburgh *Sun-Telegraph*, 12/31/1953, provided some of this information. The obituary is located in Carnegie Library, Pittsburgh, "Death Notices."

20. Amos Kidder Fiske noted in 1904 that a bank's chief clerk, the second in command under the cashier (one of the bank's officers), had usually risen through the ranks, and that

Charles Fuhr, working as an auditor in 1915, had chosen in that year to apply for employment at another bank, he might have had to start again at the bottom as a simple bookkeeper.

Two occupations held by men from the Commercial Department provide numbers large enough to examine in their own right: clerks and bookkeepers. The subsequent job changes for men beginning in these two occupations reveal both the success of the high school program in imparting specific skills to its students and the limits to significant career mobility provided by those same skills. The apparent ease with which individuals initially employed as clerks became bookkeepers and vice versa is one indication of those limits. By 1910, for example, 13 percent of the original clerks had become bookkeepers, and 19 percent of the bookkeepers, clerks. Someone with the job title of "clerk" might have a very stable position in a bank or railway office, ensuring him bureaucratic promotions at the very least; or he might have relatively insecure employment as a machine operator in a commercial or mercantile office. The fact that almost a fifth of the bookkeepers became clerks by 1910 indicates that many of those titled "bookkeeper" may have worked as "bookkeeping clerks" in offices that had already subdivided clerical tasks. The Commercial Department, in other words, had succeeded in training these men for the realities of modern offices; their skills had gained them employment in the developing office hierarchies.

Those same skills, however, moved only a handful of men beyond those offices. By 1915 only 6 percent of the students beginning employment as clerks or bookkeepers had become business proprietors of any sort, while only 4 percent had achieved professional status. Just over 70 percent remained in low-level clerical or sales positions, while 8 percent had become office managers.[21] Upward occupational mobility existed for these men to some extent within Pittsburgh's business offices, but rarely beyond the office walls. They used the experience they had gained in the school's Department of Practice not in setting up their own businesses so much as in working for others.

Despite minor differences between the experiences of male clerks and those of bookkeepers, the figures disclose the lack of significant job mobility for these clerical workers. Beginning their employment careers

---

some banks hired only at the very bottom rungs, encouraging further inside advancement. Fiske, *The Modern Bank* (New York: D. Appleton, 1904), pp. 198–199.

21. These figures are based on 229 individuals whose first occupation was "clerk" or "bookkeeper," and for whom occupations were traced to 1915. See Appendix, Description of Data.

as low-level clerical workers, the men from the Commercial Department generally stayed within the confines of that occupational rank. Both the stability of clerical employment and the sexual stratification of the office work force encouraged these young men to forgo collective action and aim for middle-management positions even though their attainment was unlikely. However disappointed these men might have been in their own failures to advance to business heights, they always enjoyed a higher position within the office hierarchy than the ever-shifting mass of female clerical workers. In their turn these women counted on their own short job tenure and on eventually leaving the labor market altogether to make their office positions endurable.

In 1916 one female advice writer reminded her readers that, "In reading business romances and applying them to one's own life, it is well to remember that business romances that are published are interesting only because they are exceptional, and the law of averages governs the careers and lives of most of us."[22] The female students of the Commercial Department probably read many such "business romances," as they became ubiquitous in almost all types of publications by the early twentieth century. The story that appeared in the February 1905 issue of the *Phonographic World* is typical of the genre. Its title, "A Christmas Dinner in a Law Office. The Stenographer Pursued the Path of Duty, and Won Out in the Good Old-Fashioned Way," sums up the story's plot. A "grumpy" old lawyer makes his office staff, consisting of a woman stenographer, a male bookkeeper, and the office boy, work on Christmas Day. But the lawyer's rich, "western," mine-owning cousin breezes into town and ends up buying them all an elaborate dinner and taking them to the theater. A few days later, just before returning west to his fortune, he proposes to the stenographer. In illustration of the story, the journal's frontispiece depicts the dinner: "She found herself seated between the westerner and the bookkeeper."[23]

Thus "seated between the westerner and the bookkeeper," most actual female clerical workers ended up marrying the bookkeeper rather than the boss's rich cousin or the boss himself. Office stories in Pittsburgh's working-class press generally depicted such realistic endings. The "Bookkeeper's Mistake," published in 1899 in the *National Labor Tribune*, told

22. Ellen Lane Spencer, *The Efficient Secretary* (New York: Frederick A. Stokes Co., 1916), p. 99.

23. Anne Guilbert Mahon, "A Christmas Dinner in a Law Office," *PW* 25 (February 1905), 91–96.

11. "She Found Herself Seated between the Westerner and the Bookkeeper." From *Typewriter and Phonographic World* 25 (1905), frontis.

of a bookkeeper's attempts to match up the typist with the shipping clerk, only to find that he was in love with her himself. After considerable misunderstandings, the typist and the bookkeeper finally declare their love for each other.[24]

These stories portrayed a relatively new way for young women to meet their future husbands: at the workplace. Unlike most other women wage earners, clerical workers often worked in close proximity with members of the opposite sex in quiet settings conducive to conversation. Before the advent of this heterosocial workplace, young women depended largely on community-based methods of meeting eligible men, from parental arrangements to social occasions sponsored by church groups or local ethnic, trade, or fraternal organizations. There were also newly commercialized social opportunities. As one recent author phrased it, "The dance hall, theater, park, and street represented the urban marriage market, definitely free enterprise in its workings but traditional in its goals."[25] Not only might a young woman's wages open up some of these locales to her, but female office workers could also become acquainted with men while they earned those wages. In this context enrollment in the Commercial Department represented not only new opportunities for wage earning, but also the introduction of a whole new group of possible marriage partners.

In some cases the Commercial Department itself directly influenced its students' marriages. Local grammar schools offered children a heterosocial space, but the high schools' programs did the same thing on a citywide basis, bringing young people together as adolescents. Eliza Miller, a widow's daughter who attended the Commercial Department during the 1891–92 school year, married a fellow student, Walter D. Rigdon, seven years after they left the program. At the time of their marriage, Walter was working as a sales agent for the same concern for which he had earlier been a bookkeeper. Other students cast slightly wider nets, marrying the siblings of high school companions. Most of the time, however, the influence of commercial education on young women's marriages was less direct, and often negligible.

The eventual marriages of the women from the Commercial Depart-

24. *National Labor Tribune [Pittsburgh]* (hereafter cited as *NLT*), 8/3/1899, "Book-keeper's Mistake." See also *NLT* 4/20/1899, "Blue-Pencil Stories," in which two court stenographers marry each other. In the *Phonographic World* the clerical worker *always* marries above her (or, in one case, his) station.

25. Leslie Woodcock Tentler, *Wage-Earning Women* (New York: Oxford University Press, 1979), p. 112; Kathy Peiss, *Cheap Amusements: Working Women and Leisure in Turn-of-the-Century New York* (Philadelphia: Temple University Press, 1985), pp. 45, 48.

ment reflect the complexity of the social structure of the time. In Pitts-burgh's offices women from working-class backgrounds interacted with "middle-class" men: the managers who dictated letters to them, the bankers they brushed shoulders with in downtown streets, the book-keepers who sat across the room from them. On November 22, 1904, Martha Voelker, daughter of a German-born carpenter, married William Rankin, a stenographer. Though we do not know exactly how they met, they lived several miles from each other, making neighborhood connec-tions unlikely. Martha had graduated from the Commercial Department in 1899 and by the next year was working as a stenographer herself. A downtown meeting between the two young people was more likely than any other. Not all of Martha's schoolmates married clerical workers, however. Another member of the same graduating class, Katy Stoerkle, daughter of the 31st-ward school director and planing-mill sawyer, mar-ried Benedict Wolff, an electrician, even though she, too, worked as a stenographer before her marriage.

Katy and Martha were fairly typical of the Commercial Department women in their marriages. As table 18 demonstrates, over 40 percent of the female students married clerical or sales workers, while about a quarter of them married manual workers. Skilled workers' daughters like Katy and Martha achieved very similar marriages; 46 percent of them married clerical workers, and 30 percent married manual workers. A quarter of the program's female students married professional men or proprietors.

A number of other factors influenced marriage choices, including parents' occupations, whether a woman actually graduated from the Com-mercial Department, and whether she participated in wage earning after leaving the high school. Annie Burns, an Irish laborer's daughter who worked as a file clerk for almost ten years after graduating from the Commercial Department, married James Speer, a downtown bookkeeper. Matilda Roesler, daughter of a Lawrenceville laborer, on the other hand, married a laborer. Although 45 percent of unskilled workers' daughters married clerical or sales workers, 32 percent of them married manual workers, and half of those manual workers were unskilled. Less than 10 percent of this group married proprietors or professional men. For these young women the possibility of repeating their mothers' lives as the wives of unskilled workers may have increased the desirability of marrying a clerical worker.

The marriages of widows' daughters suggest they had an even stronger desire to escape a financially insecure situation. Seventy percent of these

Table 18. Husbands' occupations by guardians' occupations for Commercial Department students, 1890–1903

Husbands' occupations	Guardians' occupations					
	Unskilled	Skilled	Clerical and sales	Proprietors	Unknown	Total*
Unskilled	16.1%	11.1%	5.9%	8.3%	0	10.0%
Skilled	16.1	14.3	23.5	6.3	8.7%	13.0
Foremen	0	4.8	8.8	4.2	4.3	3.9
Service proprietors	6.5	1.6	0	6.3	0	2.6
Public employees	6.5	6.3	2.9	2.1	0	3.5
Clerical or sales	45.2	46.0	32.4	29.2	69.6	43.5
Retail proprietors	3.2	6.3	8.8	8.3	4.3	5.7
Professional	6.5	4.8	11.8	12.5	8.7	8.3
Wholesale and manufacturing proprietors	0	4.8	5.9	22.9	4.3	9.2
	$N = 31$	$N = 63$	$N = 34$	$N = 48$	$N = 23$	$N = 230$

Notes: Chi square = 50.43499 with 40 degrees of freedom. Significance = 0.1248. Cramer's V = 0.25109.
*Includes supervisory, professional, public, and agricultural occupations. These occupations are not included in the statistics.

women married clerical or sales workers. Rena Garrow, who left the Commercial Department in 1899 without graduating from the program, helped support her widowed mother and siblings through her stenographic employment for almost ten years before marrying a clerk, Raymond Pollitt. Like unskilled workers' daughters, widows' daughters such as Rena sought financial security through white-collar marriages.[26]

It should not be surprising that the marriages of skilled workers' daughters come so close to approximating the marriages of all former Commercial Department students: skilled workers' children did make up the largest group within the school, and therefore their experiences often dominated, and even came close to determining, the norms. Neither should it be surprising that the main divergence from the average figures occurs at the upper end of the social scale. Only a little over 9 percent of the skilled workers' daughters married professionals or proprietors of wholesale or manufacturing concerns, compared to twice that percentage for all the students.

More intriguing are the figures on the marriages of clerical and sales workers' daughters. These young women actually married slightly more manual workers than white-collar workers. Lulu May Corbett, daughter of a toy salesman, married Samuel Allenbaugh, a passenger train brakeman who was himself the son of a Pennsylvania Railroad clerk. Cecelia Ward, however, the daughter of a railroad clerk, married a railroad clerk in 1905 after working as a telephone company clerk herself. The intermingling of skilled manual and white-collar occupations is further illustrated by the rest of Cecelia's family in the 1900 census. During that year, while Cecelia worked as a clerk, her older sister lived with the family along with her husband, an iron roll turner, and their children. These white-collar marriage patterns thus testify to the permeability of the collar line. While the children of white-collar parents overwhelmingly found work themselves in white-collar jobs, this consistency in employment status did not necessarily carry over into the presumed social status of marital choices.[27]

Proprietors' daughters followed a very different pattern in their mar-

26. Since none of the records used allow us to determine the occupations of the widows' late husbands, we cannot speculate on how many of these young women were recreating the white-collar marriages of their parents. However, the high proportion of widows' families with children employed in manual occupations (see chapter 4) suggests that many of the deceased fathers may have worked in manual jobs themselves.

27. See Seymour Martin Lipset and Reinhard Bendix, *Social Mobility in Industrial Society* (Berkeley: University of California Press, 1959), pp. 42–48, 294; David Lockwood, *The Blackcoated Worker: A Study in Class Consciousness* (London: Allen & Unwin, 1958), pp. 115–116.

riages, in large part due to a combination of economic and ethnic factors. Only 19 percent of them married manual workers, and a mere 29 percent married clerical or sales workers. More of them married proprietors (37 percent), particularly proprietors who ran wholesale concerns. The story of the Rosenthal daughters illustrates this pattern. The oldest of the sisters, Mollie, worked as a bookkeeper for the family dry-goods store before marrying a "merchant," Benjamin Wolkosky, in 1899. By 1905 the city directory listed Benjamin Wolk as the owner of the Iron City Laundry Company and the secretary of the Rosenthal furniture company. A year later the next sister, Bella, married Louis Nevins, listed in the marriage records as a merchant and in the city directory as the vice president of D. Rosenthal and Company. The third sister, Sadie, married the owner of a retail liquor store, Herman Reich, in 1909.[28] The Rosenthal women, as noted earlier in this chapter, had first used the skills they gained in the Commercial Department while working for the family business. Their marriages disclose their continued contributions to family enterprises. Two out of three of their husbands became partners in their wives' family business. Wolk and Reich also ran their own businesses. The 1900 census listed Mollie Wolk as unemployed, but she probably applied her clerical skills to her husband's businesses. Family precedent would have supported this, considering both the daughters' family employment and the mother's example. An 1882 R. G. Dun & Co. credit report on the Rosenthal company noted that the girls' mother, Hannah Rosenthal, virtually ran the business in her husband's name.[29]

The Rosenthal examples also indicate the role of ethnicity in marital choices. Virtually all of the Jewish women in the Commercial Department sample married the owners of retail or wholesale establishments. Sometimes these marriages cemented or initiated business partnerships; Phoebe Foster's husband, Louis Green, formed a scrap-metal company with his wife's brother. But within Pittsburgh's relatively small Jewish community, concentrated at this time in the city's 7th ward, even the daughters of manual workers were likely to marry business owners. Anna Stein, for example, the daughter of a 7th-ward glazier, married a dry-goods merchant. These Jewish women provide the clearest examples of

28. The fourth sister, Fannie, married Louis Schwartz in 1910; I was unable to determine his occupation. Fannie's obituary notes that one of her sons is an attorney and one a judge ([Pittsburgh] *Post-Gazette,* 7/30/1973; located in Carnegie Library, Pittsburgh, "Death Notices").

29. Pennsylvania, vol. 6, p. 225, R. G. Dun & Co. Collection, Baker Library, Harvard University Graduate School of Business Administration.

the relationship between ethnicity and marriage, but more general statistics also suggest some patterns. Women from German backgrounds were more likely than others to marry manual workers; 42 percent of them did, while 39 percent married clerical or sales workers. Irish women from the Commercial Department were more likely to marry white-collar men. Fifty-five percent of them married clerical or sales workers, while only 17 percent married manual workers and 11 percent married retail proprietors. Women with native-born parents were the most likely of any Commercial Department students to marry professionals, which some 10 percent of them did. Only 21 percent married manual workers, while 48 percent married clerical or sales workers.[30]

Young women's own occupations had less to do with their eventual marriages than did their socioeconomic backgrounds. Just over half (53 percent) of the women who worked in clerical or sales jobs married clerical or sales workers like themselves. A quarter of them (25.5 percent) married manual workers, though no unskilled workers, while a fifth married professional men or proprietors—men who might have been their bosses. The marriages of women found "at home" in the records spanned the entire gamut of possibilities. A fifth of them (21.3 percent) married manual workers, half of whom were unskilled workers, and another fifth (21.3 percent) married professional men or proprietors. Only 45 percent of these women married clerical or sales workers.[31] Although the numbers are too small for definitive conclusions, they suggest that employment as a clerical worker provided two slight marriage advantages for young women. Office employment increased a woman's chances of marrying an office worker, thereby widening the marriage market somewhat. If we could determine whether the women found "at home" had ever worked for wages, this difference between the two groups would probably increase. Perhaps more important for these women, though, office work seems to have decreased the chance that they would marry unskilled manual workers. Without these slight advantages of office employment, young women had to rely on traditional family and community connections to meet possible partners. Furthermore, the virtually identical chances of marrying proprietors or professional men experienced by these

---

30. $N = 121$. These statistics are based on fairly small numbers, because they include only women found both in marriage records and in the 1900 census. Statistics are based on forty-eight women with native-born, thirty-one with German, and eighteen with Irish backgrounds. Only ten women each from British or eastern and southern European backgrounds were identified.

31. $N = 113$.

two groups of young women indicates that the same economic conditions that kept some women out of the job market also gave them important social connections in the marriage market.

Popular conceptions of "business romances," then, may have added spice to young women's employment fantasies, but their actual work lives were quite different. One advice author in the mid-1890s warned the "Business Girl" to prepare herself for becoming the wife of a "$2500 a year man."[32] This may have been an overstatement; $2,500 was certainly a high annual salary for the clerical and sales workers who made up the bulk of the Commercial Department women's husbands.[33] It did provide a more realistic standard than the fictional bosses and heirs, however. Nonetheless, marital expectations functioned in much the same way as the prevailing assumption that young women workers would remain only temporarily in the labor market. Employers who regarded women as temporary office workers were not likely to promote them, and the women in turn were willing to accept this view of their situation. In addition, their impressions of the romantic possibilities arising from office work added glamour to increasingly rote work. Combined with office dress standards, potential business romances helped to increase the social status of clerical work within the female job market.

In 1909 a popular song published in New York City, "Go Easy Mabel," made the rounds. It told the story of a beleaguered sales clerk, Percy, whose fiancée, Mabel, thought he made much more money than he actually did. Taking her out to dinner one payday, Percy shudders as she orders more and more expensive food, until he finally cries out in the chorus, "Go easy Mabel! I'm not a Pittsburgh man!"[34] Less than a decade after the dramatic news of U.S. Steel's incorporation, the popular perception of "a Pittsburgh man" invoked by this song would have been of a corporate magnate, managing thousands of workers and investing millions of dollars. "Go Easy Mabel" suggests that this image plagued clerical and sales workers even in New York City: how much more resonance there would have been for the same group in Pittsburgh!

Pittsburghers, on the other hand, could have taken all of this with a bit

32. Ruth Ashmore [Mrs. Isabel Allderdice (Sloan) Mallon], *The Business Girl* (Philadelphia: Curtis, 1895), p. 83.

33. See discussion of male clerical workers' wages in chapter 3.

34. "Go Easy Mabel," words by Ren Shields, Ed. Moran, and Will D. Cobb, music by J. Fred Helf (Helf & Hager Co., New York, 1909). (I am indebted to Barbara DeVault for bringing this song to my attention.)

of humor; after all, they well knew that not everyone was a Carnegie, a Mellon, or a Frick. Still, the young men of the Commercial Department and the co-workers and husbands of that program's female students were, literally, "Pittsburgh men." Even without living up to the full implications of the popular phrase, the former students of the Commercial Department lived in the shadows of those implications as much as they worked in the shadows of the buildings named after the famous Pittsburgh men.

The public high school's program conveyed both specific skills and these more nebulous social values. From the school's point of view, however, the program was quite a success. The skills it imparted allowed most of its students, whether they followed the full course or not, to gain office employment. The Commercial Department's training clearly provided the skills demanded by the city's businesses. The department, then, could take pride in providing the necessary link between the two sides of the clerical equation, supplying trained workers for the most rapidly growing sector of the work force.

At the same time the students' postschool experiences—both immediate and longer term—reflect the radical transformation of this work force during these same years. The narrow skills taught in the Commercial Department translated into equally narrow employment opportunities. The program's students, both male and female, found themselves in the newly created slots below the management level. Their expectations for the future affected their perceptions of these jobs. Employers denied women advancement because of their assumption that the women's personal goals were fixed on marriage. The popular rumors of female office workers' marriages to rich and established men added glamour to otherwise unexciting jobs. The actual marriages of these women stripped away this ideological gloss, though not entirely. The fact that the largest proportion of them married men who were themselves clerical and sales workers suggests a point of intersection between women's expectations rising from clerical work and men's. For female office workers' male counterparts, dreams of promotion and independent business success substituted for dreams of marriage. In fact, most of these young men would remain in the same office strata throughout their working lives, stability and job security becoming the major benefits of male clerical employment within the developing office hierarchies.

While the former students of the Commercial Department worked in the new offices of Pittsburgh, they rarely lived in the area's newest neighborhoods. If these individuals had perceived the collar line between skilled manual workers and clerical workers as a crucial social divide, they would have acted on that perception by moving to separate neighborhoods, since, as one author put it, "social distances tend to be expressed in physical distances."[35] A study of the Commercial Department alumni provides some insight into this issue.[36] Very few of the clerical and sales workers among them moved to the burgeoning suburbs of the Pittsburgh metropolitan area. By 1915 only 6 percent of those workers lived in the suburbs, compared to 18 percent of those who owned some sort of business and 11 percent of the professionals and high-level managers. Harry Donnally, the future bank president, had already moved to the suburbs in 1900, remaining there throughout his rise in the banking world. On the other hand, David Ensell, office clerk and son of a Hill Top glassblower, not only remained in his old neighborhood, but was still living with his parents in 1915 when he was thirty-seven years old.

From the various neighborhoods of Pittsburgh, then, the former students of the Commercial Department made their daily trips into the city's offices. Once there, they were confronted by the three-tiered office work force that was just beginning to take form. Most of the Commercial Department students did not enter the highest of these three levels, that of middle management, though a few of the men did eventually become office managers. By the turn of the century, higher managerial positions were already becoming the preserve of college-educated men, leaving high school graduates locked into more routine clerical positions.[37] Male alumni of the Commercial Department thus experienced occupational mobility mostly as lateral movement between various clerical positions; job security in the developing office bureaucracies was more of a reality than was movement up the corporate ladder. The young women from the program found positions at the bottom of the office hierarchy as stenographers, typists, clerks, and office machine operators. These jobs did not offer occupational mobility in any direction, largely because of the prevailing assumption that women would eventually leave the paid labor force to marry.[38]

35. Hawley, *Urban Society,* p. 187.
36. When the city of Pittsburgh absorbed Allegheny City in 1907, the ward numbering system changed drastically. This made tracing changes in individuals' residences within the city over time virtually impossible. The figures provided here are based on 358 individuals for whom both occupations and addresses were located for 1915. Of those, 209 worked as clerical or sales workers.
37. See, for example, Edmund J. James, "The Higher Education of the Business Man," *Accountics* 4 (June 1899), 144–145.
38. U.S. Department of Commerce and Labor, Bureau of the Census, *Statistics of Women at Work: 1900* (Washington, 1907), notes that 94 percent of stenographers and

Occupying the new clerical positions at the turn of the century, the Commercial Department students formed a new group within the work force, one whose class status involved ambiguous connections with both the traditional working class and the traditional petite bourgeoisie. Existing perceptions of the class standing and social status of this group were shaped by the complex intersection of older conceptions of office work and workers, the changing situation of skilled workers, and the impact of women's entry into office jobs.

---

typists were under thirty-five years of age and that 95 percent of them were unmarried, compared to 65 percent of all female wage earners at the turn of the century (pp. 105–106).

Conclusion

Class and Clerical Work

"Did you sever your connection with the firm or were you discharged?" asked the friend.

The man out of a job gave a few minutes thought before answering.

"I'm a little uncertain about that," he said at last.

"Uncertain?"

"Yes. Of course, I know that office boys are discharged and general managers sever their connections, but I can't be sure that I was high enough up to sever my connections, and I don't think I was low enough down to be discharged. Perhaps you'd better make it that the firm and I disagreed."

—*Accountics,* April 1899

This turn-of-the-century accountant's joke captures the bewilderment of clerical workers faced with the rapid changes within offices and parallel developments in the larger economic and social world. The clerical worker's confusion about his or her position in that world matched the confusion of other social groups about how to place the new office workers. Older perceptions of office work and workers were no longer consistent with the experiences of the women and men employed in the new corporate hierarchies. What social science later enshrined as the "collar line" may have existed, but its significance was not at all clear. Rather than being a clear social delimiter, the collar line existed as a murky area invested with contradictory social meanings. If "the man out of a job" could not decide where he stood, he was not alone. Many others at the time would have shared his quandary.

172

In Pittsburgh as elsewhere the clerical sector of the labor force had begun growing in the final decades of the nineteenth century and would continue to do so in the twentieth. The former students of Pittsburgh's Commercial Department formed the new century's first generation of office workers. As such they experienced firsthand the transformation of clerical work. What they made of the experience influenced the perceptions of the families and communities from which they had come and foreshadowed the new lives they would make. Dressed in white collars and neat shirtwaists, they would live out the implications of a collar line fraught with a meaning that no one could clearly define.

Many twentieth-century scholars have downplayed the magnitude of the break between early nineteenth-century clerks and the new office workers of the late nineteenth century. This break was marked not only by the sheer increase in numbers, but also by the changes in the clerical work process itself and by the feminization of specific job categories. The resulting workplace realities contributed to the dilemma that found expression in the accountant's joke. For the growing numbers of individuals employed in corporate bureaucracies, new lines were being drawn within white-collar work. No longer could young male clerks expect to rise in the ranks and eventually run their own businesses. For them clerical work more clearly took on the characteristics of a job rather than a business apprenticeship.

At the same time, the entrance of women into office employment had contradictory repercussions. For the women themselves, these jobs offered important new opportunities, expanding their employment horizons in a positive direction. As clerical workers these women could earn more money, use their education, and meet new people, both female and male. All this would happen, furthermore, in a setting that enhanced, rather than diminished, their social status. If the development of a distinctly female stratum in the office thus had one set of implications for young women, it had quite a different set for their male co-workers. Working alongside women in a sense decreased the status of male clerical workers, further eroding any lingering questions about clerical work as an entrée to entrepreneurship. In another sense, however, the increasingly rigid sexual segregation of office employment reinforced the idea that men were not at the bottom of the office hierarchy. In effect, these men could simultaneously identify with their male employers and distance themselves from the growing numbers of female office employees.

These contradictory effects of hierarchy and gender were clearest in the burgeoning corporate bureaucracies. However, they reverberated throughout the world of clerical employment. As large corporations came to dominate the business community, the entrepreneurial promises of smaller businesses were increasingly called into doubt. In effect, the three-tiered corporate structure of male managers, male clerical workers, and female clerical workers came to define, both positively and negatively, the entire clerical world.

The development of educational programs such as Pittsburgh's Commercial Department paralleled the development of the clerical work force in important ways. The high school program reflected both the changes in the office work process and the ways in which the sexual stratification of the office hierarchy masked those changes. In the Pittsburgh school's Department of Practice, for example, students allegedly learned how to function as owners of businesses. However, both the growing numbers of female students in the program and the jobs ultimately acquired by students of both sexes suggest that the school's real value came from the concrete skills it taught as well as the knowledge it imparted of the functioning of business hierarchies.

Through the Commercial Department, then, with its many contradictory messages, Pittsburgh's young people obtained the skills necessary for them to compete in the clerical job market. Half a century later C. Wright Mills would suggest that "in American folklore, the white-collar girl is usually born of small-town lower middle-class parents."[1] The sheer numbers of new clerical workers between 1870 and 1920 belie this myth; if all the white-collar girls (or boys) had come from small-town settings and middle-class origins, there simply would not have been enough workers to meet the demand. The students of Pittsburgh's Commercial Department, then, provide an important corrective to the myth. All these young people were already part of the urban scene; they held no untested notions of the glamour of big-city life. They came from virtually all sectors of the city's population, though few were the children of the city's elite, and few came from the poorest immigrant families. The majority were the children of manual workers, well enough off to be able to afford an extended period of education for at least some of their children.

If much of the ambiguity of the social status of clerical workers arose from the mixed messages they received at work, at least an equal amount derived from the roots of many of them in the manual working class. This

---

1. C. Wright Mills, *White Collar: The American Middle Classes* (New York: Oxford University Press, 1951), p. 202. There is no similarly prevalent myth about the origins of the "white-collar boy."

second fundamental source of ambiguity becomes clearest in the case of the largest single social group represented in the Commercial Department, the children of skilled manual workers. Though the term "labor aristocracy" has had a tumultuous history, it still captures best the dynamics within the working class which contributed to the further blurring of the collar line. In Pittsburgh as elsewhere in the United States, the labor aristocracy was marked first of all by skill and its attendant economic benefits. The various ramifications of such skill levels helped endow the labor aristocracy with its own set of contradictions. These most skilled manual workers could—and did—flaunt their economic superiority over less fortunate workers. Proud of their control over the work process as well as of their semisupervisory roles on the shop floor, these workers sought to enshrine their prestige in various organizations both at the workplace and in their communities. The fact that the turn-of-the-century rise of corporate power began to erode the productive bases of this superiority only encouraged this tendency.

In the course of building their own organizations, the labor aristocrats also came to see themselves as the rightful leaders of the entire working class. In the craft unions of the turn of the century, they sought to provide a model of effective and responsible unions for their less fortunate co-workers. Later they would provide the leadership for more industrial forms of unionism. In politics and other civic matters, they similarly stepped to the fore, confident that they would know best what would benefit all workers. Within the labor aristocracy, then, contradictory tendencies toward both elitism and solidarity coexisted.

These dual tendencies of the labor aristocracy were compounded by the ethnic and racial stratification of the manual working class in the United States. In Pittsburgh's iron and steel industry, for example, the clear ethnic lines between skilled workers from the United Kingdom and Germany and unskilled workers from southern and eastern Europe reinforced the former group's sense of superiority, elitism, and leadership. These impulses gave rise to a host of tensions, as the labor aristocracy sought to understand both the erosion of its workplace power and the appearance of new—and seemingly very different—groups of workers.

In the rapidly changing economic world of the decades around the turn of the century, skilled workers had their hands full simply trying to comprehend changes in their own blue-collar world of work. The rise of the clerical sector of the work force at the same time exacerbated the difficulties even while it seemed to provide a solution to many. As the labor aristocrats' own trades seemed increasingly in danger of losing their economic advantages, office jobs appeared to hold out the promise of both equivalent economic benefits and equal social status. For both the sons and the daughters of these workers, the level of education and other appurtenances required for entry into the ethnically "pure" office ranks served both to maintain and to reinforce the labor aristocracy's social status.

Even here, however, gender dynamics further obfuscated the social significance of the new clerical jobs. As much as Pittsburgh's skilled workers wanted to believe that the city's Commercial Department fitted their sons for desirable employment, the fact that their daughters attended the same program must have been troubling. While clerical work was clearly a most desirable occupation for these young women, the very presence of women in offices called into question the fitness of such employment for young men. Only the relatively high wages, ethnic homogeneity, and sexual stratification of the office work force could begin to counterbalance this questioning of masculinity.

The collar line, then, drew its ambiguities from both the white-collar world of the office and the blue-collar world of manual workshops. These two worlds came together in workers' communities, families, and educational institutions. The resulting complexities leave us still confronting Jürgen Kocka's question: "What is the relative weight of the 'class line,' the outer boundary of the working class, in structuring social reality?"[2] Did the collar line serve as a fundamental social marker for turn-of-the-century workers?

The varied life experiences of the students of Pittsburgh's Commercial Department—and especially those from the families of the skilled workers poised on the immediate edge of the collar line—suggest that during these decades of clerical work's efflorescence, the actions of workers were not necessarily predicated on assumptions of white-collar superiority. Within the families of manual workers, both daughters and sons found employment on both sides of the collar line. Those who became clerical workers often remained in the neighborhoods they grew up in, or they moved to areas with similar mixes of blue-collar and white-collar workers. Daughters often married the clerical workers they met at work, but they also married skilled workers like their fathers. On the "other side" of the collar line, the children of clerical and sales workers were more likely to take on office jobs themselves, but the daughters married

2. Jürgen Kocka, "The Study of Social Mobility and the Formation of the Working Class in the 19th Century," *Le Mouvement Social* 111 (April–June 1980), 107.

skilled manual workers even more frequently. Given this situation, the collar line was not so much a social chasm as it was a social estuary, a site for the mingling of economic groups and social influences.

What are the implications of this for the way we think about social class in the early twentieth-century United States? Do we want to call the people located on our estuary a "working class," suggesting their commonalities as employees, as sellers of their labor power in a capitalist economy? Or are they members of an expanding "middle class," linked not only by their standards of consumption but also by their self-definitions in contradistinction both to less fortunate workers of different ethnic and racial groups and to more powerful and wealthy members of society? This very form of posing the questions provides part of the answer. Depending on the purpose of our inquiry, we can locate early-twentieth-century low-level white-collar workers in either class schema. In fact, these early clerical workers themselves could choose between these identities, opting for whichever one best fit their own purposes in a given situation.

Deeply riven by gender, the clerical sector of the work force was torn between identification with the manual working class on one hand, and with the upper levels of the white-collar stratum on the other. The "man out of a job" might not know if he had "severed his connections" or "been discharged,"but the men and women still at work in the nation's offices would be equally perplexed when they took the time to think about their social standing. As historians and social scientists we need to learn not only to accept the ambivalence these people lived with, but to find new ways of understanding how such ambiguities might work themselves out in daily life.

The students of Pittsburgh's Commercial Department brought their families' values into the high school program with them. Both in the process of that education and in their later work lives, those values were not abandoned, but transformed. Working and living in "the Smokey City," these individuals became white-collar employees, but remained the sons and daughters of labor.

Appendix

Description of Data

The Commercial Department Collective Biography

The Archives of Industrial Society of the Hillman Library, University of Pittsburgh, Pittsburgh, Pennsylvania, house the surviving records of the Pittsburgh School District. The collection includes two volumes of enrollment records for the Pittsburgh Central High School's Commercial Department. These records represent all students entering the program from 1891 through 1903, as well as students enrolled in the program in 1890 with surnames beginning with the letters K through the end of the alphabet. From these records I created my basic data set of 1,844 individuals.

The enrollment records are bound volumes of printed forms filled in by hand. The forms include the student's name, age, and previous school; the dates the student entered and left the program; and the name, address, and occupation of the student's guardian. The student's grades both for individual classes and for annual averages and final exams are also recorded. In addition to this standard information, other pieces of information were sometimes entered on the forms. Eight students had the notation "Colored" on their form, although subsequent record linkages would demonstrate that this did not appear on the enrollment forms of all the black students. Students who withdrew from the program and then returned had the dates of their withdrawal, return, and graduation (or final withdrawal). Some students' ward of residence was noted. A smattering of the forms had the guardian's place of work listed next to his or her occupation. There were also various other notations such as "left to get married," "joined the army," and "moved out of town."

I employed a stratified sampling technique in order to increase the number of women in the sample for later record linkages. I coded information on all the women (554) who graduated from the program. I then coded every other student among those remaining. I excluded from my alternate sampling pattern 150 names in the record books which were marked "Did Not Attend." The differential created by this sampling method was accounted for in the appropriate tables by weighting the variables for sex and graduation status. In weighted tables I gave female graduates a weight of one, while all other students were weighted by two. One of the only unweighted tables relying solely on the enrollment records is table 3, "Distribution of Commercial Department students by guardians' occupations." Weighting this table did not change any percentages in the table.

I coded all of the standard information from the school forms. (Only the annual averages and final-exam grades were coded from the "report card" section of the records.) In addition, I calculated the number of months a student spent in the program from the dates the student entered and withdrew. The school previously attended was entered as two separate variables, one for the type of school and one for the name of the school. I also created a variable to denote the guardian's relationship to the student. Since most of the forms did not explicitly include this information, guardians with the same last name and a male first name were presumed to be fathers, and those with a female first name, mothers. I imputed the student's sex from the student's first and/or middle name. The student's city of residence was presumed to be Pittsburgh unless otherwise noted. (This may have led to an overcounting of Pittsburgh residents. Some of the students may have been from Allegheny City, in particular; but since some forms had "Allegheny" noted on them, I assumed that all addresses were from Pittsburgh unless otherwise noted.) Later recoding grouped guardians' occupations in categories described later in this appendix.

With the Commercial Department data set in place, I created several parallel data sets using record linkage techniques.

For the years following their departure from the Commercial Department, I looked up students in the Pittsburgh city directories for 1895, 1900, 1905, 1910, and 1915.[1] A sort of early version of phone directories, the city directories list individuals alphabetically along with their

---

1. Cara Grigsby, Alice Oberfield, and James Rundle assisted in the data collection and coding for the 1910 and 1915 directories.

occupations, home addresses, and sometimes their workplace addresses.[2] I traced 1,109 of the Commercial Department students in at least one Pittsburgh City Directory edition.[3]

Those students found in the city directories did not reflect the original composition of the sample in two major respects. More of the program's graduates were found than its nongraduates. While only about 40 percent of the program's students received diplomas, 51 percent of the individuals traced to postschool employment were Commercial Department graduates. This suggests that some of the Commercial Department's students left the program to move out of town.[4]

In addition, despite the fact that the original school sample provided a larger proportion of women than the program's actual composition, fewer of the women students than the men could be found in later records. I found occupations for almost two-thirds of the men, but only about one-third of the women in my sample. The city directories list very few women, although clerical workers are more likely to appear than most other wage-earning women. For several hundred of the women, city directories turned up other members of their families, but not them. All this tells us is that the family had not moved out of Pittsburgh; no inference can be made about the presence or employment status of the young woman. Census records are somewhat more reliable; if a woman appears in the census, her employment status for the previous year is fairly accurately represented.[5] Despite this, the employed students are not far from reflecting the school's enrollment distribution; while the program contained 43 percent female students and 57 percent male students, the sample of employed former students is 37 percent female and 63 percent male.

The city directory information allowed me to code, by year, the specific

2. Workplace addresses were always given for proprietors, often given for clerical and sales workers, and never given for manual workers.

3. For each individual traced, I created a "match" variable measuring the surety of my identification of the individual. A description of this variable as well as its distribution can be found in my dissertation, "Sons and Daughters of Labor: Class and Clerical Work in Pittsburgh, 1870s–1910s," Yale University, 1985.

4. It was also harder to determine if dropouts were the people listed in the city directories, especially if they had common names.

5. Thomas Dublin discusses these problems and suggests some possible alternative sources for the study of women's occupational mobility. Unfortunately, payroll records such as those Dublin uses were not available or feasible for this project. (Thomas Dublin, "Women Workers and the Study of Social Mobility," *Journal of Interdisciplinary History* 9 [1979], 652.) Roberta Balstad Miller also discusses the topic in "The Historical Study of Social Mobility: A New Perspective," *Historical Methods Newsletter* 8 (1975), 96.

occupation, occupational category, home address, and work address of each student traced to one or more city directory. I also coded separately the student's first occupation, regardless of the year in which it was found.[6] If a member of the student's family was present in the city directory, I coded his or her specific occupation, occupational category, home address, and work address as well.[7]

I traced two groups of the Commercial Department students in the 1900 Manuscript Census, using the Soundex index for Pennsylvania located at the National Archives. I searched for all individuals, male and female, attending the Commercial Department in 1900, as well as all women whose guardians or siblings were listed in any prior city directory. These two groups provided data on family structure and ethnicity for those in school in 1900 and occupations for many of the women who otherwise would not have been found.

The 1900 Manuscript Census provides a wealth of information. Because I wanted to use the census both to provide information on the individual Commercial Department student and to describe the structure of the student's family, this data set consists of two sections. For the Commercial Department student, I coded his or her sex, age in 1900, nativity, ethnicity, years in the United States (if foreign born), order of birth, and order of birth by sex in the family. I also coded the presence of clerical and sales workers in the household (including siblings, relatives, and boarders); whether a sibling past, present, or future, was enrolled in the Commercial Department; and whether a sibling was attending high school in 1900.[8]

A second section of the data set included information on the student's family. Coded information on the student's parents included the designated head of household; the father's nativity, ethnicity, citizenship status, years in the United States (if foreign born), literacy, occupation, and the number of months he was unemployed between July 1899 and June 1900; and the mother's nativity, ethnicity, years in the United States (if foreign born), literacy, and occupation. I also coded whether the family's resi-

6. If a student had been found with an occupation listed in an earlier but different type of record, that occupation would be listed as his or her first occupation.

7. Family members included both individuals whose names I had from other record sources, especially the 1900 census, as well as individuals sharing the same last name as the former student and residing at the same address. It also includes women's husbands if the student had been found in the marriage records.

8. Any sibling over the age of fourteen listed as attending school was considered to be in some sort of high school program. Students attending post–high school programs were noted as such in the census itself.

dence was rented or owned; the number of children in the family; relatives, servants, and boarders present in the household; the total number of months children in the family were unemployed; and the ward of the city in which the family resided. All children in the family were also coded, unless there were more than ten, in which case I coded only the ten oldest. For each child the age in 1900, sex, and occupation were coded. I also created occupational categories for all family members.

Carnegie Library of Pittsburgh holds both a "Marriage License Index, 1885–1925" and the "Marriage License Docket, 1885–1906" on microfilm. I attempted to find marriage records for all of the female Commercial Department students. The index is arranged by the first letter of the surname, then by the first letter of the first name, and then by the year of marriage. I began searching for a woman's marriage in the year she left the Commercial Department.[9] Three hundred seventeen women were successfully traced to the marriage records. Of those I found husbands' occupations for only 230.[10] For each woman whose marriage I found, I coded the year of the marriage, the bride's year of birth, the husband's specific occupation and occupational category, and the husband's year of birth. From this basic information I derived further variables giving the age at marriage of both the woman and the man. Unfortunately, the marriage records provided no information on brides' occupations, even though a space for that information appeared on the form.

I combined all of these data sets in order to create the Commercial Department Collective Biography. Chapters 4 and 6 present the analysis of this data base. Additional tables for minor points of that analysis may be consulted in my doctoral dissertation, "Sons and Daughters of Labor," Yale University, 1985.

A Comparative Sample of Teenagers' Families in Lawrenceville and the Hill Top

I constructed an additional data set based on the 1900 Federal Manuscript Census for Pittsburgh's 15th, 16th, 17th, 31st, 32nd, and 35th

9. For more detail on this process, see Appendix II of my dissertation, "Sons and Daughters of Labor," pp. 352–353. This appendix also includes information on the "match" variable for the marriage record data set.
10. Some of this information came from finding the husband listed in either later city directories or the 1900 manuscript census.

wards (Lawrenceville and Hill Top). I recorded information on every tenth household containing children between the ages of thirteen and twenty.[11] If the tenth household was the family of one of the Commercial Department students, I subtracted it from the sample. This information was then coded in the same format as the census information in the Commercial Department sample.

Occupational Categories

I originally grouped the occupations of the guardians of Commercial Department students into nine occupational categories: unskilled manual workers, skilled manual workers, foremen and low-level managers, public employees, clerical and sales workers, proprietors and high-level managers, professionals, agricultural workers, and those of an unknown nature. These categories represent a combination of economic and social status at the turn of the century.[12]

The division of manual workers into unskilled and skilled was based on general information on the nature of specific occupations as well as consultations of U.S. Department of Commerce, Bureau of the Census, *Index to Occupations* (Washington, 1915), the earliest available governmental definitions of occupations. Rapid changes in the production process at the turn of the century obviously limit the precision of these divisions.[13] Although I was initially concerned about specifying semiskilled jobs as well, this turned out to be a negligible problem for these parents' occupations.

Several factors favored the development of a second occupational categorization schema. First of all, the occupations of the generation following that of the guardians of Commercial Department students called for new categories and definitions. Secondly, the accumulation of more detailed information on individuals' occupations allowed greater specificity in the categories. Accordingly, a new fourteen-part schema was set up, including the following: unskilled manual workers, semiskilled manual workers, skilled manual workers, foremen, service proprietors, public

11. Ken Pomeranz and Ken Packman assisted in the collection and coding of this data.

12. For a listing of specific occupations and my categorization of them, see my dissertation, "Sons and Daughters of Labor," Appendix III, pp. 427–452.

13. See Anthony E. Boardman and Michael P. Weber, "Economic Growth and Occupational Mobility in Nineteenth-Century Urban America: A Reappraisal," *Journal of Social History* 11 (1977), 52–74.

employees, clerical and sales workers, retail proprietors, professionals, wholesale proprietors, manufacturing proprietors, agricultural workers, juvenile workers, and unknown.[14]

The greatest change from the original categories arose from dividing the "proprietors" group into four categories: service, retail, wholesale, and manufacturing. The most important information for producing these divisions came from the city directory data. When an individual was listed in the city directory as owning a business, that business could be looked up in the business directory at the back of the city directory. Service proprietors were defined as self-employed craftspeople, selling their skills rather than a commodity. Many of these individuals came from the ranks of the skilled workers. (For example, a "contractor" might be listed as a carpenter in one year and a contractor in another.)

14. See my dissertation, Appendix III, for details.

Index

Library of Congress Cataloging-in-Publication Data

DeVault, Ileen A.
  Sons and daughters of labor : class and clerical work in turn-of-the-century Pittsburgh /
Ileen A. DeVault.
    p.   cm.
  Includes bibliographical references.
  ISBN 0-8014-2026-1 (alk. paper)
    1. Clerks—Pennsylvania—Pittsburgh—History. 2. Social classes—Pennsylvania—
Pittsburgh—History. I. Title.
  HD8039.M4U536   1990
  305.9′651—dc20
                                                                    90-55134